Pipe the Bimbo in Red

Dean Andrews, Jim Garrison, and
The Conspiracy To Kill JFK

Donald Jeffries &
William Matson Law

Pipe The Bimbo In Red: Dean Andrews, Jim Garrison, and The Conspiracy
To Kill JFK
Copyright © 2023 William MAtson Law, Donald Jeffries

Published by:
Trine Day LLC
PO Box 577
Walterville, OR 97489
1-800-556-2012
www.TrineDay.com
TrineDay@icloud.com

Library of Congress Control Number: 2023946810

Law, William Matson & Jeffries, Donald, James.
−1st ed.
p. cm.

Epub (ISBN-13) 978-1-63424-467-1
Trade Paperback (ISBN-13) 978-1-63424-466-4
1. Dean Adams Andrews Jr. 1922- 1981. 2. Kennedy, John F. 1917-1963 Assassination. 3. Presidents Assassination United States. 5. New Orleans, Louisiana
1963. I. Law, William Matson & Jeffries, Donald, James. II. Title

First Edition
10 9 8 7 6 5 4 3 2 1

Printed in the USA
Distribution to the Trade by:
Independent Publishers Group (IPG)
814 North Franklin Street
Chicago, Illinois 60610
312.337.0747
www.ipgbook.com

To the memory of my sons:

Trevit Clay Law
October 31, 1976-September 25, 2022

Ryan Matson Law
August 26, 1993-January 7, 2022

ACKNOWLEDGMENTS

The authors would like to thank the following people who helped make this book possible. William Davy's research was essential to our work, and on top of that he was kind enough to write the Foreword. Jack Roth's own groundbreaking research into the atmosphere in New Orleans made him a perfect choice for the Afterword. Paul Bleau's important work, especially on the Fair Play for Cuba Committee, deserves more recognition. Chris Graves is capable of finding things that no one else can. Gary Shaw, the dean of JFK assassination researchers, was as generous and accommodating as always. The legendary John Barbour was a fount of information on Jim Garrison. A special debt of gratitude goes to Peter Secosh, who not only helped with research, but also proofread and edited the manuscript. Gwen Ann Segal, Teddi "Cookie" Segal, Doris "Sweetie Pie" Kunitz, and Steven Voebel all were enormously accommodating in talking about their late brother Edward "Butch" Voebel, the teenage Lee Harvey Oswald's best friend. Don Jeffries would like to thank, as always, my wife Jeanne and children John and Julianna for always being there for me. And finally, my thanks and appreciation to Dean Andrews III, whose friendship and personal recollections inspired this book.

William Matson Law would like to acknowledge my wife Lori Law for understanding my great obsession. My children: Trevit, Ryan, Shawn and Haylee My grandchildren: Tristan, Christian, Trey, Tylar, Mary, Sienna, Vanessa, Zariah, Mykah, Ransom, Tuff, Riot, Colt and Bristol.

Lori Arnott Wiley and Bob Wiley. Veleka Gray for her kindness and friendship over the years.

I would like to thank my publisher Kris Millegan who is always open to my ideas and who encourages me to keep trudging the happy path. I would also like to thank the late Anne Hundley Dischler. Meeting Anne was one of the greatest pleasures of my life. We shared many conversations over the years about her work with the Garrison investigation and following in Oswald's footsteps in New Orleans. I miss her dearly. Gabby Glenn-Zediker for coming to my aid when searching for materials. Special mention to Craig Bouzarth who is an absolute genius and good friend. Finally to Dean Andrews III, his willingness to come forward for the very first time has changed our understanding of the Kennedy assassination.

CONTENTS

Lakefront Park along Lake Pontchartrain, New Orleans, 1963, with Confederate Battle Flag flying. Photo taken by Chuck Battles, shared with permission.

NOLA IN THE 1960s

S ince its founding in 1699 the city of New Orleans (NOLA) has been referred to as a melting pot, combining French, American Indian, Spanish, African, English, German, Italian, Asian, and other cultures. Its famed European architecture underlies an emphasis on music and food which have always been key characteristics of the city, but its main business was always international trade.

NOLA is also in a Southern state of the US, which was itself undergoing massive social changes in the 1960s. I will note that by 1970, NOLA had become much more like other American cities than it had been in the early 1960s. In the early 1960s, NOLA had no interstates, practically no sky line, no professional sports teams, and very little air-conditioning. Its economic life line had always been the Mississippi River, which ironically made it financially closer to cities to its north that to the rural agrarian South that surrounded it on all sides. As an international port, it imported coffee and fruits, but also tropical diseases, like Yellow Fever and malaria, and voracious termites from the Philippines.

Trade has always been the main business in NOLA. Ships full of bananas came in from Guatemala and massive amounts of sugar came from Cuba. So when Fidel Castro took over Cuba in 1959 an embargo went into effect and cut deeply into the trade with NOLA and triggered a strong Anti-Communist sentiment in the city, particularly amongst the trade community. The oil exploration industry should also be mentioned, since it was located there. The offshore oil platform was first developed there by Doc LaBorde, a retired naval officer and engineer. Crew boats were built that carried rough necks from the Louisiana coast just south of NOLA to their platforms in the Gulf of Mexico. When the elites in NOLA proved unwilling to let the Texas oil crowd into their society, the Texans set up shop in the Houston area.

Much of NOLA's famous "Gingerbread" architecture was actually milled in St. Louis and floated down the river in kits to be assembled in NOLA.

NOLA's most famous cultural contribution was jazz, which resulted when they built a French Opera house in the middle of a provincial slave colony. Song forms and European harmony combined with African rhythms to form a lively new style of American music. Classic New Orleans jazz, as it is sometimes called, flourished in the beginning of the 20th Century, but was nearly wiped out economically when the US Navy closed down Storyville, NOLA's designated prostitution district in 1917. By the 1960s, New Orleans jazz was essentially a historical relic kept alive for tourists at places like Preservation Hall. Around this same time waves of European immigrants, mostly from Italy, Ireland and Germany, settled in NOLA. They did much of the hard work of building city in the swamp. It was indeed a complex and colorful city.

* * *

In Nov. of 1963, I lived in New Orleans and went to school (7th grade) as usual. Lunch had just finished, and we returned to our classrooms for the afternoon work. Just then, the loudspeaker crackled and the voice of our Principal announced President Kennedy had just been shot in Dallas. The predictable murmur shot through the room. I was silent. The fact that someone shot JFK was hardly a surprise to me. Most of the grown ups I observed openly hated JFK. The exception was one history teacher at our school who thought that Kennedy would be remembered as one of the great Presidents. That same teacher also told us everyday that he had a talking dog. He admitted that he was trying to demonstrate a propaganda technique, saying that if he continued to repeat the lie everyday, one day we would finally believe it.

As most things in NOLA, our school was segregated by both race and gender. Ours was all white and all male. Despite this, I spent most of my lunchtimes in the basement of our school's administration building with my friend Louis with whom I worked in the cafeteria. We would go down a back stairway into the basement and throw knives with the two black janitors who had set up a target on one wall. They welcomed our company, and we were entertained by their colorful stories. I remember one day Louis asked one of the janitors if he preferred Black women or White women. He said it really didn't matter because they were all pink on the inside!

Back to the classroom. Soon the Principal's voice returned to the PA system. He announced that President Kennedy had died, and he was closing the school early for our safety. He said there was a real concern about civil unrest in the city and that we should all go home directly for the day, and stay there over the weekend. As the day wore on and the sound bites filtered through, I remember hearing the unmistakable accent in Lee Harvey Oswald's voice which indicated that he was from New Orleans.

Once we were released, I gathered my book bag together and headed out to the bus stop which was directly in front of our school. Just beyond the bus stop was a recently completed section of Interstate 10 with its endless drone of cars heading west into Jefferson Parrish. As I waited for the bus, I noticed an enormous, and menacing, black cloud in the western sky. Having been raised as a sailor, I paid attention to such things. I wondered about the motives of the people driving their cars into such extreme weather. I looked at the cars driving into the weather. I wondered who they were. It was years later I realized one of these cars contained David Ferrie, and his "young friends," who were headed to Houston "to go ice skating." Before the weekend was over, David Ferrie was arrested by Orleans Parrish DA Jim Garrison for possible involvement in the JFK assassination, only to be released by the FBI the following day.

The Summer of 1963 became known as the Civil Rights Summer all across the South. To bracket the time frame: this period began on June 11th with JFK's Civil Rights Speech and culminated on August 28, 1963 with Martin Luther King's "I have a Dream" speech in Washington. There were also events both *before* and *after* these dates, but these provide convenient markers for the tumultuous time period.

Yes, there were racial tensions in NOLA, but they were largely out-of-sight and much of the tension was held in check by the Catholic Church which played both sides of the street, as needed. On one hand, they operated "separate but equal" school systems which did provide education to black children who would not have had any. These schools were segregated both by race and gender, as is common throughout the Catholic world, and even by social class when they deemed appropriate.

The public school system, which had been segregated by law since Reconstruction, had not yet been integrated by 1960, and a public, yet legal, battle ensued. In NOLA the White Citizens Council opposed integration of the public school system and enlisted 25,000 members to raise money for their cause. Judge Leander Perez, a leader of that organization, was so upset with the actions of Archbishop Joseph Rummel who attempted to integrate the Catholic schools in the Archdiocese that he wrote a letter to the Pope suggesting that the Pope remove Rummel from his position for being out-of-step with the prevailing attitudes in the city. The Pope responded by Ex-Communicating Judge Perez and two other leaders of his White Citizens Council organization.

A cherished member of our household was an elderly black lady that we called Mama Dora. Actually, Mama Dora was 75% black and 25% Cherokee. She was a below-knee amputee due to an accident with a street car that occurred many years earlier. My father knew her from the medical circles because she worked with another doctor's family. She came to our house several times per week to help cook and clean. Mama Dora had the voice of an angel and sang Gospel hymns as she did her work. She also made fresh lemonade for me when I came home from school in the afternoon. I always thanked her with a big hug.

Mardi Gras was the ever-popular post-Christmas celebration which was a welcome relief, and the city shut down for the day so that everybody could go to see the parades and scream "Hey, Mister. Throw me something!" The parades were organized by Krewes who were almost all populated by wealthy white males. The parades carried the male krewe members from their dens, where they started drinking, to their ornate costume balls at the Municipal Auditorium on the edge of the French Quarter where their wives waited for them. The Mardi Gras balls themselves were a glittering spectacle to behold and formed the heart of elite society in this mysterious city. I always marveled at how this carnival festival managed to balance the scales between a white upper class and a variously colored lower classes by throwing cheap trinkets to the masses who gathered to watch (and hear) the parades pass by.

Today, Mardi Gras has mushroomed to be a much larger and more commercial event that goes on for several weeks. Back then, it was much smaller and a really big deal to be in one of the Mardi Gras krewes. One aspect of Mardi Gras that has endured from the Sixties has been the drag queen competition held in the French Quarter where a great deal of the gay community lived. So on this point, NOLA was clearly ahead of its time.

One story that I heard repeatedly during the 1960s was that FBI Director J. Edgar Hoover would come to New Orleans for Mardi Gras and dress as a woman during the festivities. His rationale was that he was so famous, that dressing like a woman so that no one would recognize him, was the only way he could relax and enjoy himself. It was a colorful time in a colorful city.

The Mafia ran most of the entertainment in the French Quarter (strippers, etc). Later in life, I had a client named Frank who told me that he had worked for the Mafia in his earlier years. Frank said the he had managed twelve bars for the Mafia on Bourbon Street. One day Frank told me in confidence, "You know that Oswald kid. He was with us."

What I am trying to illustrate here is how close all these people were to each other. For example, my 10th grade English teacher was a young Jesuit named Paul Piazza. The Warren Commission reported that Piazza wrote a letter to Oswald inviting him to speak on life in the Soviet Union at the Jesuit Seminary in Mobile on July 28, 1963. Piazza was attending the seminary with John Murret. Oswald was driven to the event by his uncle Dutz Murret, who was one of Carlos Marcello's inner circle. Oswald knew Dutz and his son John Murret well and had lived with them for a while as a child.

In many ways, NOLA was like many small towns that combined to form one big town. The mansions that lined the Garden District along Saint Charles Ave. were encircled by low income housing: Irish families on the river side, and black families on the lake side. The Italians and the Germans were everywhere else. This "urban plan" was known in local terms as "Salt and Pepper." But it worked reasonably well. And NOLA was not just Black and White. There were many shades of gray between the two, for which they had their own terms: Mulattoes, Quadroons, Octoroons, etc. In local language of the day, it was said that NOLA settled its racial problems in the bedroom.

It was pretty well understood that local politics were corrupt. It was said that if you controlled the voting machines, then you controlled the elections. They left no paper trail, could not be audited, and could be rigged to vote for the candidate of your choice with a rubber band and paper clip.

As the 1960s wore on, the JFK Assassination became front-page news in the city long after the assassination itself. It was learned that District Attorney Jim Garrison was investigating a conspiracy based in New Orleans, involving a connection between accused JFK assassin Lee Harvey Oswald and New Orleans business man Clay Shaw who had been General Manager of the International Trade Mart.

In the 1970s the sworn testimony of a law enforcement officer from Clinton, Louisiana, was given to the U.S. Congress in which he said he saw Oswald get out of Shaw's black Cadillac the day in Clinton.

Due to the colorful cast of characters that Garrison was investigating, his public nickname became "The Jolly Green Giant" because he was putting fruits and nuts in the can! And Dean Andrews, who is the subject of

5

this book, was one of these colorful characters. So we should all welcome William Law's and Donald Jefferies' efforts to take a closer look at the people who were in contact with both Lee Harvey Oswald and Clay Shaw in the summer of 1963.

Edward T. Haslam
Author of *Dr. Mary's Monkey*
Senior Editor of *Me & Lee* by Judyth Vary Baker

FOREWORD

By William Davy

During the course of researching and conducting interviews for my 1999 work on the Jim Garrison investigation, *Let Justice Be Done*, it was inevitable that my path would cross with veteran JFK assassination author and investigator Harold Weisberg. Inevitable because Harold had written numerous books on the assassination, was a first-generation researcher and had written, perhaps the most seminal volume at that time, on the New Orleans case, *Oswald in New Orleans*. Further, Weisberg was also a volunteer investigator for Garrison who reciprocated by writing the Forword to Weisberg's above-mentioned work. Finally, Weisberg and I were neighbors with Weisberg living just a few miles north of me in Frederick, MD.

By the time of my interview with Weisberg (ca. 1997) he had long since turned bitter towards Garrison and his investigation– which made one of his comments to me inexplicable. When I asked him about the shadowy figure of "Clay Bertrand" he confidently stated that "Bertrand was Clay Shaw. No doubt. Monk Zelden confirmed it to me." Of course, Shaw was the defendant in Garrison's case and Zelden was a New Orleans attorney who worked with one of the more colorful characters in Lee Harvey Oswald's orbit, Dean Andrews. The reader will get a very up-close view of Dean Andrews' life and times as his son, Dean Andrews III, a friend of co-author Donald Jeffries, was interviewed by co-author William Law (an ironic story in and of itself). Those who remember Oliver Stone's 1991 event film, *JFK*, will remember Andrews as colorfully played by the late John Candy, who made the statement that serves as partial title to this work: *Pipe the Bimbo in Red: Dean Andrews, Jim Garrison and the Conspiracy to Kill JFK*. The work was co-written by prolific author and researcher Donald Jeffries and William Law. As for Andrews, as I wrote in my previous work, the Andrews information can be summarized as follows:

"Sometimes described as a DamonRunyonesque character, the obese Andrews often spoke in outdated 'bebop' jargon, which lent to his flamboyantreputation. While recovering from a bout of pneumonia at theHotel Dieu Hospital during the weekend of the JFK assassination Andrews was contacted by a Clay Bertrand, who requested Andrews go to Dallas and provide representation for Oswald. This seemingly bizarre request is not so strange when one considers that Andrews knew both Oswald and Bertrand. In July of 1964, Andrews described his first encounter with Oswald to Warren Commission counsel, Wesley Liebeler:

> **Andrews:** I don't recall the dates, but briefly it is this: Oswaldcame in the office accompanied by some gay kids. They wereMexicanos. He wanted to find out what could be done inconnection with a discharge, a yellow paper discharge, so I explained to him we would have to advance the funds to transcribewhatever records they had up in the Adjutant General's office.When he brought the money, I would do the work, and we saw himthree or four times subsequent to that, not in the company of thegay kids. He had this Mexicano with him."

Later, Andrews recalled how the "gay kids" were picked up in a police sweep of the French Quarter and how he was called by Clay Bertrand to defend them. Andrews also told the Warren Commission that on one of Oswald's subsequent visits, Oswald had asked about instituting citizenship proceedings for his Russian born wife, Marina. Andrews also ran into Oswald on Canal Street as he was handing out his Fair Play for Cuba literature. Andrews asked Oswald what he wasdoing "handing out that junk." According to Andrews, Oswaldreplied that it was a job, and he was getting paid to do it. As forhis call from Bertrand, Andrews testified:

> **Andrews:** I was in Hotel Dieu and the phone rang and a voice Irecognized as Clay Bertrand asked me if I would go to Dallas and Houston - I think -Dallas, I guess, wherever it was this boy wasbeing held - and defend him. I told him I was sick in the hospital.If I couldn't go, I would find somebody that could go…. He[Bertrand] is the one who calls on behalf of the gay kids normally,either to obtain bond or parole for them. I would assume that he was the one that originally sent Oswald and the gay kid…

An obviously frightened Andrews would later offer authorities varying descriptions of Bertrand, but what is important here is the intimidation of Andrews by the FBI to retract his statement.Liebeler later asked Andrews about his claims to the FBI that thewhole thing was "a figment of his imagination":

> **Andrews:** That's what the Feebees [the FBI] put on ... I told them, "Write what you want, that I am nuts. I don't care" ... You can tell when the steam is on. They are on you like the plague. They never leave. They are like cancer. Eternal.

The "figment of his imagination" defense has been promulgated through the years by defenders of the Warren Report who cling to the Report's conclusion that Andrews was heavily medicated at the time he supposedly spoke with Bertrand. However, a careful look at the evidence proves the opposite to be true. In fact, the FBI's own reports disprove the Warren position. On December 3, 1963, Agents Regis Kennedy and Reed Jensen interviewed Andrews. Their subsequent reportstates:

> ANDREWS stated the principal reasons why he feels that thetele-phone call was not a dream was because of the action he took in contacting Mr. SAM "MONK" ZELDEN, President of the Ne-wOrleans Criminal Bar Association and a close personal friend on Sunday, November 24, 1963 by telephone, reaching him at theNew Orleans Athletic Club and discussing with him the propriety of de-fending OSWALD and asking ZELDEN if he would be interested in assisting in the defense. ANDREWS recalls this call and further recalls that it was Attorney ZELDEN who told him that LEE HAR-VEY OSWALD had been shot and that this news had just come over the television station.ANDREWS advised that in addition to talking with ZELDEN, he had discussed receiving this call from CLAY BERTRAND with his investigator, Sergeant R.M. DAVIS, United States Army Retired, and his secretary, EVA SPRINGER, as well as his wife.

Three days later on December 6th, Kennedy re-interviewedAndrews and wrote in his report that:

> ANDREWS advised that based on the discrepancy between his-memory and facts as related to him by his employees and further the fact that he cannot identify CLAY BERTRAND, he can reach only one conclusion, that is, that the call received by him while in Hotel Dieu Hospital under sedation, was a figment of his imagi-nation. But on this same day, Kennedy also interviewed Andrews' employees, R.M. Davis and Eva Springer. According to Davis,An-drews was "positive that a person named Clay Bertrand had called

him on the telephone." Further, Andrews mentioned Clay Bertrand to Davis on Sunday, November 24 and Davis was under the impression that Bertrand was well known toAndrews. Davis also recalled Andrews mentioning to him on various occasions that an individual named Oswald had been inAndrews' office. In fact, Davis remembered discussing with Andrews the procedure for upgrading an undesirable discharge from the Marine Corps. Although Eva Springer could not recall ever seeing Oswald in the office, she did recall Andrews speaking to her about amending a Marine Corps discharge. Regarding the Bertrand call, Springer told Kennedy that Andrews called her at home on November 23rd and advised her that he was going to Dallas to represent Oswald at the request of a "Bertrand" She was even able to fix the time of thecall at 4:00 PM due to the fact that she had just returned homefrom her weekly routine trip to the grocery store.

That still leaves open the question of whether Andrews was heavily sedated at the time of the call. A check of the hospital records would certainly resolve that issue and the FBI did just that. On December 5th, Special Agent Richard Bucaro reviewed Andrews' medical record. It clearly states that on November 23rd Andrews did not receive any sedation until 8:00 PM. Recall that according to Eva Springer, Andrews informed her of the Bertrand call at 4:00 PM. Thus, Special Agent Kennedy had corroborative statements from Andrews'employees regarding Oswald's visits and the Bertrand call, as well as medical records showing Andrews was not under sedation at the time of the phone call from Bertrand. Yet Kennedy falsified his report stating the opposite as fact. Even Andrews said as much to the Warren Commission. There can be no doubt at this point that a deliberate cover-up of this matter had commenced. The fear remained with Andrews for a long time. Andrews later changed his story multiple times with local restaurant worker Eugene Davis taking the place of Shaw as the mysterious Clay Bertrand. Andrews would later be charged with perjury for his continuously morphing testimony. Both Mark Lane (1967) and Anthony Summers (1980) revealed that Andrews would never confirm the key points of his narrative for fear of retribution not from New Orleans but from Washington!

However, the new research by Donald Jeffries and William Law shows that the hospital visit (and the administration of drugs) may have been more sinister than originally thought. This new compelling information comes from Dean Andrews III and is one of many shocking new revelations in this book.

I was personally glad to see the authors' use of Church Committee documentation of the INS' confirmation of Garrison's thesis based on INS' little known investigatory work on "Oswald in New Orleans" (The title of the 150-page Church Committee document). To my knowledge this was only revealed in a public forum during my 2017 speech at the George Marshall Center for Leadership and Ethics on the campus of VMI.

Jeffries and Law continue this compelling narrative by laying out what they call the "ground level" conspirators with new information being revealed in a series of interviews with names the reader may have heard before but not have associated with this ground level plot. Through these interviews they deftly lay out connections and the new information from names both familiar and unfamiliar such as Clay Shaw, Guy Banister, David Ferrie, Sergio Arcacha Smith, Kerry Thornley, Carlos Bringuier, Layton Martens, Jack Ruby and Phil Geraci (a young man in the Ferrie, Oswald, Banister nexus whose importance is highlighted in Weisberg's work especially *Never Again*). Many of these interviews were conducted by knowledgeable researcher and co-author William Law and appear here for the first time. His interview with Garrison witness Perry Raymond Russo from 1993 is illuminating. Having interviewed Russo for a full day myself just a year later I can vouch for its significance.

Additionally, the authors provide new information on the shadowy front company and obvious assassination bureau, Permindex.

In addition to the interviews, the book provides supporting documentation for the research by way of appendices that include the Warren Commission testimony of Andrews, new documentation on David Ferrie, an information laden letter from Colonel L. Fletcher Prouty to Oliver Stone and an important interview of investigator Anne Dischler who, with Louisiana State Police officer Francis Fruge investigated the "Clinton witnesses." Her interview alone is must-read information for the researcher community (The Clinton witnesses credibly tied together Shaw, Ferrie and Oswald or someone who looked very much like him).

Although there has been much good work done on the New Orleans aspect of this case (DiEugenio, Flammonde, et al), Jeffries and Law show that the Big Easy is still a rich mother lode of leads to be mined to this very day.

Clay Shaw and attorney Ed Wegamann, 3/1/67.

INTRODUCTION

In recent years... forces have developed in our government over which we have no control, and these forces have an authoritarian approach to justice—meaning they tell you what justice is.
                                                      – Jim Garrison

Why another Kennedy assassination book? With the sixtieth anniversary of the terrible events in Dallas that November weekend in 1963 looming, it seemed important to try to set the record straight about a crucial part of this case: the investigation by New Orleans District Attorney Jim Garrison. There have been other important works on the subject, most notably Harold Weisberg's *Oswald in New Orleans*, but none delved as deep as we do in this book, into the particulars of what we call the Ground Level Plot. The connections are everywhere, and they cannot be innocently explained.

The book was inspired by the close friendship between Dean Andrews III, son of the colorful New Orleans lawyer who was at the center of Garrison's initial investigation, and Richard E. Jeffries, brother of co-author Donald Jeffries. Jeffries was dubious when his brother first told him about Dean. But he invited him over for dinner, and when he brought out the scrapbooks for the New Orleans Jazz Festival, which Jeffries was aware his father had run for years, he knew he was the real deal. Dean would attend numerous family gatherings at the Jeffries home over the years, and was fascinated by how much the brother of "my main man Rich" knew about the assassination. Dean related how he'd met director Oliver Stone and lead actor Kevin Costner, while they were working on the 1991 film *JFK*. They wanted actor John Candy to follow Dean around to ape his mannerisms. Candy would play Dean's father, the colorful New Orleans lawyer Dean Andrews, Jr. in Stone's film. Dean turned them down, primarily due to his mother's objections. Dorothy Andrews had dinner at the Jeffries home in 2003. It was the first time she'd ever discussed Garrison's investigation with anyone. She had basically taken the position that her husband was crazy, and their lives were ruined because of it. Dean III related how his father had become increasingly paranoid, and despite what he'd said on the witness stand (which would result in conviction for perjury), or on the one-sided attack on Jim Garrison aired by NBC, he most definitely knew there had been a conspiracy.

Jim Garrison's interest in the JFK assassination was first triggered by reading the Warren Commission testimony of Dean Andrews, Jr., whom he knew well. Dean III would relate how Garrison would call their home on a regular basis, and greet him, with "Hello, young Dean." On the afternoon of November 23, 1963, Andrews was in the hospital when he received a phone call from a Clay Bertrand, asking him to represent the still alive Lee Harvey Oswald as his attorney. Andrews thereafter phoned his secretary Eva Springer, and told her he had been retained as Oswald's lawyer, indicating that he had accepted. He also told her that "Bertrand" had been the one who'd contacted him. Springer rather oddly told him she wouldn't come to Dallas and help him in his role as Oswald's attorney. When Oswald was killed the following day, Andrews contacted the Secret Service in New Orleans, and on November 25 he was interviewed by them and the FBI. Andrews explained that he had done business for Oswald in trying to appeal his military discharge status. He initially mentioned "Clay Bertrand" to the government agents, but would soon change his story for the first of many times. Few researchers have truly studied this call, or asked the questions they should about it. Why was Andrews contacted? Clay Shaw, calling under his alias "Bertrand," could have picked any lawyer, if he had been assigned this role by whoever his superior in the plot was. Why choose Andrews, who wasn't a high profile defense attorney? Or was Shaw being used for purposes he wasn't aware of? Didn't the plotters already know that Oswald wouldn't be needing a lawyer, since they would be silencing him? Certainly they would have wanted someone they could trust, and Andrews fit that description, but why call Andrews in the hospital, when he wouldn't even be able to meet Oswald before Ruby murdered him? Dean Andrews, Jr. was a unique character whose importance has often been overlooked by researchers.

Jim Garrison's view that Lee Harvey Oswald was on assignment at the time of the JFK assassination, for whatever intelligence agency he was working for, to infiltrate what he was told was a brewing plot to kill the president, is one we share, as do many other researchers. We believe that Garrison uncovered the first layer of the onion. He found the ground-level conspirators, who were all, in our view, being manipulated like Oswald was. We know that Jack Ruby was an FBI informant with mob connections, and that David Ferrie had both CIA and Mafia connections. Clay Shaw was an asset of the CIA, which was proven by the testimony of former Agency official Victor Marchetti, who talked about Agency honcho Richard Helms instructing that everything possible be done to "help" Shaw when Garrison prosecuted him. We don't think that Oswald, Shaw, Ruby, Ferrie, or any of the anti-Castro exiles seemingly connected to them conspired to kill President John F. Kennedy. They were all being used like pawns, by the real conspirators, "who will never let the true facts come above board to the world," to quote Jack Ruby from his explosive videotaped interview. These were forces powerful enough to get the Secret Service to stand down and let the assassination happen, to control the autopsy, lose and destroy evidence, and to prevent the entire media from ever investigating the completely ridiculous lone-assassin narrative. Anti-Castro renegades and "rogue elements" of the CIA don't have that kind of power.

Jim Garrison was attacked relentlessly by our hopelessly corrupt state-controlled media, and by politicians in both parties. He was treated more unfairly than any other guest ever had been by Johnny Carson, in the history of *The Tonight Show*. His reputation was restored somewhat by Oliver Stone's hit movie *JFK*, and that certainly must have pleased Garrison immensely, who died a year after the film's release. Our friend John Barbour likes to say that "Jim Garrison solved this case." We think he did solve it, on the ground level. Faced with witnesses who were dying unnaturally, disappearing, or afraid to come forward, and governors who broke all legal protocol by refusing to extradite others essential to his case, Garrison did the best he could. The entire establishment was aligned against him.

We've done our best to take a fresh look at Garrison's investigation, with an emphasis on the role that Dean Andrews, Jr. played. The evidence shows that, despite all the powerful forces allied against him, and witnesses dying, disappearing, or being protected from extradition to Louisiana, the New Orleans district attorney's work unearthed some remarkable information. As Garrison said, "It is important to know who killed Jack Kennedy and why." The two of us have been seeking the answer to this crucial question for a very long time. Jim Garrison was on the right track, as you will learn in the book you are about to read.

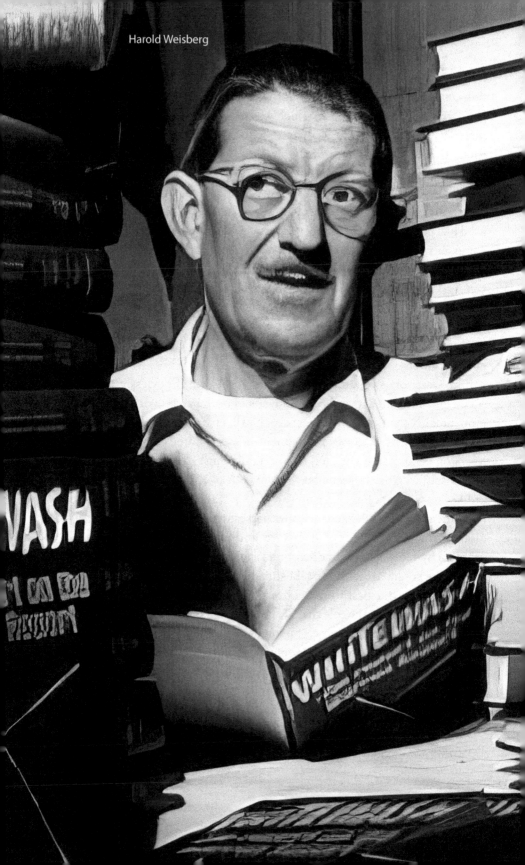
Harold Weisberg

CHAPTER ONE

HAROLD WEISBERG IN NEW ORLEANS

In view of Weisberg's character, he should not be given the information he requests, and there is legal ground for our position.

– J. Edgar Hoover

Harold Weisberg was perhaps the most cantankerous of all the often difficult JFK assassination researchers. But he also produced
the most work, and left behind an invaluable legacy. One of his
most often overlooked books is *Oswald in New Orleans: Case for Conspiracy
with the CIA*, published in 1967 by an actual publisher, unlike most of his
other works, which he was forced to print and market himself. It featured
one of the oddest Forewords you'll ever see in a book, by none other than
Jim Garrison himself. For unknown reasons, Garrison never mentioned either Weisberg or the book itself in the Foreword. Weisberg would turn on
Garrison, like several other prominent Warren Report critics, and was so
bitter towards him near the end of Garrison's life that he leaked an advance
script for Oliver Stone's 1991 film *JFK* to none other than the *Washington
Post's* veteran Warren Commission apologist George Lardner, Jr.

In the Foreword to Weisberg's book, Jim Garrison mentions that "the
only notes known to be taken during the long twelve- hour interview of
Lee Oswald after the assassination appear to have been burned."[1] This is
an intriguing reference, which seems to exist nowhere else in the assassination literature. Critics initially were understandably critical of the fact
that the Dallas Police had failed to record any of the interrogation sessions
with accused JFK assassin Lee Harvey Oswald. Years later, notes taken
by Dallas Police Captain Will Fritz belatedly emerged, but many critics
were dubious about their authenticity. Were the notes Garrison referred
to from Fritz, or some other unknown party?

Former Warren Commission member and future President Gerald
Ford spoke for the entire Establishment when he told UPI that New Orle-

ans District Attorney Jim Garrison should "immediately" send all the information he had on the case to "officials in Washington."[2] Garrison elicited a kind of vitriol from the mainstream media that had never been seen before. NBC News produced such a biased attack on him (prominently featuring the revised fanciful testimony of Dean Andrews, Jr.) that they were forced to give him thirty minutes of air time to respond. Reporters like Hugh Aynesworth and James Phelan took particular delight in ridiculing Garrison's investigation, and demeaning his character. Following document releases from the JFK Records Act passed in the wake of Oliver Stone's *JFK*, it was revealed that Phelan reported to the FBI after his early 1967 interviews with Garrison. Phelan's freelance work appeared in all the biggest mainstream outlets, and he was a staff writer for the *Saturday Evening Post* during the crucial years of 1963-1969. Aynesworth's credibility is best reflected in various claims he made over the years, from being a witness in Dealey Plaza to JFK's assassination, to being at the scene of the murder of Officer J.D. Tippit later that day, to being at the Texas Theater when Oswald was arrested, and finally to being present in the basement of the Dallas Police Department when Jack Ruby shot Oswald, despite the lack of any credible evidence. He grew close to Marina Oswald for a time and supposedly bragged to friends that he was sleeping with her. Assistant Dallas D.A. Bill Alexander leaked the dubious, alleged diary of Oswald to his friend Aynesworth, and they both went on to profit handsomely from selling it to *U.S. News and World Report* and *Life* magazine. In 1966, when *Life* magazine conducted its own investigation into the assassination, led by Richard Billings and Holland McCombs (a good friend, coincidentally, of Clay Shaw), Aynesworth became involved and went on to inform the FBI of the findings of the investigation. He also attempted to smear prominent Warren Commission critic Mark Lane by telling the FBI he was a homosexual. Aynesworth actually openly helped Clay Shaw's defense team. As author Jim DiEugenio wrote, "It would not be hyperbole to write that no other reporter in recorded history had as much to do in opposing a DA both covertly and overtly as Aynesworth did in New Orleans from 1967-71."[3]

A rough draft of Aynesworth's May 15, 1967 *Newsweek* article, "The JFK Conspiracy," is in the Lyndon B. Johnson Library. There is also a cover letter addressed to LBJ's press secretary George Christian. Aynesworth wrote, "I am not offering this for comment of any kind, nor a check of the validity of any part.... My interest in informing government officials of each step along the way is because of my intimate knowledge of what

Jim Garrison is planning ... I intend to make a complete report of my knowledge available to the FBI, as I have done in the past." What is an "independent" journalist doing essentially seeking approval from the White House, regarding a story about the investigation of the murder of the previous occupant? It is known that Aynesworth once had a keen interest in working for the CIA.[4] There are also many letters between Aynesworth and the lawyers for Clay Shaw, in the National Archives. These include examples of Aynesworth trying to intimidate witnesses at the Shaw trial. This "reporter" also used files that were stolen by Garrison staff turncoat William Gurvich. Even some of his fellow mainstream journalists chastised both Aynesworth and Phelan, charging that "Jim Phelan and Hugh Aynesworth, both fiercely anti-Garrison, became in effect special advisors to the defense... The two of them, says chief defense attorney F. Irvin Dymond, were 'extremely valuable' to the defense case..."[5]

Aynesworth also aided the efforts of Walter Sheridan, a former aide to Robert F. Kennedy in the Justice Department, whose journalistic career seems limited to the work he did for NBC News in trying to destroy Jim Garrison. In the 1990s, when the Assassination Records and Review Board requested Sheridan's files from the aforementioned monstrously biased NBC special attacking Garrison, his family sent the files to NBC, which they refused to release. ARRB chairman Judge John Tunheim was so angry at the television network that he had the Board's legal counsel prepare a subpoena. However, the Bill Clinton Department of Justice wouldn't serve the subpoena. Lyndon Larouche's organization would later tie Sheridan to the shadowy, international assassination bureau Permindex. Garrison was rumored to be interested in Permindex, and Clay Shaw's supposed position on its board. Sheridan worked on planting infiltrators inside Garrison's investigation, the most notable being New Orleans private investigator William Gurvich. Garrison would hire Gurvich but never trust him, explaining that "we soon learned that he was having meetings with Walter Sheridan."[6]

In a June 19, 1967 memo to Garrison, Assistant D.A. Andrew J. Sciambra described how Sheridan had tried to bribe their key witness, Perry Raymond Russo. "Russo said that Walter Sheridan of NBC News told him that the President of NBC contacted Mr. Gherlock [Russo's boss] at Equitable's home office in New York and Gherlock assured the President of NBC that if Russo did cooperate with NBC in trying to end the Garrison probe, that no retaliation would be taken by Equitable against Russo by the local office, on instruction from the home office." The memo read,

"Russo said that he told Sheridan that he needed a rest as the news people have been bothering him day and night and that he would take a seven-to-ten day vacation in California ... Russo said that Sheridan then told him that if he did side up with NBC and the defense and bust up the Garrison probe that he would have to run from Garrison and move from Louisiana. Sheridan said that they could set him up in California, protect his job, get him a lawyer and that he could guarantee that Garrison could never get him extradited back to Louisiana. Sheridan asked him if he would like to leave now and Russo told him no ... Russo said that Sheridan told him that what he wants Russo to do is to get on a NBC national television show and say, 'I am sorry for what I said because I lied, some of what I said was true, but I was doctored by the District Attorney's staff into testifying like I did.'" Sciambra continued, "Perry said James Phelan of the *Saturday Evening Post* told him that he was working hand in hand with Townley and Sheridan and they were in constant contact with each other and that they were going to destroy Garrison and the probe. Three weeks later, Walter Sheridan was indicted for bribery in relation to the Russo tampering. Two weeks later, Sheridan posted a $5,000 bond, but began a series of legal maneuvers to protect himself from appearing before the Orleans Parish grand jury. On Aug. 19, 1967, a hearing was held in Chicago Federal District Court by order of the U.S. Supreme Court to determine whether illegally obtained wiretap evidence had been used to convict Jimmy Hoffa and six associates. One of the defendants, Zachary "Red" Strate, testified that 'Walter Sheridan offered me evidence of government bugging so I could get a new trial at my hearing in Chicago, in exchange for helping discredit Jim Garrison... I gather Sheridan was working for Robert Kennedy. He said he was interested in stopping the probe of Kennedy's death in New Orleans.'"

Tom Bethell was another infiltrator inside Garrison's ranks. He was accused of taking a memo for the prosecution, which contained the names of each witness in the Shaw case, and summing up their testimony while sharing it with Shaw's lawyers. Bethell's reputation was unscathed by his duplicity, and he would go on to become editor of *The Washington Monthly* in 1975, and then the Washington editor of *Harper's Magazine*. He became an editor and columnist for *The American Spectator*, was associated with the neocon powerhouse American Enterprise Institute, and a media fellow for Stanford University's Hoover Institution for twenty-five years. Bethell took contrarian views on topics like AIDS and evolution, which were included in his book *The Politically Incorrect Guide to Science*. Curiously, Penn Jones claimed that after meeting Bethell, who traveled from London with a photographer associated with Black Star Publishing, in response to Jones obtaining a letter purportedly smuggled out of prison from Jack Ruby, the future Garrison turncoat wound up staying with him from the end of 1966 until early 1967. Sylvia Meagher, who would be among many Warren Commission critics to later oppose Garrison, was rumored to have recommended Bethell to the New Orleans D.A. Bethell would perhaps even more oddly stay at Mary Ferrell's home for a period after fleeing New Orleans after he'd been exposed. Ferrell's motivation for stockpiling a voluminous amount of JFK assassination evidence remains murky. She admittedly never liked the Kennedys, and some researchers grew suspicious of her. Another spy in Garrison's ranks was Bill Boxley, a former CIA staffer whose real name was William Wood. Garrison accused him of stealing files from his office. In another of those endless connections associated with this case, Bethell's friend Warwick Reynolds just happened to be the roommate of Lee Harvey Oswald's fellow Marine Kerry Thornley, whom we will be discussing at length later.[7] Yet a third infiltrator in Garrison's ranks was his investigator Pershing Gervais, an IRS informant who would testify in a bribery trial against Garrison in 1973, from which the former New Orleans D.A. emerged victorious. And there was Alberto Fowler, a Bay of Pigs veteran who was Director of International Relations for the City of New Orleans. Fowler became one of Jim Garrison's investigators, and the entire time was reporting on the progress of the investigation to none other than Carlos Bringuier, whom we will also be closely scrutinizing.

Garrison evoked, and continues to evoke, hatred in not only the mainstream media and court historians, but in many of those who claim to dispute the official story of the JFK assassination as well. Anthony Summers, author of the widely regarded book *Conspiracy,* blasted Garrison's investigation as having "long been recognized by virtually everyone— including serious scholars who believe there was a conspiracy—as a grotesque, misdirected shambles."[8] Paul Hoch lambasted Oliver Stone's use of the real (and dying) Jim Garrison, playing the role of Earl Warren in *JFK,* noting that he "did much to discourage or co-opt other investigations." David Lifton called Garrison "intellectually dishonest, a reckless prosecutor, and a total charlatan."[9] The previously mentioned Sylvia Meagher, author of *Accessories After the Fact,* still one of the most respected books on the assassination, also inexplicably turned against Garrison. Most interestingly of all, Harold Weisberg, in a bitter letter to Oliver Stone, wrote,

21

"You have every right to play Mack Sennett in a Keystone Kops *Pink Panther,* but as an investigator, Jim Garrison could not find a pubic hair in a whorehouse at rush hour."[10] He trashed Stone's film and was quoted by his supposed long-time adversary George Lardner, Jr. in the hit piece "On the Set: Dallas in Wonderland," that appeared in the *Washington Post,* on May 19, 1991, as saying, "I think people who sell sex have more principle." In fact, a good deal of Garrison's investigation revolved around the research of Harold Weisberg. So why did he come to essentially discredit his own work?

Jim Garrison zeroed in on David Ferrie very early. But Ferrie's name was coming up just as early in the government's "investigation." On November 24, 1963, immediately after Oswald was killed, his wife Marina was subjected to a grueling interrogation by the Secret Service. Among the questions they asked was if she knew a "Mr. Farry." Since David Ferrie, to whom this unquestionably referred, wasn't arrested and questioned by Garrison's office until November 25, how did anyone in Washington, D.C. know about Ferrie before that?[11] Weisberg discovered an FBI report of December 2, 1963, describing agents Eugene P. Pittman and John C. Oakes interviewing NBC cameraman Gene Barnes. The interview reads, "Barnes said Bob Mulholland, NCB [sic—should be *NBC*] News. Chicago, talked in Dallas to one Fairy, a narcotics addict now out on bail on a sodomy charge in Dallas. Fairy said that Oswald had been under hypnosis from a man doing a mind-reading act at Ruby's 'Carousel.' Fairy was said to be a private detective and the owner of an airplane who took young boys on flights 'just for kicks.'"

Weisberg appeared on many talk radio shows while he conducted his investigation in New Orleans. At the end of a December 15, 1966 interview with Oakland, California radio station KNEW, a caller asked Weisberg if he could speak to him off the air. The caller claimed to have served in the Marines with Oswald, and had been debating for three years about going public. He said he didn't believe a single thing that had been reported about Oswald during this time period. The man, who insisted on remaining anonymous out of fear for his family, remembered Oswald as a bright, quiet, and serious guy. He never heard him say anything about communism. He claimed Oswald held a favored position in the Marines, and possessed a special "crypto" top security clearance level. Weisberg talked to the man for over an hour and a half, and finally asked him to write his key points in a letter. The man was paranoid that his writing—or even the typewriter he was using—could be traced. He said he'd consider getting a trusted friend to copy his handwriting, but Weisberg never heard back from him.[12]

Dean Andrews, Jr.'s testimony is, unlike virtually all others in the Warren Commission's volumes of Hearings, intriguing, entertaining, and valuable. Andrews talked about Oswald's connections with "Latinos," "Mexicanos," and "Cubanos." He referenced these Hispanics being "gay" or homosexual. He stated that he wanted to find Clay Bertrand, the mysterious caller who'd attempted to get him to represent Oswald as his attorney. As noted, it was that November 23, 1963 phone call, which Andrews claimed to have received at the hospital where he was a patient, that would later help reignite Garrison's interest in the assassination. He said that his secretary Eva Springer didn't remember Oswald at all. Counsel Wesley Liebeler clearly attempted to get Andrews to say he'd been doped up and imagined the phone call. At one point saying, "you finally came to the conclusion that Clay Bertrand was a figment of your imagination?" Andrews scoffed back, "That's what the Feebees [FBI agents] put on." He said he'd told them, "Write what you want, that I am nuts. I don't care." He stated, "They are on you like the plague. They never leave. They are like cancer. Eternal." Andrews described "Bertrand" as "about 5 feet 8 inches. Got sandy hair..." This was obviously not the tall, distinguished Clay Shaw. Liebeler confronted Andrews with the FBI report of an interview he had with Regis Kennedy on December 5, 1963, in which he remembered Bertrand as 6 feet 1, or 6 feet 2 and "well dressed." Andrews replied, "I don't play Boy Scouts and measure them." Andrews claimed Bertrand was a bisexual "swinging cat." Andrews testified that Oswald had come into his office a "Minimum of three, maximum of five" times.

Andrews' most memorable statement came when he suddenly blurted out, "There's three people I am going to find: One of them is the real guy that killed the president; the Mexican; and Clay Bertrand." Liebeler replied, "Do you mean to suggest by that statement that you have considerable doubt in your mind that Oswald killed the President?" Andrews boldly responded, "I know good and well he did not. With that weapon, he couldn't have been capable of making three controlled shots in that time." When a predictably dismissive Liebeler questioned his qualifications, Andrews declared, "I am basing my opinion on five years as an ordnanceman in the Navy." He later reiterated, "This boy couldn't do it ... I think he is a patsy. Somebody else pulled the trigger."[13] Andrews stressed that it was Clay Bertrand who sent Oswald and the "Mexicanos" to him. Andrews noted that "I said that I wasn't in shape enough to go to Dallas and defend him and I would see what I could do." If this was the case, then why did he immediately contact both Eva Springer and attorney Monk Zelden, and ask them to come to Dallas and help him out with Oswald's defense? Dean Andrews couldn't produce any records of Oswald visiting him and engaging his services, but claimed that these files were among those stolen from his office. As Dean told the Warren Commission, "My office was rifled shortly after I got out of the hospital, and I talked with the FBI people." Andrews' private investigator Prentiles or Preston (Sarge) Davis said he was also told by Andrews that he would be going with him to Dallas to represent Oswald. Davis was noticeably nervous when questioned by Garrison's office. Davis recalled a break in to Andrews' office, while Eva Springer did not. Davis even said that Springer (whom he called "an old maid") was the one who discovered the break in. As Harold Weisberg noted, "In Whitewash where for the first time Andrews's sensational testimony was brought to public light and its probable meaning set forth, I pointed out that one simple way of confirming part of his testimony or disproving it would have been to call Zelden as a witness and ask him if Andrews had phoned to request him to defend Oswald. This was not done."

In a February 26, 1967 three-way interview with Harold Weisberg and Dean Andrews, Harv Morgan of KCBS confronted the New Orleans lawyer with some of his provocative statements before the Warren Commission. Andrews denied making them, then suddenly said, "Say, is this being taped?" When informed it was being broadcast on live radio, Andrews exclaimed, "Somebody's out of his mind!" then hung up. To Boston radio host Bob Scott, Andrews explained that "I like to live. If a guy can put a hole in the President, he can just step on me like an ant." Repeating what he said before the Commission, when he declared that he wanted to find out who really killed Kennedy, Andrews told Scott that regarding Oswald, "Oh, he never killed him. All the people know that. He ain't nothing but a decoy.... You can't win for losing in this game.... He's just a patsy." He noted, "Well, I got the shortest memory in the world. Round about a minute." After detailing how he thought there'd been three assassins, Andrews closed with, One day we'll write a book. If you're ever down here, 'Who Killed Cock Robin?'"[14]

During Garrison's investigation, both UPI and the *Washington Star* simultaneously reported that the Warren Commission had investigated David Ferrie and found nothing suspicious, but Ferrie's name doesn't appear in the Commission's records.[15] The day after their stories were published, on February 24, 1967, George Lardner, Jr. in the *Washington Post* reported the same thing, that Ferrie had initially been cleared by the FBI. The *Los Angeles Times* echoed this theme the same day. Where are the FBI files relating to any investigation of Ferrie? On March 3, 1967, the *New York Times* quoted Warren Commission counsel Wesley J. Liebeler as saying that a "very substantial" FBI investigation had cleared Ferrie from being involved in any conspiracy. Liebeler claimed to have gone through "a substantial stack" of FBI reports on Ferrie, but again none of this made it into the Commission's record. Liebeler assured the *Los Angeles Times,* in that February 24 story, that in regards to Jim Garrison, "I personally don't think he has anything, because everything I have seen so far was aware to us then." On November 27, 1963, Ferrie told the FBI that he never loaned his library card to Oswald or anyone else. That was one of the persistent rumors connecting the two men. Ferrie produced his New Orleans library card, which had "N.R." for non-resident, stamped on it. The card had expired in March 1963. The Secret Service also questioned Ferrie about this library card, shortly after his dubious skating trip to Houston, with two young friends, on the evening of November 22, 1963. They asked him whether he ever lent his library card to Oswald, leading to logical speculation that perhaps the authorities had found Ferrie's card on Oswald. There is evidence that this indeed is what happened; in a November 25, 1963 FBI report, Layton Martens (another of Ferrie's endless supply of young companions) claimed that he'd been told by Ferrie's attorney and employer G. Wray Gill that Ferrie's library card had been found on Oswald when he was arrested. When Wray himself was questioned by the FBI, he said he'd talked to bail bondsman Hardy Davis, who had "informed him that he had learned through hearsay when Oswald was arrested by the Police Department in Dallas, Texas, he had in his possession a library card of David Ferrie." When the FBI spoke to Davis, it turned out his source had been Guy Banister associate Jack Martin, who seems to have been the source for a good many things. Oswald's landlady in New Orleans and another neighbor would tell Jim Garrison's office that Ferrie had visited them personally and inquired about a library card.

Discovered in a November 27, 1963 New Orleans FBI report, was the fact that in the days immediately following the assassination, David Ferrie was looking for something else; a particular photo. It was the Civil Air Patrol group picture, from a 1955 cookout, in which both he and Lee Harvey Oswald could be seen. The photo wasn't shown publicly until 1993, on a PBS *Frontline* special. Ferrie called a former CAP member, Roy McCoy, to see if he had a copy of the incriminating photo. McCoy and his wife later contacted the FBI and revealed the strange tale of Ferrie's desperate search for the photo. The man who snapped the picture, Chuck Frances, stated that he had told the FBI about Ferrie and Oswald knowing each other.

In his final days, Ferrie trusted Garrison's Chief Investigator Lou Ivon enough to admit that he knew both Oswald and Clay Shaw, and that Shaw hated Kennedy. Ivon told author William Davy that Ferrie was petrified: "… very scared – a wild man."[16] During their last time together, Ivon stayed at Ferrie's talking until 2 A.M. When he returned in the morning to check on Garrison's top witness, Ferrie wasn't there. Ivon and others searched New Orleans, especially Decatur Street, where both Carlos Bringuier's store and Orest Pena's bar were located, places Ferrie was most likely to have gone, without success. Ferrie would be found dead three days later.

As he himself predicted, David Ferrie died under exceedingly strange circumstances on February 22, 1967. His body was found by a "blonde haired boy with long sideburns, not identified by the police," who claimed he didn't know Ferrie but "just happened to wander in." Among Ferrie's collection of 3,000 books was "a full assassination library." Coroner Nicholas Chetta found that Ferrie had to have died before 4 A.M., which makes *Washington Post* reporter George Lardner, Jr's presence there until 4 A.M. a bit difficult to explain. "Ferrie was certainly living when I said goodbye to him Wednesday shortly before 4 A.M.," Lardner declared, and saw "nothing inconsistent" about it.[17] Lardner would claim that Ferrie told him that night, before he died, that he feared Garrison's "witch hunt."[18] What was Lardner doing there until nearly 4 A.M.? Is this a normal time for reporters to conduct interviews? As Harold Weisberg asked, "Lardner stayed to 4? Sounds pretty strange under any circumstances. Lardner doesn't notice Ferrie's distress?" Lardner was a unique character. He won a Pulitzer Prize for reporting on the 1992 murder of his own daughter. Some have suspected that he was part of the CIA's notorious Operation Mockingbird plan to infiltrate the media with sympathetic assets. That would be a perfect description for Lardner's decades of dishonest reporting on the JFK assassination. Despite the presence of two typewritten, unsigned suicide notes, Ferrie's death was ruled to have come from a brain aneurysm. There were supposedly no signs of a struggle. Coroner Dr. Nicholas Chetta, who initially ruled that Ferrie had died before midnight, but dutifully changed the time to fit with Lardner's story, would die at only fifty years of age, supposedly of a heart attack, on May 25, 1968. Chetta administered sodium pentothal to key Garrison witness Perry Raymond Russo and hypnotized him, and testified that he "definitely was not faking" and "fulfilled all the requirements of legal sanity." Chetta found Russo to be a "very rational, controlled and well-disciplined individual."[19] Russo claimed to have heard Oswald, Ferrie, and Shaw plotting to kill President Kennedy.

There were other mysterious deaths connected to just this one aspect of Garrison's investigation. Nicholas Chetta's brother-in-law Henry De-laune was murdered in early 1969. Jules Delaune (presumably his broth-er), a pallbearer at Chetta's funeral, died at only forty-eight in January, 1971 (no cause of death listed).[20] Dr. Mary Sherman, who'd allegedly been working with David Ferrie on cancer research, died in a suspicious fire, in March of 1967. As author Ed Haslam revealed in his 2014 book *Dr. Mary's Monkey*, in the bedroom where her body was found, the curtains, furniture, books, carpet and blanket showed no signs of fire, despite the fact her charred body had been found on the bed. And as happens in most fires, the cause of death was actually due to a stab wound to the heart. There were several other stab wounds found to have been added after her death, presumably for indecipherable staging purposes. Perhaps most incredibly, Eladio del Valle, another anti-Castro exile leader, was shot through the heart on the same day Ferrie died, with a hatchet through his head leaving a suitably terrifying exclamation point. He supposedly had used David Ferrie as a pilot. Del Valle was a prominent figure in his native country, being an ex-Cuban congressman. Former Havana news-paperman Diego Tendedera claimed to have been friends with del Valle, and wrote about his highly suspicious death in the Spanish newspaper *El Tiempo*. His work was reprinted in the April 30, 1967 *National Enquirer* where he was quoted as saying, "On February 22, a Cuban refugee named Eladio del Valle was brutally murdered in Miami. I knew the victim well. And I am convinced he was executed because he had information about a conspiracy that led to the assassination of President John F. Kennedy. I do not say this lightly. For I believe that del Valle's killers plan to silence me, too. Anonymous callers have threatened my life." Tendedera contin-ued, "It was there (Miami) that I met Ferrie. As a freelance pilot, he was flying scores of missions with del Valle to drop bombs on Cuba. For six months I saw Ferrie and del Valle together almost every day. They'd take off two or three times a week in del Valle's twin-engined Apache to drop incendiaries on strategic targets and rescue anti-Communist Cubans who wanted to escape. Del Valle told me he gave Ferrie $1,000 to $1,500 per flight, depending on whether they would just drop bombs or would have to land on some highway to pick up refugees, a far more dangerous mission. I never really trusted Ferrie. And del Valle didn't either. He once told me: 'Ferrie has guts. We've saved dozens of our friends. But I don't fully trust him. He'd sell us out if he could.'" Tendedera conducted his own investigation, and reported, "Five days after del Valle's death a highly reliable informer confided in me that del Valle had been murdered in the Miami house of a woman who subsequently disappeared. The police are still looking for her. I drove to the house and neighbors told me the police already had been there. Neighbors also told me del Valle had been a frequent visitor at the house before his death. He played cards there with other refugees. The neighbors recalled how police carted away a sofa and bathtub, complete with plumbing, from the murder site. And one man told me how at 6:30 a.m. the morning following the murder he glanced out the window and saw the woman of the death house load a suitcase and two heavy lamps into her car and drive off with a companion." Some researchers have linked Del Valle to the CIA, mob boss Santo Trafficante, and Florida Senator George Smathers, close friend of JFK's who was rumored to be replacing LBJ on the 1964 presidential ticket. Del Valle had supposedly been show a photo of Oswald in the company of two persons, at the time that the Fair Play for Cuba leaflets were being passed out in the street. Del Valle identified one of the men as Manuel Garcia Gonzales, who according to the *National Enquirer*, was "now target of a world-wide manhunt." Like so many others involved in this case, the article notes that the married del Valle "was well known as 'bisexual.'" Evidently, the first person to identify this man as Gonzales was Dean Andrews, Jr. Apologists for the official story maintain that Andrews created this fictitious character, and Garrison seems to have been unable to find him. He was being assisted by another anti-Castro Cuban, Bernardo DeTorres, working as a private investigator. Garrison came to distrust DeTorres, writing across a memo from him on January 11, 1967, "His reliability is not established." DeTorres would be questioned by a federal grand jury in 1976 about the assassination of Chilean politician Orlando Letelier.

Yet another anti-Castro Cuban, David Morales, is suspected of involvement in the assassination by some researchers. Morales supposedly told friends, "I was in Dallas when we got the son of a bitch, and I was in Los Angeles when we got the little bastard." In his deathbed "confession," legendary CIA agent E. Howard Hunt named Morales, along with the CIA's Cord Meyer and David Atlee Phillips, and Watergate figure Frank Sturgis, as organizing the plot to kill Kennedy, at the behest of Lyndon Johnson.

Filmmaker Shane O'Sullivan would identify Morales as being near RFK in the Ambassador Hotel on the night he was shot. Some researchers quickly and predictably tried to debunk this, but O'Sullivan stood by his story. Morales died at just fifty two, right in the midst of the HSCA investigation. Quoting from the Spartacus Educational Forum: "David Morales made his last trip to Washington in early May, 1978. Ruben Carbajal had a drink with Morales a few days later. Carbajal told him he looked unwell. He replied: 'I don't know what's wrong with me. Ever since I left Washington I haven't been feeling very comfortable.' That night he was taken to hospital. Carbajal went to visit him the next morning. As Carbajal later recalled: 'They wouldn't let no one in, they had his room surrounded by sheriff's deputies.' Later that day (8th May) the decision was taken to withdraw his life support. Morales's wife, Joanne, requested that there should not be an autopsy." Morales had expressed fear of his "own people" because "I know too much." In a drunken rant witnessed by businessman Bob Walton, Morales once raged at JFK as "that no good son of a bitch motherf***er" and bragged, "Well, we took care of that son of a bitch, didn't we?"

Philip Geraci was a young associate of Oswald's who was questioned by the Warren Commission. Accompanied to the hearing by his mother Varola, Geraci made it clear that he didn't want to publicize the fact he was testifying. He described meeting Carlos Bringuier at his New Orleans radio shop the Casa Roca, when he was just fifteen. Geraci saw Oswald there "about the fourth time," later corrected to perhaps the fifth time, he met Bringuier. Geraci solicited donations and gave them to Bringuier. When he met Oswald there, he was accompanied by his friend Vance Blalock. Geraci described Oswald as seeming "nervous," claimed that Oswald questioned Bringuier "like he was connected with the Costa Nostra." In Vance Blalock's Warren Commission testimony, Liebeler refers to it as Casa Nostra, a Cuban organization. Strangely, Oswald offered to give Geraci his Marine Corps manual. The future patsy shared some provocative thoughts to Gerarci and Blalock, regarding what he'd learned about guerilla warfare, derailing trains, and "He said the thing he liked best of all was learning how to blow up the Huey P. Long Bridge." Geraci estimated he'd met Oswald in late July 1963, and didn't recall seeing Bringuier again until he looked him up after the assassination, "to get things straightened out and talk with Carlos a little about him, you know." In typical Warren Commission fashion, Liebeler asked no questions about why Geraci went to see Bringuier, or what they discussed. Mrs. Geraci broke in to ask, after

29

Liebeler said he had no further questions, "Do you have a record of me reporting Carlos to the FBI? Do you have that in the record anywhere where I found out – he told me he was going to collect money for Cuba, but I didn't know he was giving out these little tickets as he called them, and then when I found out he had collected $10 and brought it down and I saw the receipts and he had more tickets, we forbade him to go down there, and Carlos called the house to try to get him a – what is it – a license or permit to go from house to house and collect money."[21]

Garrison interviewed Geraci for hours on December 14, 1968, where it was inferred that he had to have seen Oswald at Bringuier's place (presumably the Casa Roca) much earlier than the August 5, 1963 first encounter Bringuier testified to. In his report summing up the interview, it is noted, "My impression is that he was trying to protect Bringuier…" This report (perhaps from Garrison himself – no author is credited) is dated December 15, 1968, and includes the interesting tidbit: "He told of a strange incident his mother confirmed, that at 2 A.M. the night David Ferrie died, meaning that early morning after it, he was awakened by Sgt. Borne of Jefferson Parish Sheriff's office, who had worked on his juvenile case, taken from Orleans into Jefferson Parish to the home of an uncle, and severely interrogated about Ferrie (he had been in Civil Air Patrol also but in 1962-3, and was looking for a proper shirt the first time he went to Bringuier's). He was told this questioning was for both parishes – specifically that it was for Garrison and would keep Garrison from troubling Geraci. He was reminded that '20 people' had met mysterious deaths – frightened – and kept in Jefferson Parish a week. He was reinterviewed on tape and told a copy would be given to Garrison's office. Neither Sciambra nor Ivon know anything of this. Why anyone would question Geraci about Ferrie is not clear. I suggest the possibility something else was sought." Harold Weisberg would suspect Fred O'Sullivan, an officer with the New Orleans Police vice squad, as being behind the odd late night/ early morning interrogation of Geraci. He also thought that O'Sullivan had recruited both Oswald and his high school best friend Edward Voebel into Ferrie's world. O'Sullivan had been one of Ferrie's "boys" in the Civil Air Patrol. Perhaps it's just clumsy wording, but is it being suggested here that Geraci was trying to buy a "proper shirt" at Bringuier's radio shop?

A May 6, 1965 FBI memo describes how the aforementioned Don Borne (then a deputy sheriff) notified the New Orleans office of the FBI that Geraci was a "mentally disturbed youth" who had "an interest in guerilla warfare, explosives, and the organizing of groups." He also stated that

Geraci "must hate his father with intense passion." He claimed that Geraci had tried to join the notorious Alpha 66 anti-Castro group, but was refused. There is a reference here to Geraci knowing a "Mario," who was thought to be a homosexual, almost certainly Mario Bermudez, a friend of Clay Shaw. It is more than intriguing that Bringuier attempted to connect the then sixteen-year-old Geraci with Oswald, when he was questioned by the authorities, stating that "he knew of no associates of Oswald with the possible exception of a Philip Geraci, III." Vance Blalock was more certain than Geraci that it was Oswald they had met, and specified that it was associated with the Cuban Student Directorate, an anti-Castro group, which met in Bringuier's Casa Roca store. He had the impression that Bringuier was the leader of the CSD. He testified to the same things Geraci had regarding the conversation with Oswald; guerilla warfare, how to derail a train and blow up bridges.

What is really bizarre is that Geraci, described in many online lists of mysterious witness deaths as "Perry Russo's friend," and often reported to heard a conversation between Oswald and Clay Shaw, among many other things, supposedly died from electrocution in August of 1968. This would, of course, have been four months *before* the interview quoted above. We found a Philip Geraci, born in New Orleans in 1926, who died there on August 17, 1968. Looking further into Garrison's files, there was a reference to "Phil Geracy (sic) father was electrocuted yest. Was not accident. Dept. of Justice is interested. Connected his son with other people who are important to invest." It is then clarified that the father was Philip Geraci II and Philip III the son. As noted, Bringuier had mentioned Geraci as the only possible associate of Oswald's he knew of. There are notes in both Garrison's and Weisberg's archives, to Geraci's father reporting him missing in 1965. Weisberg interviewed Geraci's parents, about a month before the father was electrocuted. Weisberg included the obituary of the elder Geraci in his archives. Weisberg's archives include a letter of condolence he sent to the widow, and a reference to "The paper says Philip is returning from Vietnam," and "I would like very much to talk to him." On the Find a Grave site, Geraci's wife and two daughters are listed (both died fairly young), but not his son or two other daughters. So "conspiracy theorists" were a bit sloppy here, confusing the father with the son, but Garrison certainly felt the death was mysterious, and Geraci remains an interesting and largely overlooked character.

In an FBI memo dated October 11, 1968, another reference is made to Geraci being in Vietnam. The memo concerns testimony from Bringuier, who in another memo is described as having provided information to the

New Orleans FBI office in the past. Bringuier notes that a woman named Dione Turner had received a letter from Geraci, in which he asked her to tell Bringuier that he had been contacted by Harold Weisberg, "author of the book *Whitewash*, who has been assisting New Orleans District Attorney James Garrison in his investigation of the assassination of President John Fitzgerald Kennedy." Geraci claimed that Weisberg told him he would be subpoenaed by the New Orleans Grand Jury "if he did not state that he had previously been hired by Carlos Bringuier and that he, Bringuier, and some other Cubans had gone to a training camp for Cubans in the New Orleans area." Weisberg supposedly told Geraci that his mother "had been cooperating with Garrison and had made some type of deal with him." Turner intimated that an unnamed "agency" was "building a case against Weisberg," for "spreading KGB propaganda in the United States." On November 6, 1968, Weisberg wrote to Garrison's aide Jim Alcock, recounting his recent meeting with Lillian Cohen, an attorney representing the Geracis. Weisberg noted, "She appears to be less than 100 percent certain the father's death was only accident. She had known him; he had done work in their home. The mother's interest, she thinks, in to protect her son…." On January 31, 1969, Cohen sent a letter to Mrs. Geraci, in which she stated, "I was very disturbed last week to learn that you had allegedly advised several persons (one of whom was Mr. Melvin H. Wright) that you personally did not want to prosecute any civil claims relative to your husband's death, but that you doing so because I had 'solicited' you in this matter. Further, I was advised by Mr. Wright that allegedly according to you I had persisted in calling you until you decided to go ahead with this case – otherwise, you would not have bothered with this case at all; except for my persistence and insistence you would not have done anything in the case. This, of course, is completely untrue as you well know, and it is personally offensive to me since I have gone out of my way to assist you in anything that I could without one cent of compensation."

Cleary the Geracis had been scared: Weisberg wrote a letter to Philip on February 12, 1969, in which he wonders why he hasn't heard from him. Weisberg was still looking into Bringuier and Dione Turner in 1978. Weisberg's records on Geraci are extensive. There is a bizarre reference to Geraci being "gangbanged" at a gay club, after Bringuier arranged for him to stay at a "dive" known as the Silver Dollar (interestingly, this was mentioned in a 1984 letter to researcher Gary Mack, who had yet to go over to the dark side at that point). There also seemed to have been some connection between Geraci and the previously mentioned "gay" Mario Bermudez, who was supposedly friends with Shaw. There seems to be no information available about Giraci's middle initial, but on May 25, 2011 a Philip A. Geraci was found guilty in a Lafayette, Louisiana courtroom of child pornography, obscenity, and sexual battery charges on an un-named underage victim, who is described in two places as both male and female. Geraci is listed as being forty-three-years-old, which makes him too young to be Oswald's friend. But it is certainly possible that it is Paul Geraci III's son.

The aforementioned Nicholas Chetta is another enigmatic figure here. After first claiming that he smelled poison on Ferrie, he ludicrously con-cluded that he had died from "natural causes," despite the presence of two suicide notes. But he was a character witness for Perry Russo, one of Garrison's crucial witnesses. Jack Martin, whom we will discuss at length later, commented that Chetta was notorious for selling "natural causes" verdicts "just like a prostitute." Martin had told Jim Garrison, in reference to the death of Ferrie's mother, that there "are a lot of ways of killing a guy without showing in an autopsy." We could find little on Ferrie's mother, other than that she died in 1962 at age eighty-two, in Pennsylvania and was buried in Ohio. Martin maintained that David Ferrie was "the key to everything." Of great interest is the fact that none other than Robert F. Kennedy phoned Nicholas Chetta, to find out the cause of Ferrie's death. Chetta had been getting so many calls about Ferrie that his teenage son at first believed it was a prank call, and slammed the phone down.[22]

Harold Weisberg claimed that 36 of the 40 pages in FBI File 75, just one of those on David Ferrie, were being suppressed. It is difficult to de-termine whether more of File 75 has been subsequently released. Such was the absurd coverage of the Garrison case that Associated Press, treat-ing David Ferrie like some kind of real psychologist and expert on the assassination, reported on February 23, the day after he died, that "Ferrie said it was fruitless to search for an accomplice for Oswald because 'my assessment of Oswald is that he would be incapable of any interpersonal relationship, especially anything as delicate as a conspiracy to kill.'" At the same time, AP reiterated that Ferrie had consistently denied knowing Os-wald. But he was still somehow an "expert" on him. One seldom reported tidbit in the records, which can be found in Warren Commission Exhib-it 75, consists of a November 27, 1963 FBI report, from Special Agent Nathan O. Brown, which recounted a mysterious long distance phone call on November 24, 1963 by Covington, Louisiana telephone operator Yvonne Cooper, that she had handled "two or three days previously." It was a person-to-person call to Lee Harvey Oswald at the "Texas State Book Depository." The person placing the call was an adult female, and when the Depository was reached, the person answering "advised she did not know who Oswald was." After being told Oswald was a new employee, with Cooper seeming to recall him being identified as a janitor, "at this point the answering party said 'oh' as if she knew who it was, and the call was completed." Cooper thought the call had originated from Slidell, Louisiana.

On March 2, 1967, Attorney General Ramsey Clark, adhering to a persistent anti-Garrison agenda, stated that the FBI had already investigated and cleared Clay Shaw. But in the same article, former Warren Commission Chief Counsel J. Lee Rankin was quoted as having said, "As far as I know, we've never heard of this person (Shaw)." Clark claimed that Shaw "was included in an investigation in November and December of 1963" and "We have the evidence ... there was no connection found."[23] Where is this "evidence?" Shaw's name doesn't appear in the Warren Commission's records. Of all people, George Lardner included this in a March 3 *Washington Post* story: "The Attorney General's remarks consequently amounted to an acceptance of Garrison's charge that Clay Shaw and 'Clay Bertrand' are one and same. 'It's the same guy,' said one source in the Justice Department." The only indication in the record that the FBI investigated Shaw is a November 27 FBI report from the busy Regis Kennedy, in which he reported that a cab driver with "extensive contacts in the New Orleans French Quarter, particularly among the homosexual element," claimed that Clay Bertrand was unknown to him or any of the sources he'd questioned. Interestingly, when Weisberg obtained the document, the sentence "CLAY BERTRAND was unknown to him" featured a blue "un" handwritten between "was" and "known." Regis Kennedy supposedly hounded Dean Andrews, Jr. to such an extent that Andrews told him to put whatever he wanted in his report.[24]

Weisberg quotes an unspecified news story about Oswald's enigmatic one time best friend Edward Voebel as saying, "A New Orleans florist, Edward Voebel, had seen Lee Harvey Oswald's picture on television and reported he and Oswald had served in a Civil Air Patrol squadron under Ferrie."[25] Voebel's Warren Commission testimony was wishy-washy on the subject, and Weisberg rightly condemned counsel Albert Jenner for his typical Warren Commission-style inept questioning, writing, "questions that should not remain, exist only because Jenner allowed it." Researchers might assume that the first reference to a connection between Oswald and Ferrie came in the statements of the enigmatic Jack Martin, as previously noted an associate of former-FBI-man-turned-private-investigator Guy Banister. Papers like the *Times-Picayune* disclosed that FBI reports revealed that Jack Martin had repudiated his statements about Ferrie and Oswald, but "Martin said he never told either the FBI or the Secret Service that he made up the story about Ferrie's association with Oswald."[26] According to the FBI report by Anthony Gerrets, which casts dispersions on Martin (calling him an alcoholic, claimed he had a reputation for giving bum information to police), Ferrie "had a very good idea who had reported him as having associated with Oswald, training him in the use of rifles with telescopic lenses, etc." He then provided Martin's name and home address. However, Weisberg traced the initial reports of a relationship between Ferrie and Oswald to Voebel (who like Ferrie died under very suspicious circumstances), and then Martin. Voebel was rushed to New Orleans's Oschner Clinic on May 16, 1971, feeling "mildly ill." The doctor asked if he'd been around any poisons. He died a few days later at just thirty-one. Researchers have linked Dr. Alton Oschner to the CIA.[27] Oschner injected his own grandchildren with the polio vaccine, tragically killing his grandson and resulting in his granddaughter developing polio.[28] Interestingly, a young Oschner was one of Huey Long's numerous political enemies. The Oschner Clinic specialized in treating wealthy South American dictators like the Somozas in Nicaragua, and Argentina's Juan Peron, with the CIA generously paying their bills.[29] Another notable patient was Dallas oilman Clint Murchison. Finally, Oschner was close friends with Clay Shaw, and president of the International Trade Mart's sister organization, the International House. According to author William Davy, there is a photograph in the New Orleans Public Library of Shaw and Oschner together in Shaw's office.

Weisberg closely scrutinized Orest Pena, who owned the Habana Bar and Lounge on Decatur Street in New Orleans. Pena read Weisberg's first book, *Whitewash: The Report on the Warren Report,* and sent him an unsolicited letter on March 25, 1967. He wrote "It is true," regarding what Weisberg called The False Oswald in the book.[30] Pena was an FBI informant who reported to agent Warren de Brueys. When he was deposed by the House Select Committee on Assassinations (HSCA), Pena revealed that he had "worked in some capacity for another United States government agency, which he refused to identify." Pena spoke of seeing Oswald at a restaurant with "other federal agents from the Customs House Building.

He refused to say if he'd ever seen Oswald and de Brueys talking to each other, but believed they knew each other 'very, very well.'" Interestingly, when Oswald moved to Dallas, so did de Brueys. A 1978 HSCA memo notes "Pena believes that Oswald was an agent of the U.S. government." Of greater significance is the statement in the memo that reads, "Pena did not testify on all relevant issues before the Warren Commission, because de Brueys had threatened him before he was scheduled to testify, and because Commission Counsel Wesley Liebeler did not cooperate." Pena had declared that Oswald was an FBI informant on CBS television in 1975. Interestingly, it was Pena who posted bond for Carlos Bringuier after his fight with Oswald while he was handing out Fair Play for Cuba pamphlets.[31]

The HSCA naturally believed de Brueys' denial of Pena's allegations. Pena's HSCA testimony from June 23, 1978 was finally declassified in 2017. In it, he claimed that David Ferrie was close to Bringuier, and had taught Pena how to fly. He revealed that Ferrie was good friends with Sergio Arcacha Smith, who had also worked with Guy Banister. When asked if Warren de Brueys ever attended Cuban Revolutionary Front meetings, Pena replied, "He was very frequently in the office talking in private with Mr. Sergio Arcacha Smith." He described how, after the assassination, "The FBI used to come to my place of business" to "aggravate and to give me a hard time." He detailed how de Brueys himself used to frequently visit his business "talking to all the customers." Pena called de Brueys "the most important person in the Kennedy assassination." He clarified that de Brueys had actually been transferred to Dallas shortly before the assassination. When pressed to talk about his possible relationship with the CIA, Pena answered, "Maybe if you investigate and get the real facts of the training camp that was run by the FBI and the CIA of the United States in New Orleans, the camp in New Orleans. Maybe I will remember something else later on." Clearly out of fear, he refused to say whether Oswald knew David Ferrie and Sergio Arcacha Smith. He mentioned that "Arcacha Smith will come around and start suing me. I have spent over $20,000 in attorneys' fees." Pena recounted how a frightened Ferrie came to his Habana Bar about twelve hours before he died, telling him it was very important that he see two people, one of whom was Arcacha Smith. Pena didn't specify who the second person was (and he wasn't asked by HSCA counsel Robert Genzman), but related how Ferrie had left the bar to talk to Carlos Bringuier, and came back to tell Pena that Bringuier denied knowing anything about Arcacha Smith or the other person.

Pena's testimony before Senator Frank Church's Committee, along with the testimony of other witnesses, has incomprehensibly disappeared. In the Weisberg Hood College archives, a letter from Weisberg to "Dick" dated September 26, 1991, mentions that Pena had telephoned him on an unspecified date, and said he couldn't talk long because he was at the hospital awaiting x-rays on his head. Weisberg wrote, "He said he'd been lead piped and he suspected it was because he had phoned me." Weisberg and Pena subsequently spent every night together in New Orleans during the week that MLK was killed. He told Weisberg that "'they' had tried to kill him, by staging an auto accident. His car was totaled. So he decided that if they were going to kill him, "Fuck it! I live it up." One night, after going to the Playboy Club, Pena found his parked car with all four tires slashed. No other cars were touched. This goes a long way towards explaining Pena's reticence with the HSCA. He was particularly unwilling to say anything regarding Oswald's connections to any of the prominent players in New Orleans.

An unnamed bartender at Cosimo's in the French Quarter told Garrison's assistant Andrew Sciambra that Bertrand was a regular customer and the alias for Clay Shaw. He recalled seeing Bertrand/Shaw on television often, "usually with important people." He recognized Clay Shaw instantly as the man named Bertrand who frequented his club so often. At around the same time, Sciambra questioned Shaw, and found that his testimony conflicted with other evidence they'd gathered. When asked where he was at the time of the JFK assassination, Shaw claimed he'd been traveling on a train to San Francisco. Garrison's office would subsequently find that Shaw was already in San Francisco when JFK was killed, in the company of San Francisco Trade Mart Director J. Monroe Sullivan. Shaw would later give yet another account of his whereabouts, telling the *New Orleans Times-Picayune* that he was in the St. Francis Hotel when he heard the news about Kennedy. Sullivan would dispute Shaw's claim that he'd invited him to speak, telling author William Turner that Shaw called him weeks earlier to ask him to set up a lunch gathering. Sullivan claimed that Shaw exhibited no reaction when they learned that JFK had been shot in Dallas, and insisted on going ahead with the lunch.[32]

In some of his finest, seldom touched upon research, Weisberg located the outfit that had printed up the Fair Play for Cuba leaflets Oswald passed out in New Orleans. Douglas Jones ran the small print shop that was located only a short distance from the Reily Coffee Company where Oswald had worked. When Weisberg went to interview Jones, Bill Boxley went along with him. Asked to identify the man who had picked up the handbills after they were printed, Jones selected four photos (out of approximately a hundred), all of the same individual: Oswald's strange fellow Marine, Kerry Thornley. Boxley would deny the identification of Thornley, but Weisberg had tape recorded the interview, and he was forced to admit he'd been "wrong." The tape of the conversation was suspiciously lost. Weisberg would later interview Jones' secretary Myra Silver, and she independently identified Thornley as well. Weisberg described how the government handled Jones after the assassination: "On December 3, 1963, Special Agent Donald C. Steinmeyer went to see Jones. His brief report of only 13 lines was dictated that day. Steinmeyer reports showing a picture of Oswald only to Jones. Steinmeyer's first sentence includes Jones as saying after examining that Oswald picture, 'that although he could not be positively sure, he said he did not believe the person ordering the printing on the handbills relating to Cuba last May 29 was OSWALD.' Steinmeyer's last sentence begins, "He [Jones] again stated that he could not positively say the person ordering the handbills was not OSWALD but he did not think it was." Silver was interviewed by the FBI as well, and also couldn't identify the man as Oswald. Weisberg casually mentions that "Jones was killed in Hurricane Camille, but not until I had interviewed him two times."

The history of the Fair Play for Cuba Committee was thoroughly researched by Paul Bleau. The FPCC was started in 1960 by CBS reporters Robert Taber and Richard Gibson, along with New Jersey contractor Alan Sagner. Among those who initially supported the organization were Truman Capote, Norman Mailer, and Jean-Paul Sartre. Taber and Gibson ran a full page ad for the FPCC in the *New York Times* on April 6, 1960. A FBI program called AMSANTA targeted the FPCC as a subversive outfit, but seems to have abruptly stopped in the fall of 1963. Bleau found an FBI file dated November 22, 1963, which noted that Oswald was the organizer and chairman of the FPCC in Texas. The same document states that Oswald was being polygraphed on the day of the assassination. If this ever happened, there is no record of it. And he unearthed a letter from Guy Banister, who from the letterhead appears to have been a 33rd degree Freemason – the highest rank in the shadowy order, to the FPCC in 1961. The CIA was also involved in the AMSANTA project, and David Phillips and James McCord monitored the FPCC for the Agency. Oswald, already notorious as a defector to the Soviet Union, would have stood out starkly to the government when he opened a chapter of the FPCC in New

Orleans in 1963. Bleau raised the question of finances here, something few have considered. Oswald was supposedly living on a shoestring budget, with his consistently low-paying jobs, with a wife and small child to support. Yet he had to factor in FPCC membership dues, the renting of a space, the costs of printing the leaflets, and the use of a post office box, among other things, without anyone to help with the costs, since he was allegedly the only member of his chapter. Oswald did tell Dean Andrews, Jr. that he was being paid $25 a day to pass out the leaflets. Bleau pointed out that the FBI, while infiltrating FPCC chapters all over the country, did not assign an informant to the New Orleans chapter. It seems obvious because they already had someone working there, as the president, Lee Harvey Oswald.[33]

As was pointed out so memorably in Oliver Stone's *JFK,* the address printed on Oswald's FPCC pamphlets, 544 Camp Street, housed Guy Banister's office in the same building, and was literally surrounded by offices of the CIA, Office of Naval Intelligence, FBI, and Secret Service.[34] Researcher William Davy discovered a letter Oswald had written to the Fair Play for Cuba Committee's New York headquarters, describing his street altercation while passing out the pamphlets. The difficult thing to explain about this letter is the fact it was written on August 4, 1963, five days *before* the incident took place. We knew that Oswald very strangely asked to speak to the FBI after the altercation. But according to Joan Mellen's research, he asked for agent Warren de Brueys specifically. The government had no explanation as to why both Marxist defector Lee Harvey Oswald and ultra anti-communist Guy Banister both shared the same 544 Camp Street address. On August 27, 1978, Banister's secretary Delphine Roberts was re-interviewed by HSCA Investigator Robert Buras. She told Buras that she "believes that LEE OSWALD came into the office to be interviewed for a job, but doesn't remember anything specific, because so many people came in for interviews. At a later date Banister introduced Marina and OSWALD to her in his office, but they walked right out and she did not talk to them. She could not recall hearing Marina speak, or how they were dressed. On several occasions LEE OSWALD would come in and go into Banister's office and she could not hear any conversation from that room. She believed that OSWALD was either working, or attempting to work, for Banister. She does remember hearing Guy Banister holler at Jim Arthus and Sam Newman about letting OSWALD the second-floor room and about keeping the Fair Play for Cuba Committee literature from his office. Arthus used to come into the office and put leaflets on Banister's leaflet table as a joke because all the other literature was anti-communist." Earl Golz of the *Dallas Morning News* would later quote Roberts as identifying Oswald as "an undercover agent" in an office above Banister's, which the ex-FBI man had arranged for him. The HSCA would conclude, in their typically milquetoast fashion, "there was at least a possibility that Oswald and Guy Banister were acquainted."

Paul Bleau's research also exposed the fact that among those linked to 544 Camp Street was William T. Walshe of the Mississippi Valley World Trade Center, an outfit whose secretary was none other than Clay Shaw. This organization was important enough that, during a visit by the First Deputy Premier of the Soviet Union in the Eisenhower years, it was debriefed along with John Foster and Allen Dulles, and President Eisenhower himself. Yet another intriguing figure associated with the address is Richard D. Reily, of the same family who owned the Reily Coffee Company, where Oswald had worked. It is of interest that Bleau refers to the enigmatic figures Jack Martin and David Lewis as being roommates.[35]

In a December 3, 1975 memo for the Senate Committee chaired by Frank Church, counsel Paul Wallach reported on his telephone conversation with Wendall Roache, head of IN&S' New Orleans Border Patrol Station. Wallach wrote, "IN&S New Orleans was charged with the responsibility of surveilling various Cuban 'groups' in New Orleans.... Included in this surveillance was the group of 'nuts' headed by David Ferrie.... He stated that Ferrie's office – on a side street between St. Charles and Camp … was under surveillance (although he never surveilled it, another inspector drove him past it and identified it); that Lee Harvey Oswald was seen going into the offices of Ferrie's group and 'Oswald was known to be one of the men in the group.' Wallach noted that Roache maintained both the New Orleans Police and the Sheriff's office had reports regarding Ferrie's group. Roache had only seen Oswald once himself, passing out handbills at a spot not too distant from Clay Shaw's New Orleans Trade Mart. Roache related the story of how Oswald, while in custody of the New Orleans Police, "would only speak Russian and the NOPD deduced that he was Russian." Roache claimed that Ron Smith (position not identified, but presumably an employee of the Border Patrol) went to the police station and identified Oswald as an American citizen. "After that, Oswald spoke in English."

Among the personal attacks and petty jealousy, there are some important finds in Weisberg's huge, unpublished *Inside the Assassination Industry*, which is available online in his Hood College archives. After describing meeting Dean Andrews' niece Pat Young in his office (he clearly was thrilled when she unexpectedly kissed him "full on the mouth"), Young informed them that she was leaving for Washington, D.C., to work for an unnamed intelligence agency. Weisberg raved about Andrews' Warren Commission testimony, in particular his critique of Oswald's marksmanship. He wrote that, with all his own years of experience on the subject, "There is no testimony at all that compares in its dependability and informativeness with Andrews.'"[36] At one point, Weisberg curiously writes, "I had no interest in Clay Shaw." He also said he had no interest in Carlos Bringuier, despite recounting being almost assaulted by him on one occasion. Weisberg, always a curmudgeon, grew increasingly bitter in his old age. His revisionist views are everywhere in this rambling memoir. Here he matter-of-factly states that Geraci's father "killed himself by accident in the course of his work."[37] Weisberg recounts making an agreement with Garrison, that he'd leave Geraci and other unspecified "youngsters" alone, if he questioned him and reported the results back to the D.A. Weisberg unfairly attacks Garrison for being uninterested in what he calls the "kidnapping" of Geraci by O'Sullivan and the NOPD. In fact, this is mentioned in memos from Garrison's office, and someone (perhaps Garrison himself) was skeptical about the death of Geraci's father.

Weisberg had fallen so sharply that on November 11, 1991 he penned a long, bitter and self-serving letter to the *New York Times,* which had (and has) consistently been in the forefront of covering up the truth about the assassination. In it, he blasted Jim Garrison personally, along with Oliver Stone's film. He spoke glowingly of the probable CIA Mockingbird asset George Lardner, "having known him for 25 years." He notes that he warned Oliver Stone that Garrison's book was a "fraud" and a "travesty." He calls Garrison "an egomaniacal fraud and poseur." He suggested the *Times* ask Lardner about his credibility. The revisionist Weisberg is on full display here. He dismisses the infamous "Tramps" as "winos." He ridicules the notion that Bill Boxley was a CIA plant. He smears the esteemed researcher Gary Shaw, and inaccurately claims that the co-author of his immensely underrated book *Cover-Up* was the late Larry Howard of the Assassination Information Center, when it was in fact Larry R. Harris, who died in a suspicious car crash. He terms Jim Marrs' invaluable book *Crossfire* a "compendium of nutty theories." Weisberg, who once called Penn Jones a friend, refers to him as "paranoidal," and dismisses any notion that there were mysterious deaths associated with this case. He declares, "None had any connection with the assassination and none took any secrets to the grave. Most died of natural causes." Of particular interest, Weisberg blasts Marrs for including Geraci in the Body Count. Marrs, like many, was technically wrong here, but Geraci's father did die unnaturally, as related earlier. Weisberg scoffs at this, telling the *Times*, "The relevant Philip Geraci was not electrocuted. His father was, non-conspiratorially, in an industrial accident for which he was responsible." That's an odd way of describing being found in the attic of a home where he'd been working. He also claims that there were three Philip Geracis in New Orleans. One contrasts this dismissal of the "mysterious deaths" with the way his friend Orest Pena was "lead piped," and had his tires slashed. Was that from "natural causes?" One can only imagine how pleased the cover-up artists at the *Times* were with this excessively lengthy and whiny letter. Weisberg's jealousy over Stone choosing Garrison as his protagonist instead of him comes through loud and clear with every word.

Weisberg followed this pathetic letter up with a personal one to Tom Wicker of the *New York Times* on December 22, 1991. Wicker epitomized the kind of Establishment reporter who swallowed every absurd bit of information doled out to our "free press" by the government. Weisberg notes that "I have long opposed the multitude of conspiracy theories presented, as Oliver Stone now does, as solutions to the crime." He congratulates Wicker on his "excellent review and commentary" of Stone's *JFK*.

The compelling connections, and unnatural deaths (despite the older, excessively bitter Weisberg's claims to the contrary), were everywhere. George Piazza, Jr., allegedly a close friend of Ferrie's in the Civil Air Patrol, eventually became an assistant on Garrison's staff. He was the attorney for James Lewallen, a former roommate of Ferrie's. Piazza was killed in a plane crash on March 31, 1967. There were no signs of or calls of distress, and the night was calm and clear.[38] Weisberg (when he was younger and more skeptical) claimed that the thirty-year-old Piazza's sole heir was Alvin Beauboeuf, a close Ferrie friend who was one of his two teenage companions during the bizarre car trip from New Orleans (Ferrie was sitting next to his employer Carlos Marcello in a courtroom on the day of the assassination) to Dallas on November 22, 1963, allegedly to go ice skating. Lewallen was discovered by Garrison to be living next door to Clay Shaw on Dauphine Street. Residing with Lewallen was Dante Marachini (alternate spelling Marochini), whom Garrison's staff had staked out and learned that he'd frequently visited David Ferrie. Marachini was one of several former co-workers of Oswald's at the Reily Coffee Company, who all strangely went on to work for NASA. Incredibly, so did Lewallen.

And they both just happened to wind up as next door neighbors to kindly philanthropist Clay Shaw.[39] Yet another notable individual connected to Ferrie through the Civil Air Patrol was Barry Seal, the infamous pilot tied to the activities at Arkansas's Mena Airport, during Bill Clinton's reign as Governor.[40] Seal would die unnaturally, in a plane crash, like so many others linked to the Clintons. Fellow CAP member John Odom would claim that Seal met Lee Harvey Oswald during a CAP training session.

Clyde Johnson, another key Garrison witness, was hidden for his own protection, but still was found and beaten severely, preventing him from testifying. Johnson, a thirty-seven-year-old preacher, would be shot and killed on July 24, 1969.[41] The fear is still palpable, not only in witnesses, but to those even tangentially connected to this case. Veleka Gray is an actress who starred in soap operas like *As the World Turns* and *The Young and the Restless*. She became friends with William Law, and talked about her sister Monya, who was an independent court reporter. While it was never specified, *something* terrified her at the time of the Shaw trial. "My sister was scared to death. Dymond told her to keep her mouth shut because there were people dying and I don't want you to get in trouble," Veleka told Law decades after the fact.

Leander D'Avy was a doorman at the Court of the Two Sisters in New Orleans. D'Avy would tell the HSCA: "in 1962 this young man walks up to me and asks me if there was a Clay Bertrand working there. I told him I don't know any Clay Bertrand. [I asked the] night manager, Eugene Davis in the tavern, 'Gene, do we have a Clay Bertrand working here?' And Eugene said 'Send the young man in here, I'll talk to him.' Clay Bertrand, that's probably a code name. Just like that. So I sent him on in, about an hour later the young man walks out, Eugene Davis comes up to the door where I'm standing, talks to one of the waitresses in there, and he says 'See that young man? He's just come from behind the Iron Curtain.' Well, I didn't put no assassination n' that together—it hadn't happened yet.' Two weeks before the assassination I was called one Saturday morning to pick up my check. I walked into the patio and asked where Eugene Davis was, they said he's up there in the store room. So I went up there and it wasn't no storeroom, they had a little apartment up there, had a bed in it, had five men in it. One of them was OSWALD, I recognized him after the assassination. He was laying across the bed. One of them was David Ferrie. When I went up to Jim Garrison's office I knew it was going to get back to CARLOS MARCELLO or one of them, that I'm talking. And my life won't be worth a plug nickel if they find out.

Right then and there I moved out of New Orleans, right the next day. I went to Jackson, Mississippi. I have seen pictures of the other two men [with OSWALD, David Ferrie and Davis] in the Enquirer, the tramps, the little one in that picture was the guy that had the whiskers... I could identify [two] tramps. I don't know their names. All I know is I can identify 'em when I see 'em. One—ah, two of the tramps was, I'm pretty sure, CIA—former CIA men, or something. I never heard no talk [the tramps were HUNT and STURGIS]. I'll take a polygraph test on everything I told you, that's just the way it was, the way it is. I believe there was at least two guys who used to belong to the CIA ... two CIA men that were members of the Bay of Pigs, along with a bunch of Cubans. I think them Cubans were from the Bay of Pigs invasion." According to researcher A.J. Weberman, "Leander D'Avy tried to sell his story to the tabloid, *Midnight*. The HSCA asked him if he had received psychiatric care. He said he had not."

Again quoting Weberman, "In December 1977 Leander D'Avy was interviewed by HSCA investigator L.J. Delsa. This time he said he had inquired of the bookkeeper, Margaret Tannenbaum, if Clay Bertrand worked there, and Eugene Clair Davis overheard him. Leander D'Avy stuck to his tale about having seen the tramps, and stated that Nick Karno owned the Court of Two Sisters. L.J. Delsa reported: 'Nick Karno is a MARCELLO associate and is alleged to have his names on businesses in the French Quarter that are actually CARLOS MARCELLO'S. In 1959 a confidential source indicated that Nick Karno was going to South America, and seemed to be helping procure arms for Fidel Castro. Nick Karno is presently fighting trial dates which his attorneys have been successfully putting off since his murder indictment in 1974...' A distant cousin of Leander D'Avy was contacted: 'I thought he had died. He was an individual that had been inflicted by encephalitis as a child and he roamed a lot. He was a merchant seaman in his younger days. It's been 30 years since I've seen him.' The brother of Leander D'Avy, Nuby D'Avy, was contacted: 'Leander died February 1986 in Jackson, Mississippi. He went in the hospital for a checkup and the nurse left him with something, and she went back, and he strangled on himself, and he went into a coma. He told me he might come into some money because he knew something about the Kennedy assassination. And he had heard about it, he had nothing to do. ... My brother was in Navy. He's got three boys in Mississippi. Charlie, Nuney and Philip. He told me he had information about it, and he was going to talk with the FBI, and he might not live long. Somebody was going to be after him to kill him or something. He said he knew something. That's all he told me. No details.'"

It's still a mystery as to why Weisberg, who provided so much material for Garrison's investigation, wound up turning so bitterly on the former New Orleans district attorney. In a 1999 interview with Barry Ernst, author of *The Girl on the Stairs: The Search for a Missing Witness to the JFK Assassination*, Weisberg said of Garrison, "I don't know if he became crazy or just irresponsible." He stated that Garrison's claim that it was Senator Russell Long (son of the great Huey Long) that "gave him the idea about the assassination" was dubious. Weisberg cited an interview Long supposedly gave with the ever-present George Lardner, where he said he first heard of this over the radio. He also shared an interesting anecdote about Dean Andrews, telling Ernst, "I'll tell you a story about Dean Andrews. I was in his office on a Saturday afternoon when the telephone rings. It was from one of his homosexual clients calling and saying that he was coming up from Texas to kill him. I won't try to imitate his [Andrew's] accent – nobody could – but he says to me, 'When he comes to New Orleans he'll be on *my* turf.' This was on a Saturday. In the papers on Monday or Tuesday, the evening paper, had a banner headline across the whole top of the page that this guy was captured in New Orleans. A remarkable coincidence that Dean knew what he was talking about. That's impressive."

It was a sad and inexplicable transformation for a man who was clearly angry at the world, and felt he'd been cheated out of a prominent place in the history of JFK assassination research. There is no question that he was one of the greatest, if not the greatest researcher into the events of November 22, 1963. We certainly own him a huge debt for his enormous work in sifting through the conspiratorial connections in New Orleans.

Endnotes

1   Harold Weisberg, *Oswald in New Orleans: Case for Conspiracy with the CIA,* New York, Canyon Books, 1967, p. 11

2   Ibid, p. 52

3   *Kennedys and King,* December 3, 2006

4   CIA Biographical Data Sheet on Hugh Aynesworth, October 10, 1963, document #100-300-17

5   *Columbia Journalism Review,* Spring, 1969

6   *Executive Intelligence Review,* December 29, 1981

7   William Davy, *Let Justice be Done: New Light on the Jim Garrison Investigation,* Reston, Virginia, Jordan Publishing, 1999, pp. 61

8   Anthony Summers, *Conspiracy,* New York, Paragon House, 1989, unnumbered first page

9   Paul Hoch, *Echoes of Conspiracy,* Vol. 13, no. 1

10   Robert Sam Anson, "The Shooting of JFK," *Esquire,* November 1991

11   Weisberg, p. 24

12   Weisberg, pp. 85-90

13   *Warren Commission Hearings & Exhibits,* Vol. XI, p. 330

14   Weisberg, pp. 139-141

15   *Washington Star,* February 23, 1967

16   William Davy interview with Lou Ivon, April 7, 1995

17   Weisberg, pp. 163-164

18   *Washington Post,* February 25, 1967

19   *New York Times,* March 17, 1967

20   *New Orleans States-Item,* January 11, 1971

21   *Warren Commission Hearings & Exhibits,* Vol. 10, pp. 74-80

22   David Talbot, *Brothers: The Hidden History of the Kennedy Years,* New York, Simon & Schuster, 2007, p. 322

23   *Washington Star,* March 2, 1967

24   Weisberg, pp. 219-220

25   Weisberg, p. 176

26   *Times-Picayune,* February 28, 1967

27   *The American Chronicle,* February 10, 2017

28   *New York Times,* May 5, 1955

29   E. Howard Hunt, *Undercover,* New York, Berkley Publishing, 1974, p. 99

30   Weisberg, p. 252

31   Memorandum from Robert Blakey to staff counsel Robert Genzman, July 31, 1978

32   Letter from William Turner to William Davy, October 17, 1995

33   Paul Bleau, *Kennedys and King,* "Exposing the FPCC," Parts I-III, August 7, 2021

34   *Kennedys and King,* August 7, 2021

35   *Kennedys and King,* September 10, 2022

36   Harold Weisberg, *Inside the Assassination Industry,* Unpublished manuscript, p. 300

37   Ibid, p. 321

38   *Avalanche Journal,* March 31, 1967

39   Jim Garrison, *On the Trail of the Assassins,* New York, Warner Books, 1991, pp. 114-116

40   *New Orleans Times-Picayune,* July 27, 1955

41   *New Orleans Times-Picayune,* July 24, 1969

CHAPTER TWO

THE GROUND LEVEL PLOT

I am as innocent regarding any conspiracy as any of you gentlemen in the room.

                     – Jack Ruby, Warren Commission Testimony

A s noted, it is almost a certainty that Lee Harvey Oswald was working in some capacity for an intelligence agency. There is evidence that he was associated with both the CIA and FBI. If his assignment was to infiltrate what he was told was a brewing plot to kill the president, those who were identified as potential conspirators would have been David Ferrie, Jack Ruby, Guy Banister, Clay Shaw, Sergio Arcacha Smith, Jack Martin, Kerry Thornley, and various anti-Castro Cuban figures. To clarify, these were *not* the real conspirators in our view, although certainly most of them would have approved of Kennedy's assassination. They may have all been told the same thing, and were essentially spying on each other, while being manipulated by the true conspirators. Dean Andrews, Jr. was connected to all these men, and his role is murkiest of all.

To show how deep this rabbit hole goes, consider that someone was seemingly engaged in impersonating Oswald *years before* the JFK assassination. On January 20, 1961, the same day that JFK was being inaugurated, two men arrived at the Bolton Ford Truck Center in New Orleans. They identified themselves as members of the Friends of Democratic Cuba. One of the men identified himself as Oswald and insisted that his name appear on the bid for ten vans, because he was "the man with the money." Manager Fred Sewell gave a description that resembled the future alleged assassin, and also recalled that his first name was Lee. The problem here is that the real Oswald was winding up the final months of his defection in Russia at that time. The Truck Center's assistant manager Oscar Deslatte actually contacted the FBI three years later, upon seeing Lee Harvey Oswald on television. Garrison would investigate this incident in detail.[1] Garrison's office questioned Bolton Truck manager Fred

Sewell. He told them that "he didn't use the Harvey, just Lee Oswald if I remember right." He said the man with Oswald was named Joseph Moore, was "kind of heavy-set ... curly haired ... had a scar over his left eye ... he had a Cuban accent and looked like a Cuban." Researcher John Armstrong, author of the book *Harvey & Lee*, theorized that the "Oswald" in this encounter was actually the southern-born Lee, as opposed to the Russian-born Harvey, who was eventually framed for the assassination of President Kennedy. Armstrong unearthed the initial November 25, 1963 interview with Oscar Deslatte. In contrast to Sewell's later interview with Garrison, this FBI report states that Deslatte had no information on Joseph Moore, "whose description he cannot remember, nor can he furnish any other identifying data ..." It is claimed here that "Oswald" provided no first name, and "Deslatte was exhibited a photograph of Lee Harvey Oswald and he said he cannot recall ever having seen him before nor could he say this was the individual who had come in with Moore." Deslatte felt he couldn't describe either man since it "was almost three years ago that they were there and only spent a short time with him." Deslatte rather ludicrously claimed he only remembered the incident because of the name of their organization, Friends of Democratic Cuba; not because of Oswald.

So why did Deslatte even bother to contact the FBI, if he couldn't associate the man who put a bid on trucks with the alleged assassin? As Sewell told Garrison's office, "So when the President was assassinated and the name came out, OSCAR come in either the next morning or the morning after and said, 'Say, Fred, do you remember those two guys who was in here from Cuba trying to get some buses cheap?' and I said, 'Yes.' He said, 'I think that one of those men was the one who killed the President.' I said, 'Aw you're kidding' and he said 'We've got a piece of paper around here somewhere with a bid on it.' He went and hauled that piece of paper out and the[n] OSCAR called the FBI." Sewell recalled that the "two young FBI agents" who visited the dealership didn't show them any photos of Lee Harvey Oswald, and declared, "Oswald wasn't even in the country at that time. He couldn't be." The FBI never called them back. In a December 19, 1963 FBI memo from the Special Agent in Charge, New Orleans (no name listed, presumably Warren de Brueys), it was noted that Carlos Bringuier had called John Rice, Agent in Charge, U.S. Secret Service, to inform him that a "Mrs. Cusco, who worked for the Graham Paper Co., had been told by her boss that a friend of his who works for a trucking concern had been contacted by Oswald and Oswald said he was trying to get trucks for Cuba. The boss in question, Charles Pearson, subsequently stated that "the friend who had been contacted by Oswald was Oscar W. Deslatte, assistant manager, Truck Sales, Bolton Ford Co., New Orleans."

The Friends of Democratic Cuba was also associated with Sergio Arcacha Smith, and an informant told Garrison that the outfit was "an undercover operation in conjunction with the CIA and FBI." Intriguingly, the vice president of FDC was Gerard F. Tujague, for whom sixteen-year-old Lee Harvey Oswald had worked as a messenger from November 1955 to January 1956.[2] Another officer of FDC was Guy Banister. The Bolton Ford incident fits in nicely with the memo that FBI Director J. Edgar Hoover sent to the State Department even earlier in 1960, in which he raised the possibility that someone was impersonating Oswald. As co-author Donald Jeffries wrote in his book *Hidden History: An Expose of Modern Crimes, Conspiracies, and Cover-Ups in American Politics,* "FBI Director J. Edgar Hoover asked the State Department for current information on Oswald, on June 3, 1960, since 'there is a possibility that an imposter is using Oswald's birth certificate.' In March, 1961, the Passport Office informed the State Department that '… it has been stated that there is an imposter using Oswald's identification data …'"[3]

Guy Banister, who harbored extreme right-wing views, retired from the FBI in 1955, and found his way to New Orleans, where he was quickly promoted up the ranks to the number three man in the police department, as Deputy Superintendent of Police. In 1957, one of Banister's characteristic violent outbursts in a bar ended his police career. He founded the private investigative firm Guy Banister Associates, Inc. a year later. Banister was close enough to J. Edgar Hoover to talk to him regularly on the telephone. Unlike all the others mentioned as seeming ground-level plotters, Banister was never questioned by Jim Garrison, having conveniently died of a heart attack on June 6, 1964. It bears repeating that Delphine Roberts, Banister's secretary and mistress, and several others recalled seeing Oswald in Banister's office, and that he in fact had his own office there. This included Banister's associate Dan Campbell, who also curiously saw Oswald's aforementioned talkative Marine buddy Kerry Thornley in Banister's office. Thornley, it may be recalled, was writing a book about Lee Harvey Oswald *before* the JFK assassination. His Warren Commission testimony is much longer than any of Oswald's other fellow Marines, and was used to paint the picture of a Marxist Private "Oswaldovitch." In another strange coincidence, on the day of the JFK assassination, Thornley was in the company of Dan Campbell's brother Allen, who also worked for Banister.[4] Thornley, whose hatred of JFK was such that he wanted to urinate on his grave, becomes even more suspect, given the two witnesses, cited in the previous chapter, who identified him as the man who picked up the Fair Play for Cuba leaflets Oswald passed out in New Orleans. Dan Campbell claimed that "Banister was a bagman for the CIA and was running guns to Alpha 66 in Miami." He called him "one of the most frighteningly violent persons I have ever known" and described those around him as "the worst kind of fanatics." Campbell recalled being in Banister's office when a young man came in to use the telephone. "I knew he was a Marine from his bearing and speech pattern the minute he walked into 544 Camp Street," he stated, and identified him as Oswald after seeing his picture on television.[5]

Delphine Roberts, who Banister's investigator Vernon Geddes identified as his boss's mistress (and as noted, called her "a nut"), discovered his body. Banister's widow supposedly told Delphine Roberts that she was going to burn Banister's "communist files." Mary Banister indeed burned an unknown number of files – Roberts described seeing the smoke coming from the "trash burner" outside her home. She also sold some files to the Metropolitan Crime Commission and the State Police, out of financial necessity. Jim Garrison was unsuccessful in his efforts to retrieve these files.[6] Mary Banister told Garrison investigator Andrew Sciambra that she'd seen some Fair Play for Cuba leaflets in her husband's office. Geddes claimed Roberts went into Banister's office right after his death, and removed some files which she allegedly took to attorney G. Wray Gill's office. Gill was a powerful New Orleans attorney whose most notorious client was mob boss Carlos Marcello. David Ferrie worked as a private investigator for Gill. Still more suspicious deaths were related to Banister. On May 23, 1964, a month before Banister died, Hugh Ward, a private investigator working for him, was killed in a plane crash. Banister's friend Maurice B. Gatlin, Sr. served as general counsel to the Anti-Communist League of the Caribbean, to which Banister belonged. Gatlin either fell or was pushed out of a hotel window in San Juan, Puerto Rico in 1964.[7] At least eleven people testified to seeing Banister in the company of Oswald in New Orleans during the summer of 1963. Needless to say, a relationship between the avowed anti-communist and the Marxist defector to Russia was something impossible to explain innocently. As was so colorfully recounted in Oliver Stone's *JFK*, Banister's business was run out of the same building that featured the address on

Oswald's Fair Play for Cuba pamphlets. Jim Garrison would rather oddly say, in his October 1967 *Playboy* interview that he had no evidence Banister was involved in killing Kennedy.

In a May 22, 1967 letter to Garrison, in which she offered to be interviewed, Banister's part-time employee Mary Brengel referred to "several rather strange or unexplained things (to me)" which had occurred "from the latter part of October until about the 10th of December, 1963." She stressed that these things were "however not *associated with Cubans." She confessed that "though naturally I would like to stay out of the limelight." She alluded to some suspicion about Delphine Roberts, writing,* "I do question that she would speak freely and if she may have omitted mentioning any persons I might mention, I surely would not want her to know I offered information until after you had my information." Brengel then volunteered, "Is there a question about whether Mr. Banister's death in June 1964 was from natural causes? I do question this as well as the roles of others in connection therewith." Lou Ivon summarized Brengel's statement to Garrison's office in a June 1, 1967 memo. Brengel mentioned that the ever-present FBI agent Regis Kennedy was part of a group Banister formed to help attain a contract to guard the Mississippi Test Sight (presumably spelled incorrectly). She recounted how Banister didn't come into the office on the day of the assassination, and that when JFK's death was announced, Delphine Roberts "jumped with joy and said, 'I am glad.'" Brengel inferred that Roberts seemed to have advance knowledge of Banister's death, as she seemingly overreacted when he didn't answer the phone, by getting "an FBI man" to accompany her to his home. In an April 6, 1978 interview with the HSCA, Brengel testified that *she believed both Banister and his secretary Delphine Roberts knew that JFK was going to be assassinated on November 22, 1963. Growing a bit bolder in her suspicions, the HSCA noted* "she has wondered if BANISTER was not in Dallas on 11-22-63 and in fact was one of the men with a high-powered rifle there." She revealed even more to the ARRB in 1994, stating, "Delphine told me that both Lee Harvey Oswald and David Ferrie, as well as others who figured in the government hearings, had been in the office many times while I worked there." She was also interviewed for the BBC by well known researcher Anthony Summers, who told her that he'd been unable to locate Delphine Roberts, which Martin Daly of the HSCA had told her as well. She went on to tell the ARRB that "It is my personal belief that there will never be a true solution, that for every truth uncovered, there will be innumerable 'debunking' teams, more unexplainable deaths. Until and unless our government is some day free of every vestige of corruption, I do not believe the people will ever know the truth."

Guy Banister was also one of several characters who crossed over into the UFO field. As Joseph Farrell wrote, **"For one thing, Guy Banister was at one time the FBI agent in charge of the Butte, Montana FBI field office in 1947, and was thus intimately involved in the FBI's covert investigation of UFOs, beginning with the famous Kenneth Arnold sighting in June of 1947, the Maury Island UFO affair, and of course, the Roswell Incident in July of 1947."**[8] **Recently declassified FBI files show a number of telexes from Banister, all pertaining to UFO phenomena, and some even claim that he originated the term "X-Files" to describe them. Fred Lee Crisman was a central figure in the Maury Island UFO incident, which seems to have been the first to feature the notorious "Men in Black." Watergate attorney Douglas Caddy is among those who have claimed the Crisman was one of the infamous three tramps arrested after the assassination. Jim Garrison was deeply interested in Crisman, and connected him to Sergio Arcacha Smith. Richard E. Sprague, in his book** *The Taking of America 1-2-3,* **cast Crisman in a central role in the assassination conspiracy.**

As touched upon earlier, one of the most curious things Garrison uncovered was the fact that almost everyone who had worked with Oswald at the Reily Coffee Company, makers of Luzianne coffee (Oswald was there briefly, from May through July 1963), had gone on to work for NASA. The Reily Coffee Company was located only two blocks from Banister's office. In addition to all the bizarre employee relocations to NASA that Garrison discovered, a CIA memo dated January 31, 1964, stated that "This firm (Reily's) was of interest as of April 1949." The memo listed an Agency number assigned to William Reily, whom soldier-of-fortune and CIA contract employee Gerry Patrick Hemming would claim had worked for the CIA for years. Both Reily and his brother were active in anti-Castro politics. Adrian Alba, whose garage was next door to the Reily Coffee Company, told the HSCA in 1978 that he'd witnessed an FBI agent hand Oswald an envelope through the window of one of the government cars that were contracted to park there. Alba described how the FBI agent wanted an FBI vehicle, but took a Secret Service car because none were available. The man had displayed credentials of a Washington, D.C. FBI agent, but he "wouldn't remember his name, even what he looked like."Alba witnessed another encounter between Oswald and the same car two days later, which only consisted of conversation. Oswald had visited Alba's office frequently while employed at Reily. They talked about guns, and Alba loaned him some gun magazines, some of which were later found in Oswald's room. Alba oddly didn't remember the incident until years later, but offered to take "truth serum" or a lie detector test. FBI agent Warren de Brueys predictably stated that "it seems kind of asinine" since the Bureau "had our own garage," separate from the Secret Service.[9] Alba also reported that Oswald had told him that he expected to soon be working for NASA at a New Orleans plant.[10] Where, of course, so many of Oswald's fellow employees at Reily went on to work.

Louise Decker was briefly employed by Banister, from October 1961 until January 1962. She found out about the job from the wife of the doomed Hugh Ward. Decker stated in a January 28, 1968 interview with Garrison's detective Douglas Ward that "she had once seen some of BANISTER's files in which the names of numerous political persons and influential person names were mentioned . MRS. DECKER further stated that she thought if these files fell into the wrong hands they could be used to blackmail some of these persons mentioned in them." She'd seen David Ferrie, Jack Martin, and Sergio Arcacha Smith in Banister's office. Banister warned Decker that Martin "was the type of man to be afraid of." She claimed that Martin pulled a gun on Banister in his office on November 22, 1963, and threatened to kill him "over some words about the assassination of President Kennedy." She was told about this incident by the aforementioned Vernon Geddes, Banister's business associate and friend. She also alleged that Banister was far behind in his rent. Decker corroborated Geddes by stating that Delphine Roberts had removed files from Banister's office after discovering his body.

Jack Martin is one of the most puzzling of all the characters in this great drama. Delphine Roberts said that Martin called himself "Reverend" and was a regular presence in Banister's office. As far back as February 10, 1961, Jack S. Martin contacted the New Orleans FBI office and "advised that two of his clients in South America, who were in the oil business, had requested him to check on a Charles F. Riker, 2610 S. Mac-Gregor Drive, Houston, Texas, who reportedly was in Venezuela and on various occasions had represented himself as an FBI agent or Central Intelligence agent. Martin advised that he was a private detective and wished to obtain any data the Bureau could give him regarding Riker on behalf of his client. Martin was unsuccessful in obtaining any information." The FBI seems to have been unaware of the sort of background information on Riker that the CIA would receive a few weeks later. "[informant number] MM T-1 advised that C.F. Riker, 2610 MacGregor #2, Houston, Texas...was in Miami and claimed to represent a group of assassins that operate exclusively against Communists. Riker is described as being well educated, and claims to have attended a number of Government schools having to do with arms, demolitions and languages. Riker claims he lived in Mexico during his youth, and speaks Spanish." Needless to say, it is intriguing to find Jack Martin seeking information about a man representing assassins nearly three years before the assassination of President Kennedy.[11]

On December 13, 1966, Martin was interviewed by Pershing Gervais of Garrison's office. Mimicking Dean Andrews' beatnik lingo, Martin told Gervais, "There is a local cat around who is mixed up in a narcotics deal and he has been pardoned and he is Ferrie's godson. You could probably sweat him out. His name is Morris Brownlee. He plays with a bunch of queers in the Quarter." Martin said, regarding Brownlee, "I don't know what the hell this man does." He claimed Brownlee had been to medical school (where he was booted out for narcotics), and "has a hell of a chemical laboratory," and remarked, "He could be making LSD right now." Martin described Brownlee as a Jew whom Ferrie converted to Catholicism, but who "looks Latin American and speaks Spanish." Brownlee was Ferrie's godson, according to researcher Ray Evans. Brownlee supposedly stated that Ferrie had a long association with the CIA. Interestingly, Brownlee was in the same 1956 graduating class with the elusive Gordon Novel, at East Jefferson High School. Martin alleged that "Ferrie was in Dallas when Lee Harvey Oswald was, but he lied about it and he knew he lied about it." Martin asserted here that he first met Ferrie through Sergio Arcacha Smith. Martin spoke of meeting Oswald in Ferrie's house, in the presence of his mother, "who is now dead. She died a very quick death." After Mrs. Ferrie provided Martin with details about Ferrie's association with his version of the Catholic Church, Ferrie put her on a plane back to Philadelphia, "and two weeks later that woman died. She was in pretty good health. There was nothing wrong with that old lady." Martin disclosed that "I can't tell you how I know, but it's damn reliable, that Ferrie was in Dallas, at least in Fort Worth, two days before the assassination of President Kennedy." He named "Arcacha" when Gervais asked him "Who was the head man for the Cuban movement?"

A Secret Service memo, signed on December 4, 1963 by Anthony Gerrets (there are multiple spellings of this last name in the record) and John W. Rice, mentions that barely an hour after Kennedy was shot, Lillian L. Rhyan, of "our Dallas office," called the New Orleans office at the request of Special Agent Robert A. Steuart, regarding an individual named Jack Martin. About a half hour later, Ryan called again, "advising that at the time it was thought that possibly Jack Martin might have been the assassin of President Kennedy." This record is part of the Harold Weisberg collection at Hood College. Weisberg wrote in the margins of this memo, "Once Oswald was arrested, all interest in this Jack Martin disappeared. The matter is ignored in the Report and in the testimony." Martin the enigmatic private investigator, played memorably by Jack Lemmon in Oliver Stone's *JFK*, claimed to have been pistol whipped by Guy Banister (portrayed by Ed Asner) on the night of November 22, 1963. In an August 17, 1967 memo from Assistant District Attorney Anthony Sciambra, to New Orleans D.A. Jim Garrison, we learn that Jack's grandfather Charlie Martin was a member of the notorious Bonnie and Clyde gang. A few years after turning state's evidence against the gang, Martin was discovered cut in half on a railroad track. A fellow researcher combed the records and found out more intriguing information about Martin. His birth name was reportedly Edward Suggs. He was associated with the Flying Tigers, which is known to be connected to the CIA, and gave HSCA investigators a letter from the airlines' founder General Claire Chennault, requesting him to work for Chiang Kai-shek. Martin obviously wanted to be a cop, as he applied for positions with several police departments. He had an extensive arrest record, the most serious being a 1952 murder charge, in Houston. Those charges were subsequently dropped.

In a November 28, 1963 teletype sent by the New Orleans FBI office to the Director and the Dallas Office, Martin's claim that Oswald and Ferrie were associated was dismissed thusly: "all allegations against Ferrie stem from Jack S. Martin who was previously confined to the psychiatric ward of Charity Hospital, New Orleans, for character disorder. Martin is well known to New Orleans office and is considered thoroughly unreliable." A July 6, 1967 Dallas Police department memo written by D.K. Rodgers, addressed to Captain W.F. Dyson, notes how Jack S. Martin "had a dispute with William David Ferrie, deceased principal in the assassination conspiracy." The memo states that Martin was aware that Ferrie had flown into Dallas on November 22, 1963, accompanied by Alvin Beauboeuf, and grasped the "chance to make trouble for Ferrie" by reporting this information to an assistant district attorney named

Holman. Martin told Holman that Ferrie "had personal knowledge of Lee Harvey Oswald." The memo notes, "This is reported to be the basis for the assassination conspiracy case of Jim Garrison against Ferrie and some of his associates." The memo goes on, "Information has been received from a confidential source that the true name of Jack S. Martin is Edward Stewart Suggs…" Martin, as Edward Stewart Suggs, was involved in a bizarre plot to blow up a sheriff with nitroglycerin, in relation to the 1952 murder charge.[12]

There is an intriguing, but little reported on April 7, 1967 "General Statement and Affidavit Regarding Garrison Probe" by J.S. Martin. Martin is described as "a resident and duly qualified elector within the state of Louisiana." Martin states, "Shortly after the assassination of President John F. Kennedy and the murder of Lee Harvey Oswald, a professional acquaintance of mine with the FBI that I'd known rather well for the past few years came by to see me at home, per my request." Martin continued, "It was at this time that I first mentioned David William Ferrie, and the details contained in a 1961 news article of the *Times-Picayune*, authored by a former reporter Herman S. Kohlman, who at the present time (1963) was as assistant district attorney." Martin spoke of "Ferrie's potential capabilities and activities," including "the probability and feasibility of having once known or associated with Oswald…" The affidavit then goes on to mention another interesting character: "A short time later, either that evening, or the next day, it seems a subject said to be Edward Voebel, a local florist, reported that he had 'served in the same CAP Metairie Falcon Squadron with Oswald under the command of a Captain David W. Ferrie.'" Martin described seeing the report about Voebel on a local television station, and notified Kohlman, who "assured me that he would certainly look into this matter at once…" Martin's FBI friend returned to his house the following day, "but his attitude appeared somewhat hostile." He told Martin, "You know Jack, drinking as you were, you may not remember it but you called WWL-TV and then Kohlman." Martin declared he hadn't been drinking at the time, and sought to quickly end this "unpleasant" interview. The following day, Martin was visited by two men "who said they were from the Secret Service." Evidently, they were hostile to Martin as well, and he "was forced to advise them of the fact they appeared to be exceeding the bounds of their authority," and summarily showed them the door. Martin goes on to say that "with minor exception, this is the last we ever heard from any of these people until this year (1967)." Martin protested that he "had no idea what had been reported in our name to the Warren Commission, as to date, we've been denied this legal privilege of ever seeing a copy of any statements allegedly filed with such a legal body in our name." Martin swore that in all the interviews he'd given, "never did I observe a note being taken." Which begs the question if FBI agents, like the Dallas Police who interrogated Oswald, utilized this curious practice of not recording anything that was said by other witnesses. Martin also stressed that "nor did I, or have I ever, 'taken back' anything I had to say. In short, I categorically deny even an implied reversal of any comment made to these people at this (or that) time. In short, I take nothing back now, and I took back nothing then."

In Part II of Martin's fascinating affidavit, he relates, "On or about December 5, 1966, I received a call one morning from the office of the Orleans Parish District Attorney." Garrison's representative explained that he wanted to talk with him, to which Martin replied, "If Jim wants anything of me, all he's got to do is ask … he knows that." Garrison then got on the phone and explained that a car would be sent to pick him up. He appears to state that there is no doubt that Ferrie knew Oswald, but the page is cut off at the top, so this couldn't be verified. Martin seems to have been regularly involved here, as he states, "I am in contact daily with some members of this office by telephone. But there is nothing unusual about this, as not a day goes by that I'm not in touch with either some sheriff, the police, the press, or other such people…" This hardly fits the image of the shadowy figure other evidence depicts Martin as being. Part III of the affidavit basically consists of Martin dancing around any comment one way or the other on the Warren Commission. In Part IV, Martin defends his own character. Another document in the Mary Ferrell database discloses that Martin was often known as "Colonel," and had been commissioned as such by the "Staff of the Governor of Louisiana, under two administrations." Yet another document reveals that Martin was ordained as a priest in the Holy Syro-Byzantine Order of Saint John, by the Catholic Apostolic Church. Still another file reveals that Martin was later ordained as a Bishop by this sect.

Jack Martin, referred to here as Edward Suggs, spoke to the HSCA. In a document detailing this, it was reported, "Edward Suggs had seen OSWALD with Ferrie in Guy Banister's office, located at 544 Camp Street. On the day that President Kennedy was assassinated, Suggs saw a rifle (Mannlicher-Carcano) on TV and remembered that he had seen one just like it in David Ferrie's apartment. Suggs called friend who was an Assistant District Attorney, Herman Kohlman, and told him about seeing OSWALD with Ferrie and about the gun. Suggs feels this was the first call anyone made to the New Orleans District Attorney. As a result of that call David Ferrie's apartment was raided by Special Investigators of Jim Garrison. Ferrie was later arrested and released." (HSCA 1801007810416). It is then ludicrously added, "Had Mr. Banister had previous contact with OSWALD before the assassination, he would have immediately contacted us and reported this information." In contrast to Martin's fascinating affidavit quoted from above, researcher A.J. Weberman published a document that appears to have come from the FBI, on his web site, where it was revealed, "Edward Suggs telephonically contacted S.A. Regis L. Kennedy on January 27, 1967, and demanded that the FBI stop Jim Garrison from harassing him. Edward Suggs told S.A. Regis Kennedy "the scope of Garrison's investigation is that there was a conspiracy which originated in the room above W. Guy Banister's (deceased) office in New Orleans and that there was a second assassin firing at President Kennedy in Dallas, Texas…. No investigation is being conducted by the New Orleans Office." Weberman also published the following on his website, "About the time David Ferrie was found dead in his apartment on February 22, 1967, Suggs reportedly left town. The CIA reported: "Sugg's wife, when interviewed during the period of his disappearance, stated that such a disappearance was not unusual, as he takes off alone for several months every year. She admitted that he drinks a great deal, but maintained that he is a 'plain, ordinary man who makes model planes for his (9-year old) son and a chapel (a religious chapel in the house) for his wife and hundreds of ecclesiastical heraldry for his friends."

We were also very interested in David W. Lewis, or David Franklin Lewis (appears in the record as both), a former employee of Guy Banister's, who according to a May 5, 1967 FBI report, "furnished information to District Attorney Garrison concerning persons allegedly involved in assassination plot." Lewis is perhaps even more enigmatic than Martin. In what seems to have been his first statement to Garrison's office, dated December 15, 1966, David F. Lewis revealed how, while working as a private eye for Guy Banister & Associates (January 1961-1962), he saw Sergio Arcacha Smith, Carlos (Lewis said he didn't know his last name—presumably Bringuier) and someone who was introduced to him as "Lee Harvey" at Mancuso's Restaurant, located in Banister's building. As he stated, "It has now been determined by me through photographs that this man was Lee Harvey Oswald." He described Oswald as quiet, and "highly nervous with boundless energy." He said it appeared that Arcacha, Carlos and Oswald were involved in some "racket" business deal involving Cuba. He noted "Arcacha Smith to me appeared to be the boss." He also saw David Ferrie in Banister's office while "a slim, sandy-haired young man" who could have been Oswald was there, and also witnessed Ferrie in the presence of Arcacha and Carlos. In a December 15, 1966 interview with Lou Ivon, Lewis said he'd seen Oswald "No more than four times, each time in the company of Carlos." He once went to Ferrie's house on "unknown business—just went along for the ride" along with Jack Martin, Joseph Newbrough, and Louise Decker. Ivon asked Lewis if the Carlos in question was Carlos Corega, and Lewis said the name sounded familiar. Lewis was married April 4, 1962, and his son was born on January 21, 1963. According to information published on A.J. Weberman's website, Lewis was born on May 12, 1940, and had been interviewed by the FBI in 1961 regarding "voting irregularities" in New Orleans. They received his information from none other than "Edward Suggs, part time private detective," and seemingly Lewis's close friend. Weberman also lists an incident where Martin (referred to consistently in these documents as Suggs) telephoned Lewis and asked him about Oswald and Ferrie, while recording the call. He then attempted to sell an excerpt from the call to Ray Berg, President of Pacesetter Publishing, located conveniently at 107 Camp Street. Weberman also included this fascinating tidbit: "The FBI reported: "(Deleted) a private investigator and reliable source of the New Orleans Office, advised that on January 27, 1967, that he had been conducting investigation for the Trailways Bus Line regarding thefts from the New Orleans terminal, and was one of the individuals under investigation is David Lewis. (FBI 62-109060-4539)." Of even more interest is what comes next: "The FBI (1995) withheld information on David F. Lewis. Reports of television broadcasts of David F. Lewis were deleted. (FBI 62-109060-4527). "In 1968, while applying for a job with Avis Rent-a-Car, Lewis was described as "either a mental case or on narcotics." He also told the interviewer that he had four children, "but their whereabouts are unknown."

In early March, 1967, long-time Establishment reporter Haynes Johnson claimed to have received phone calls from both Martin and Lewis. Johnson predictably took an anti-conspiracy spin, and depicted them in a less-than-credible light. He accused them of being publicity seekers, with Lewis bragging that he was going to be on NBC's *Huntley-Brinkley*

Report (he never was), and Martin claiming that the *Washington Star* was considering offering him a retainer to provide them with "insider" information. That never happened either. Martin, again adopting the lingo of Dean Andrews, disparaged the CIA and FBI, and referred to Secret Service agents as "squares." Martin wouldn't swear to having seen Oswald in Banister's office, but Lewis was certain he'd been there. Martin admitted he had only "circumstantial" evidence of a conspiracy to kill JFK. Lewis said he "may know several who were connected with the plot," and declared that "A lot of strange stuff went on in that office."[13] Lewis reacted to Ferrie's death by telling news reporters on February 23, 1967, "Well, it did shake me up. I can tell you it's more fear for myself other than for my family. The possibility is there I don't know if they might want to get me or they might get at me through my family. And this thing is something that really irritates me. I think I've been exposed quite a little too much... They know what I look like. They know who I am. They know where I work." Lewis did state that Ferrie was not one of "the several" he knew of who might have been involved in the conspiracy. In the February 20, 1967 edition of the *Washington Daily News,* a front page headline announced, "Says Five Aided Oswald." The story went on to detail how Lewis, identified as a former private investigator now working as a bus station express handler, knew the identities of those involved in the assassination, but had promised Jim Garrison not to reveal them until granted permission. He did say they all still resided in New Orleans.[14]

Jack Martin and Dave Lewis were given the byline for an article that appeared in *The Houstonian* on August 13, 1968. It was provocatively headlined, "The White Wash is Over! Not the Who, but the Why of J.F.K. Assassination." The article starts with a note from the editor that says "Martin and Lewis are two of the few remaining original Banister agents alive." In the story, Martin is described as the person who "triggered the Garrison investigation," and both he and Lewis are said to have "worked with Garrison on the probe." Martin and Lewis link Bobby Kennedy together with Allen Dulles and Kim Philby, a British intelligence officer who worked with the CIA and was allegedly a Soviet spy, in a confusing scheme that involved Cuba and financial payoffs. The authors clearly have no love for Bobby Kennedy. In an April 2, 1967 article in the *Washington Post,* George Lardner had written that "The D.A., however, has assiduously sought to avoid identification with the Martin and Lewis team."

After that article, David Lewis seems to have vanished. As noted, he was born in 1940, and had at least four children. In a chilling postscript

here, *The Houstonian* published an announcement, found in the voluminous files at the Mary Ferrell database, but undated, in which the public
was told, "'Not The Who, But The Why,' a series behind the facts of the
Garrison probe were discontinued last April 26. Our reason for doing
so was based upon a demand made by one George G. Wyatt, who at the
time identified himself as an agent of the U.S. Justice Dept. Amongst other things Wyatt told us was, 'Your reporter Jack Martin, will be killed if
these are continued.' He also stated that we'd 'Be Sorry' that the first of
these were ever published, as Bobby (RFK) didn't like them, etc. However, as we have since learned that Wyatt is a complete FRAUD, we are
continuing these last installments for all to read." However, the dates
here make no sense. The article in question by Martin and Lewis, which
is described as "continued from a previous issue," was published on August 13, 1968. So how could they have discontinued the series (and there
seems no available record of the "previous issue") before that, in April?
It's possible the actual date of the article was April 13, instead of August
13, but the Ferrell database has "8-13-68" off to the side of the story.

An intriguing CIA memo titled "The Oswald Case – Jack S. Martin aka John J. Martin(?)" (question mark is in original), written by
M.D. Stevens, was dated April 5, 1967. In it, it is noted that Martin is
also known as Edward Stuart Suggs, Colonel Martin, and Bishop Martin. One paragraph states, "About the time Ferrie was found dead in his
apartment on 22 February 1967, Martin was reported as being quite ap-
prehensive about his own safety and as having 'left town,' but on about
1 March was said to have returned to New Orleans and gone into hiding.
Within a few days he was being quite vocal again in connection with the
investigation…"

Even the most basic information about Jack Martin is unclear. Sources
have him born anywhere from 1915 to 1920, as Edward Stewart Suggs.
The claim has been made that Suggs was at Pearl Harbor on December
7, 1941. Suggs was interviewed about what he witnessed at Pearl Harbor
a few years later, and declared, *"I was in the barracks and the Japs hit a PX
[post exchange] nearby. We crouched in the stairway until the attack ended,
and then I hurried to Bellows Field, my home station. I got back there in time
to see the Japs hit a B-17 just taking off and then get two P-40's."*15 Starting
*in 1944, Suggs compiled a lengthy arrest record. One of the things he was
wanted for was a botched abortion (as "Dr." Suggs) which resulted in the
death of a woman in Dallas. As mentioned earlier, he was also wanted for
murder in conjunction with a plot to blow up a sheriff with nitroglycerin, but*

mysteriously wasn't tried in either case. It wasn't until he moved to New Orleans in the mid-1950s that Suggs assumed the Jack Martin identity. He wrote for a small regional newspaper, and was the "Police Editor" of the West Bank Herald. His request to have his name legally changed to Jack Martin was first denied in 1957, by none other than future Warren Commission counsel Leon Hubert, but an appeals court granted his request. Guy Banister took over management of the West Bank Herald in August, 1958. UPI correspondent Merriman Smith, who won a Pulitzer Prize for his JFK assassination coverage, predictably dismissed Martin, declaring, "Martin, an episodic drunk and no stranger to jails and mental wards has a pattern of talking and recanting. He told the Secret Service the lurid story about Ferrie being the get-away pilot, then took it all back as being nothing but a fantasy." Smith killed himself in 1970.

Another Establishment journalist, Rosemary James, co-author of the anti-Garrison book *Plot or Politics*, summed up Martin thusly: "He is as full of that well known waste material as a yule hen. On the other hand, he is many times a very competent investigator who has the friendship and confidence of reputable, well-placed individuals. He drinks, often to excess, but bears no evidence of being an alcoholic. He desperately wants to be loved, and this is his downfall. Often, he wants to please everyone, everywhere so damn much that he ends by hurting the people who have befriended him. He must be taken with a grain of salt leavened by a grain of confidence. If you listen to him for two hours, often you will receive two minutes of useful information. I suppose to sum him up, he is like a muddy river. You have to use a very fine filter! It's more than possible that Garrison's staff were using that fine filter on Martin who knew all of the principals who have been mentioned in the case thus far and names of others Garrison is trying to piece together."

As if Martin wasn't a complicated enough figure, there are others with nearly the identical name connected to this case. A John Martin Jr. filmed the motorcade just a moment before shots were fired. From a March 25, 1964 memo by Dallas FBI agent Kyle Clark, "USA Barefoot Sanders telephonically advised 10:15 A.M. this date that he had received a call from Mr. John Martin, Jr... advising that he was standing near the reflection pool at the time the President was shot ... Martin told the USA he was positive the shots came from the Texas School Book Building and that he had so informed an unnamed police officer of this fact." In an April 2, 1964 FBI report, which became Commission Document 897, it is detailed, "Martin said he ran north on Houston Street and stopped at the north end of the reflection pool which lies west of and is adjacent to Houston Street ... Martin said he took some movie shots of the President as he passed by on Elm Street. A few seconds after the President had passed and was departing from his view, he heard a loud report and at first thought that it was a firecracker and a few seconds later heard two more reports and then knew it was rifle fire ... the shots sounded to him like they came from the Texas School Book Depository."

And there is yet *another* Martin here, John T. Martin, who filmed both the house of General Edwin Walker and Oswald in New Orleans passing out leaflets on the street. Both of these, we are supposed to believe, just coincidentally appeared on the same roll of film. One of these Martins, presumably the one who filmed the motorcade, supposedly told Richard Trask, author of the book *Pictures of the Pain*, that he'd seen Oswald get into a car about fifteen minutes after the shooting. Was he yet another witness to the infamous Rambler incident, which was all but ignored by the authorities? In one of his last acts as director of the Sixth Floor Museum in Dallas, the late Gary Mack published Jack T. Martin's home movie online for free. In 1996, researcher Martin Shackelford provided the following synopsis for the Jack Martin film: "The Jack Martin Film (8-9-63) In another of those aforementioned ironic twists, a tourist named Jack Martin was in Dallas in August 1963. His film records his view from the airplane. Next, he visits General Edwin Walker, under whom he had served, allegedly target of an assassination attempt by Lee Oswald in April of that year. The film documents the scene of that attempt: the window through which the shot was fired, the bullet hole, and the wall from behind which it was most likely fired, ending with shots of Walker's flag and mailbox, and a nearby building under construction (allegedly also photographed by Oswald prior to the attempt!). Then we see the entrance to a movie theater, cypress trees, a seal at the edge of a pool, and the statue of Andrew Jackson in Lafayette Park in New Orleans. Aroused by a commotion on Canal Street, Martin crossed to see what was happening, and began filming. We see Lee Oswald, leaflets in hand, standing on the sidewalk, being harangued by anti-Castro militants including Carlos Bringuier. Four police officers are seen arriving. The film ends with a view of the yellow leaflets scattered on the sidewalk after Bringuier knocked them out of Oswald's hands, and a brief aerial view of a subdivision. ... A still from this film was finally published in Robert Groden's 1995 book, *The Search for Lee Harvey Oswald*, an essential photo archive on Oswald." It seems that this Jack T. Martin was a teenager in 1963.

In 1968, Harold Weisberg and his assistant Gary Schoener, received the Jack Martin home movie, from Jack Martin himself, and then met him personally. According to Schoener, when Gary Mack later put Martin's film up online, it was under the condition that Martin never be contacted by anyone. An April 6, 1967 memo by CIA analyst Marguerite D. Stevens, concluded that Jack S. Martin and John J. Martin were probably the same person. (File 201-289248 crossed out, changed to 100-300-17). The memo noted, "According to the individual who made the allegation concerning John J. Martin, one Carl John Stanley, aka 'Most Reverend Christopher Maria Stanley,' self-styled archbishop of the Metropolitan Eastern Province, American Orthodox Catholic Church, he and 'Bishop' John J. Martin in July 1961 had, on Martin's recommendation, consecrated (David Ferrie) as a bishop in Stanley's church. Ferrie, according to Stanley, had subsequently been 'deposed' as bishop in January 1962, when Stanley learned that (Ferrie) had been discharged by Eastern Airlines for homosexual activities. According to Stanley (who the Louisville Police Department believes is a mentally unbalanced con-man) John J. Martin drank a great deal and on one occasion, while drinking, said that Lee Harvey Oswald and Ferrie 'were buddies' and that he (Martin) was connected with them. Stanley added that Martin told him that he (Martin), Ferrie, Jerry de Pugh (allegedly a relative of Jimmy Hoffa), George Augustine Hyde – 'a bishop in another church' … who Stanley characterized as a homosexual, and Lee Harvey Oswald lived together, worked together, were close friends and were involved with some Cuban organization. Stanley said that John J. Martin in 1963 … was a writer for a newspaper … during this period Martin corresponded with him from New Orleans as well as from Houston…. According to Stanley, John J. Martin claims to have been in the Air Force during WW II, to have worked for CIA, and to carry out numerous police 'commissions' … Jack S. Martin … appears to be of unsound mind and who in all probability is John J. Martin regarding who (Carl Stanley) reported."

Carlos Bringuier was questioned by Garrison's office on February 16, 1967. Interestingly, he mentioned that both he and Edward Voebel were interviewed by WDSU radio on the night of the assassination (it does not clarify whether they were interviewed together). It is curious that Oswald's close boyhood friend should be appearing on radio that quickly, and on television as well, according to Jack Martin. Was it related to what seems to have been Voebel being the first to point the finger at David Ferrie? Bringuier also mentioned that Donald Savery, a friend of Ruth Paine's who was also a Quaker, "may have been involved with Oswald." Savery was referenced as being "connected with the New Orleans Committee for Peaceful Alternatives," but there is nothing else about him anywhere in the official record. Bringuier's New Orleans clothing store Casa Roca became the gathering spot for anti-Castro Cubans in the area. He would memorably confront Oswald on August 9, 1963, as he was passing out Fair Play for Cuba pamphlets at a Canal Street intersection, and a fight broke out after he denounced the future patsy as a Castro-supporting communist. Oswald, Bringuier, and three other Cubans were arrested for disturbing the peace. On August 17, eight days after the altercation, Oswald was interviewed on WDSU radio. Bringuier seems to have been the one to arrange the interview. A few days later, Oswald, Bringuier, and Edward Butler of the anti-communist outfit Information Council of the Americas, took part in a debate on the same radio station, moderated by William Stuckey, who had been the one who interviewed Oswald. By August 16, Oswald was back passing out his leaflets, in front of the International Trade Mart, whose director, of course, was Clay Shaw.

Bringuier was born in 1934, and is still alive at the time of this writing. In a revealing 2013 interview, we learned that he and his wife had operated a grocery store on Magazine Street in the 1990s, and he had been both a salesman and manager for Radio Shack after that. Bringuier liked being a salesman, saying, "I don't want responsibility." Regarding Lee Harvey Oswald, Bringuier declared, "I distrusted him—I don't know what was the reason—but I distrusted him." Interestingly, in this article, the Casa Roca is described as a "dry goods store," selling things like blue jeans and "new underwear." When Oswald first walked into his store, Bringuier claimed, "He didn't sell himself to me 100 percent. And I had a feeling inside me—that I don't know if the man was a communist or somebody from the FBI that wanted to find out about me." Bringuier talked about journalist Jefferson Morley attempting to talk with him, saying he threatened to call the police, because he didn't want to be interrogated by "conspiracy theorists." He called all the speculation about him in connection with the assassination, "Lies, lies, lies."[16] Bringuier apparently still has Oswald's USMC handbook, and reportedly has been trying to sell it for six figures over the years. An FBI report, dated June 19, 1964, from Special Agent Edwin D. Kuydendall, claimed that in a talk given on May 5, 1964 in Plano, Texas, Carlos Bringuier "said the name shown inside the cover of that book was HIDELL." A.J. Hidell is the alias that Oswald supposedly used to order both the alleged assassination weapon and the gun allegedly used to kill Officer J.D. Tippit, and was the name listed as the President of the Fair Play for Cuba Committee. Bringuier has a profile on Linkedin, where he promotes his latest book, *Crime Without Punishment – How Castro Assassinated President Kennedy And Got Away With It*. He also boasts about all the "very interesting people" he has met, including Spiro Agnew, General Edwin Walker, and Dr. Alton Oschner. His seemingly lengthy career at Radio Shack isn't listed, but he does list working as a supervisor for United Homecare in Miami, from 1995-1998. He also lists the store referred to as Casa Roca by other sources, as Casa Cuba, which he ran from 1964-1983. He refers to himself as "Dr. Carlos Bringuier," but his education centered around law school.

An FBI memo dated March 24, 1967 describes Gordon Novel having contacted their New Orleans office, without giving the location he was calling from. The memo reads, "Novel stated he has thirteen questions he wants Garrison to answer which if he asks will destroy Garrison's investigation." It further describes Novel as having been "in contact with one of Shaw's attorneys," with the claim that "Garrison is trying to force him to say that Shaw and Dean Andrews have met which he refuses to say." Garrison was being blocked by Ohio Governor James Rhodes, as he was by several other governors, from extraditing important witnesses (like Novel) to New Orleans. Incredibly, Rhodes stipulated that he wouldn't extradite Novel unless Garrison promised not to question him about the assassination.[17] Garrison alleged that Novel, along with Sergio Arcacha Smith, David Ferrie, and others, had conspired to burglarize a Louisiana munitions bunker in 1961. Novel would claim that Attorney General Jack Gremillion "had been told who killed David Ferrie and how it was done." According to author William Torbitt, Novel was witnessed meeting with Jack Ruby and Oswald lookalike William Seymour in the Carousel Club in October and November 1963. Shortly after Novel left New Orleans, two young women cleaning his old apartment found a letter hidden in the kitchen. Addressed to a "Mr. Weiss," (who Garrison would conclude was Novel's CIA handler), it read, "I took the liberty of writing you direct and apprising you of current situation, expecting you to forward this through appropriate channels. Our connection and activity of that period involves individuals presently about to be indicted as conspirators in Garrison's investigation."[18] According to researcher Robert Charles-Dunne, in the early 1980s, Novel was hired as a bodyguard by *Hustler* magazine's Larry Flynt, who was famously shot and paralyzed himself, and offered a million dollar reward to anyone solving the JFK assassination.[19] In another curious connection, Novel would assist former Attorney General Ramsey Clark, when he was representing some of the survivors of the Waco massacre.[20] In a video now removed from Google, Novel made several interesting comments, including "Oswald was a patsy," "RFK was killed by a Manchurian candidate," and "I am a fan of Jim Marrs."[21]

Reporters Hoke May and Ross Yockey of the New Orleans *States-Item* told Jim Garrison that Novel's lawyers were being paid by the CIA. As Richard Billings wrote, "At this point, Hoke May came to Garrison's office; he had a report about Jerry Weiner, the Novel lawyer in Columbus, who, according to Hoke May, has admitted being paid by the CIA. This makes two lawyers who told reporters they were on the CIA payroll, the other being Plotkin, who is Novel's lawyer in New Orleans, who told *States-Item* reporter Ross Yockey of his CIA retainer."[22]

In a June 25, 2005 post on the Education Forum, the late Jack White, in my estimation a sadly neglected researcher into several important subjects, wrote, "Novel once phoned me long distance from Florida, berating me for saying he was the Umbrellaman. He talked for 45 minutes; I got in about a dozen words. His every third word was 'motherxxxx er.' He claimed that he was in a meeting at the Stork Club in New York at the time of the assassination, and had at least a dozen witnesses who would say so. He threatened to kill me, then changed his mind to suing me for a 'motherxxxxing million dollars and ruining my life so I would suffer more than death.' Mary Ferrell was on friendly terms with Novel and other such people, believing in the theory of the 'Godfather' ... be closer to your enemies than your friends. Mary played both sides of the street to gather her vast information. It was she and Robert Cutler who arranged a lie test for Novel about whether he was in the Plaza on 11-22. He flunked the test." White didn't make it clear whether Novel's threats against him came before or after he actually was attacked in his home and severely wounded by an intruder. Novel would pop up again during Watergate, when Jack Anderson reported that Charles Colson had asked him to build a "degaussing gun" that could erase tapes stored at the CIA and the White House that might be incriminating to President Nixon. In a 2006 interview, Novel declared, "I'm not a CIA agent. I'm affiliated, I work with, and we have a mutual admiration society based upon my relationship with the individuals I work with.... The CIA has multiple sides but it's been my experience over the years that they're basically the only good guys in the entire United States government. They're really patriots. Most of 'em are patriots and I've never known ... I personally have never known them to do anything criminal, ever. And they didn't kill John Kennedy and they didn't kill a lot of people that they've been accused of causing the death of but I don't know that to be true. So I can tell you that my experience with 'em has been like dealing with Eagle Scouts."

Oliver Stone, in a December 22, 1991 letter which appeared in the *New York Times*, in response to Tom Wicker's unsurprising attack on his film *JFK*, wrote, "A declassified CIA memo dated June 1, 1967, says that then NBC correspondent Walter Sheridan was 'coaching (witness) Gordon Novel to get maximum publicity before picturing him on a TV program intended to destroy Garrison's act.' The show did not air until several weeks later – how did the CIA know its point of view?" Sheridan did more than perhaps anyone else to undermine Garrison's investigation, but many continue to believe that he was working at the behest of his supposed close friend Robert F. Kennedy. Sheridan, in fact, put Novel on a $500 a day retainer, especially great money at that time, while prepping him for the NBC hatchet job on Garrison. He encouraged Novel to flee to avoid indictment, and gave him an additional $750 after he arrived in Columbus, Ohio.[23] Dean Andrews claimed to have been offered a recording studio. Sheridan had worked for the National Security Agency, and had ties there that were still evident at the time of the NBC television hit piece on Garrison. A CIA memo noted that, "Richard Lansdale, Associate General Counsel, has advised us that NBC plans to do a derogatory TV special on Garrison and his probe of the Kennedy assassination; that NBC regards Garrison as a menace to the country and means to destroy him. The program is to be presented within the next few weeks. Mr. Lansdale learned this information from Mr. Walter Sheridan of NBC."[24] Sheridan used Turkish bath house owner Fred Leemans, who had claimed Shaw used the name Clay Bertrand while frequenting his business, to say on air that Garrison's office had offered him $2500 for his testimony. After the show aired, Leemans explained that he had only participated in the one-sided special because of the threatening phone calls he'd received, "relative to the information that I had given Mr. Garrison." He also said he'd been visited by someone wearing a badge who said they were checking around for income tax violations, and that it was "not smart" to be involved in the Garrison case "because a lot of people that had been involved got hurt." He further stated that Shaw defense attorney Irvin Dymond offered him a lawyer and bond if he was charged with giving false information to the district attorney.[25]

Jack Anderson, the reporter with an undeserved reputation as a muckraker, interviewed Jim Garrison in April of 1967. Afterwards, before submitting anything to the *Washington Post* which published his column, he went straight to the FBI. In a memo touching on this, Cartha DeLoach described how Anderson went into the interview prepared to be strongly opposed to the D.A., but was swayed by Garrison to such a degree that he accepted "there is some authenticity to Garrison's claims." Despite this, the wildly dishonest Anderson blasted Garrison just like the rest of the mainstream media, and began pushing the absurd fallback notion that Fidel Castro had Kennedy killed in retaliation.[26] At the same time, the CIA responded to Garrison's probe aggressively. In a September 26, 1967 "survey of possible courses of action," they suggested getting someone friendly to the Agency to convince Senator Russell Long not to endorse Garrison's investigation, and sought to persuade former CIA director John McCone to "exert influence in Catholic and Republican circles." They mentioned talking with John Daly, best known as the long-time host of the television show *What's My Line?*, who was the director of USIA and the son-in-law of Chief Justice Earl Warren.

One of Walter Sheridan's close friends was Carmine Bellino. Bellino had worked with RFK on the McClellan Senate Select Committee on Improper Activities in Labor and Management, and assisted Sheridan in his work for RFK during the Kennedy administration. Bellino had once shared an office with the shadowy Robert Maheu. More significantly, Bellino had worked for none other than Guy Banister, performing background checks for the Rand Corporation, linked to the CIA. He became an investigator for the Watergate Committee.[27]

The government continued to be concerned with any further prosecution of Clay Shaw. In 1971, Judge Herbert Christenberry made the unprecedented move of permanently restraining the District Attorney's office from prosecuting Shaw. Christenberry refused to recuse himself, even though he had sent an astonishing letter to Shaw following his acquittal, in which Caroline Christenberry (Herbert's wife), wrote: "Our most sincere congratulations! We shared your anxieties over the past two outrageous years. Should your case have eventually found its way to federal court and been allotted to my husband you most certainly would have had a <u>fair</u> trial. He felt we should not risk the possibility of being considered 'prejudiced' in advance. This is our reason for not openly expressing these sentiments much earlier. ..."[28] Christenberry would go on to preside over the laughable prosecution of Garrison in 1973.

The raid on the Houma, Louisiana bunker of the Schlumberger Wells Company took place in August of 1961, according to Garrison, while Novel claimed it was earlier, probably prior to the April Bay of Pigs invasion. Houma Police department records showed that the burglary was reported on August 22, 1961. One witness questioned by Garrison testified that those participating in the raid included Novel, Ferrie, Sergio Arcacha-Smith, Layton Patrick Martens, and several other Cubans. This unidentified witness told Garrison's office that the reason behind the raid was to "secure ammunition and other explosives" for purposes unknown to him. According to researcher William Kelly, the munitions and arms taken from Houma eventually found their way to Guy Banister's 544 Camp Street office. The owner of the Schlumberger company, Jean DeMenil, was connected to the White Russian community in Texas, which included Oswald's much older close friend with powerful connections, George de Mohrenschildt, who were instrumental in helping Oswald and his wife when they arrived from the Soviet Union. Novel would later bring a libel case against Garrison over Houma. Luis Rabel Nunez, former head of the New Orleans Cuban Revolutionary Council, was rumored to have been another participant in the Houma raid. A.J. Weberman described how, "...in a telephone interview Luis Rabel Nunez denied he met David Ferrie or Guy Banister, but said he knew Sergio Arcacha Smith." When asked about the Houma burglary, Nunez replied, "Well, I used to run a dry cleaners, and I had a truck that I used to loan to about 40 or 50 exiles here. Arcacha asked me to loan him the truck to move some furniture. Whether the truck was used to move anything other than furniture is beyond me." From his safe refuge in Ohio, Novel cryptically called the Houma incident one of "the most patriotic burglaries in history." At a party, where alcohol had made him more uninhibited, Novel claimed the arms were intended for use at the upcoming Bay of Pigs, which would have put the date months earlier than Garrison had it. Novel claimed he was given a key to the bunker by his CIA contact. He identified others in the "CIA group" which raided the bunker as David Ferrie and Sergio Arcacha Smith. A major newspaper story appeared to support this, noting that a reliable source close to Banister had seen 50 to 100 boxes marked "Schlumberger" in Banister's office, in early 1961, prior to the Bay of Pigs. The boxes contained grenades, land mines, and "little missiles."[29] Some of the Houma material would resurface on

August 1, 1963, when the FBI raided the Cuban exile training camp on Louisiana's Lake Pontchartrain. Jack Martin would allege that Banister contacted the manager of the Schlumberger Well Services Company, M.E. Loy, to confirm that the FBI or CIA would be supplying the group with keys to the bunker.

Sergio Arcacha-Smith's attorney Frank Hernandez stated, "It was a CIA operation. It was set up so that Schlumberger could report it (the weapons transfer) as a robbery, and be reimbursed by their insurance company. They went in at midnight and the material was waiting for them on a loading dock. We later verified that the CIA indeed reimbursed the insurance company."[30]

Sergio Arcacha-Smith was born in Havana, and graduated from the prestigious Columbia Law School. Arcacha was Cuba's counsel in India under Fulgencio Batista. After Castro obtained power, Arcacha fled to Venezuela, where he was the assistant manager of the Lago Hotel in Caracas, from 1954-1957. While an assistant manager of a hotel in Houston, Arcacha became friends with both General Edwin Walker and oil baron H.L. Hunt. He eventually wound up in New Orleans, where he interacted with the other ground level conspirators. Two witnesses would testify that Arcacha was with them in a Houston office, where he worked as an air conditioner salesman, at the time of the assassination. Sergio Arcacha-Smith was perhaps David Ferrie's closest associate. Jack Martin claimed that the Office of Naval Intelligence helped to reunite Arcacha with his family in Louisiana. Arcacha became the New Orleans delegate to the Cuban Democratic Liberation Front, which a CIA memorandum unearthed by William Davy revealed had been created by the CIA in 1960. The same memo acknowledges that the Cuban Revolutionary Council was formed by the Agency as well, and absorbed the other outfit in 1961.[31] When questioned by Louisiana State Police Lt. Francis Fruge, Mac Manuel, owner of the Silver Slipper bar in Eunice, Louisiana, identified Arcacha-Smith as one of the men seen in the company of the ill-fated Rose Cheramie. Arcacha-Smith was protected from extradition in Texas by John Connally, who of course had been sitting in front of President Kennedy in the limousine on November 22, 1963, and was wounded himself. An intriguing comment by Mary Ferrell on her extensive online database notes that "When Sue Blake, teller preferred by Jack Ruby at Merchants State Bank, moved out of the Lake Gardens apartment, Arcacha moved in." Oswald visited the Mexican Consulate in New Orleans, on September 17, 1963, where he was issued a fifteen-day tourist card. According to a May 14, 1976 summary document from Harold Weisberg's Hood College archives, written by Mark A. Allen, "The man whose tourist card was apparently issued directly before Oswald was William George Gaudet, who told the FBI on 11/27 that he was a former employee of the CIA (C.D. 75, Pg. 588). After twenty years with the Agency, Gaudet went on to work for the International Trade Mart, where Clay Shaw was the director." William Gaudet told author Anthony Summers, "Another vital person is Sergio Arcacha Smith. I know he knew Oswald and knows more about the Kennedy affair than he ever admitted."[32]

Gaudet had another intriguing connection; his *Latin American Reports* newsletter was co-funded by the previously mentioned Alton Oschner. The weekly journal was published out of a practically rent-free office at the International Trade Mart, where Clay Shaw was director. There are strong indications that the CIA may have helped finance Gaudet's publication as well.[33] Researcher Mark A. Allen pointed out that "all of the 19 people who appeared at the Consulate on 9/17 had their names listed in C.D. 75 in the order first name, middle, last name except for Oswald and Gaudet. The former's name was mistakenly inverted Harvey Oswald Lee and the latter's is listed Gaudet William George." He further noted that "Curiously enough, Gaudet's name appears in the Hearings and Exhibits on a completely different matter. CE 2880, an FBI report relates that William George Gaudet telephoned the New Orleans FBI office on 11/27 stating 'he had heard Jack Ruby from Dares, Texas had purchased Paintings from one Lorenzo Borenstein.'" When Gaudet was interviewed by Warren Report critic Bernard Fensterwald on May 13, 1975, he denied ever giving any information about Ruby to the FBI. Also appearing at the consulate on the same day as Oswald was one David Pearce Maygar, whom Allen claimed in his summary document, told the FBI he was a friend of Ferrie. Allen also dropped a reference to the passengers list for the bus Oswald allegedly took to Mexico that "disappeared under suspicious circumstances."

Jim Garrison started out confidently, declaring that the assassination had been "solved beyond any shadow of a doubt," and called Lee Harvey Oswald "a decoy, a victim, and a fall guy." Garrison objected to the right of Supreme Court Chief Justice Earl Warren and associate justice Abe Fortas to "pass on efforts of Clay L. Shaw to avoid trial on charges of conspiring to assassinate President John F. Kennedy," to quote from an August 14, 1968 FBI teletype. Garrison stated that Warren should be barred from any involvement due to his role as head of the Warren Commission, whose work Garrison was essentially debunking. Garrison was opposed to Fortas because he was a "long time personal friend of President Johnson." Garrison was quoted as saying, "Once again the federal court has reached down and prevented us from going to trial in the case of Clay L. Shaw. We do not agree with the court's position that there is any basis for more federal interference with the processes of justice in this case." The New Orleans D.A. charged that Johnson "has participated actively in concealing vital evidence with regard to the murder of his predecessor." Garrison noted that Fortas "would not be free to look at the case objectively, nor would any other man who had received his judge's robes from President Johnson." Garrison was responding to the fact that a day earlier, on August 13, 1968, a special three-judge panel had barred Garrison from prosecuting Clay Shaw, until the Supreme Court ruled that he could be tried in New Orleans. Although Shaw would eventually be tried and acquitted, when Garrison sought in 1972 to indict him for perjury, the Supreme Court stepped in to protect him, rejecting Garrison's attempt.[34]

Behind the scenes, Jim Garrison was telling people that he thought then-Vice President Lyndon B. Johnson was involved in the assassination. Then acting Attorney General Ramsey Clark alluded to this, in a February 20, 1967 phone call to LBJ, during which he said, "I had heard that Hale Boggs was sayin' [that] he – Garrison – was sayin' that ... or privately around town [was saying] that it [the assassination] could be traced back [to you] ... or that you could be found in it someplace, which ... I can't believe he's been sayin' that. The Bureau says they haven't heard any such thing, and they got lots of eyes and ears. 'Course, that was a [credible] fella like Hale Boggs. But Hale gets pretty emotional about people [like Garrison] that he really doesn't like, and people who have fought him and been against him, and I would be more inclined to attribute it to that. Either that, or this guy Garrison [is] just completely off his rocker." After Clark identified aide Marvin Watson as the man Boggs had said this to, LBJ confronted Watson, who was in the room, asking, "[Did] Hale tell you that—Hale Boggs—that this fella [Garrison, this] district attorney down there, said that this is traced to me or somethin'?" Watson replied, "Privately he [Garrison] was using your name as having known about it [the assassination]. I said [to Boggs], Will you give this information to Barefoot Sanders? Ramsey was out of town—this was Saturday night. [Boggs] said, I sure will. So I asked the operator to get Barefoot and Ramsey together, and they did."

Oliver Stone's *JFK* shows how some witnesses were scared to come forward and testify in Garrison's investigation. One such witness was Jean Hill, the schoolteacher who was wearing red, and standing closer to the presidential limousine when the president was shot than any other witness except her companion, Mary Moorman. An FBI airtel [a letter, to be typed and mailed on the same day], dated August 9, 1968, notes that Hill had reported being contacted by Garrison's aide Tom Bethell, about being questioned at her home. The airtel states, "She does not want to testify in New Orleans and is upset over this matter." The airtel continues, "Mrs. HILL stated it is a strange coincidence that these men contacted her today as just night before last two men attempted to break into her home... She does not know if this had any connection with this matter, but she has considered the possibility. Hill, apparently pretty astute, questioned whether Bethell was a legitimate representative for the District Attorney. Both former Dallas Deputy Sheriff Roger Craig and Dealey Plaza eyewitness Richard Carr survived attempts on their lives before testifying at Shaw's trial. Julia Ann Mercer, who identified Jack Ruby as the man she saw on the Grassy Knoll earlier on the day of the assassination, told Garrison the government had not recorded her statements accurately, and was too frightened to testify. She would also refuse to appear before the HSCA. Richard Giesbrecht related a fascinating account of overhearing a conspiratorial conversation at Winnipeg International Airport on February 13, 1964. He heard detailed conversations relating to the assassination of JFK. One of the participants, who was unforgettable due to his singularly odd physical appearance, would later be identified by Giesbrecht as David Ferrie. He was set to testify at the trial of Clay Shaw, but after receiving one too many threats, he backed out.[35]

Garrison faced a barrage of vicious negative coverage by the entire mainstream media. There was a front page story in the *New York Times,* on June 12, 1967, which accused the D.A. of offering enticements to witnesses, and fabricating evidence. This would culminate in an NBC special that made no pretense at being anything other than a Garrison hit piece. Garrison actually won his first trial associated with this case, when Dean Andrews, Jr. was convicted of perjury in August of 1967. In trying to prevent the trial from taking place, Andrews claimed that the "only conspiracy existing is the conspiracy planted in Perry Russo's mind through the use of hypnotic suggestion." As Richard Popkin, author of the early conspiracy classic *The Second Oswald,* pointed out in defending Garrison, he was being denied some forty pages of classified material in the National Archives, on David Ferrie alone. As Popkin further stated, in addition to other key witnesses being refused extradition orders, "Another potential witness, Sandra Moffitt, fled or moved to Iowa, a state from which she cannot be extradited. She has been willing to 'testify' on NBC, but not as yet before the New Orleans Grand Jury. Recently, a Vermont judge turned down a summons for J. Wesley Liebeler, the lawyer who had conducted the New Orleans investigation for the Warren Commission, to appear as a witness in the Andrews trial." He recounted how infiltrator William Gurvich appeared on CBS's disinfo series defending the Warren Report, where he charged that Garrison's methods were "very illegal, and unethical." Popkin noted that both Perry Russo and Marlene Mancuso (former lady friend of Gordon Novel), had accused NBC of attempting to bribe them. Popkin wrote, "Miss Mancuso's statement predates the NBC program by a month (it is dated May 20, 1967), and describes how she was treated by the NBC people when they tried to induce her to give them an interview. Russo, in a statement made public right after the NBC program, claimed Walter Sheridan had offered to move him to California, protect his job, get him a lawyer, and guarantee him against extradition if 'he did side up with NBC and the defense and bust up the Garrison probe.' Townley (NBC's Richard Townley) has been charged with attempting to bribe Russo by offering him lodging in California, employment, payment of legal fees, protection and immunity from the state of Louisiana and Garrison's office, and influence on the defense lawyers in their forth coming cross-examination of him (*States-Item*, July 11)." Sheridan claimed it was "harassment" when the New Orleans Grand Jury attempted to subpoena him, and was charged with contempt when he failed to appear when summoned.[36]

Largely because his other witnesses either died unnaturally, were shielded from extradition by several governors, or were just too frightened to testify, Garrison was ultimately left only with Clay Shaw to prosecute. As we've seen, Shaw was connected to several of the players who were members of the Ground Level Plot. Given his standing in the community, it seems unlikely that someone like Shaw would have consorted with figures far below him economically, except perhaps for sexual purposes. If there was a player overseeing these manipulated figures at the ground level, it would have been Shaw. Although it is probable that Shaw, too, was being manipulated by greater powers, the real conspirators in the JFK assassination. If Shaw was just a kindly philanthropist who was persecuted by an overzealous Jim Garrison, then why are his military records still classified?[37] On at least two occasions, Shaw slipped up and admitted he was Clay Bertrand. On his official arrest record, under "Alias," it is clearly printed "Clay Bertrand." According to researcher Paul Bleau, he also used the Bertrand alias in an airport lounge. As was dramatized in Oliver Stone's *JFK*, Judge Edward Haggerty refused to permit New Orleans police officer Aloysius Habighorst to testify to Shaw admitting under his questioning that he'd used the Bertrand alias. Witness Jessie Parker testified that Shaw had signed the name "Clay Bertrand" on a registration book on December 14, 1966. Bleau sent copies of Shaw's signature, and Bertrand's (on a library card about which there seems to have been little curiosity – if it wasn't Shaw using as alias, then why wasn't the real library patron with the name of Clem Bertrand identified?), to a handwriting analyst. The expert replied, "I have reviewed the signatures you sent me. I must first tell you that these signatures are not of good quality. They are copies of copies of copies.... Ideally, I should examine originals or first-generation copies, i.e. made from the original. Despite everything, I can tell you that there are several similarities between these signatures on several levels. ...." Handwriting expert Elizabeth McCarthy had testified at the Shaw trial, and was able to examine better quality originals. She too testified to there being obvious similarities.[38]

The aforementioned Permindex may be crucial here. Short for Permanent Industrial Expositions, this mysterious outfit is very real. Originally located in Basel, Switzerland; after protests in Switzerland, France, and Italy, it relocated to South Africa. It was chaired at the time by Montreal Major Louis Mortimer Bloomfield. Some researchers, including those associated with Lyndon Larouche's organization, believe that Permindex orchestrated the assassination of President Kennedy. According to Larouche's *Executive Intelligence Review*, "The Garrison investigation and trial also revealed that some of the same Permindex officials involved in the Kennedy assassination were involved in the attempts on Charles de Gaulle. According to testimony at the trial, the Permindex funds which financed the 1961 Bastien-Thiry attempt had been conduited to Europe by Guy Banister, a former FBI agent residing in New Orleans and a close associate of Shaw, who had also played a major role in the Kennedy assassination." The reference here is to Col. Jean-Marie Bastien-Thiry's September 1961 assassination attempt against French President de Gaulle. *EIR* claimed that Prince Philip's World Wide Fund for Nature, initially created as the World Wildlife Fund in 1961, was the agency behind Permindex. Bloomfield had founded the WWF's Canadian branch. Bloomfield had served as a recruitment agent for the FBI's counterespionage division during World War II. He was directed by the shadowy Sir William Stephenson, another Canadian. Oddly, Stephenson ran all British intelligence operations from his base in New York City. He would be instrumental in the creation of the CIA, and many consider him to be the model for the James Bond character. Bloomfield's law firm represented the powerful Bronfman liquor empire, connected to both organized crime and British intelligence. Stephenson also founded the World Commerce Corporation, which would eventually evolve into Permindex. World Commerce Corporation worked closely from the beginning with the International Trade Mart in New Orleans, which Col. Clay Shaw had established in 1945, after serving as OSS liaison officer to Winston Churchill's headquarters.[39]

There seem to be no updates available, but circa 2007, there was some legal wrangling in Canada over the LM Bloomfield papers. Bloomfield died in 1984. A few years before his death he donated 31 boxes of documents to the Library and Archives of Canada. This included correspondence with well-known politicians such as George H.W. Bush. The one condition Bloomfield placed on the donation was that public access to the papers would be restricted for 20 years after his death. However, when researcher Maurice Phillips attempted to gain access to these materials in 2004, he found that Bloomfield's widow, Justine Stern Bloomfield Cartier, was still refusing permission for them to be released into the public domain. It's reasonable to speculate that his widow was concerned that release of the letters would damage her husband's reputation.[40]

Shaw was also a member of the Board of Directors for Centro Mondiale Commerciale, the Rome Word Trade Center, sitting alongside CIA and Mossad assets. Another CMC board member was Prince Gutierrez di Spadforo, who'd been Benito Mussolini's under secretary of agriculture. CMC was connected to the notorious Italian Freemason lodge Propaganda Due (P2), and the Banco Ambrosiano scandal, which led to "God's banker" Roberto Calvi, being found hanged under London's Blackfriars Bridge on June 17, 1982. The anti-Catholic bigotry that JFK's presidential campaign incited among Freemasons in America was apparently international in scope. A September 24, 1960 letter from the Italian Grand Master of the Freemasons, Enzio Milone, to Christian Democratic Member of Parliament, Elio Rosati, instructed, "... propagate as much as possible the protestant idea—influence Italian immigrants in the USA to vote against Kennedy ..." An informant would tell Garrison that FBI agent Regis Kennedy had confirmed that Shaw was a CIA agent who had done work "of an unspecified nature" for five years in Italy. Supposedly, Shaw set up an official Permindex display in the New Orleans Trade Mart. In a May 5, 1959 letter to Mrs. Ann Carnahan, Shaw admitted his connections, writing, "I am a member of the Board of Directors of Centro Mondiale Commerciale which is a PERMINDEX subsidiary...."

A very curious member of the Permindex board was Hjalmar Schacht, who was president of the Central Bank of Germany under Adolf Hitler, and also served as his Minister of Economics. He would break with Hitler, and was arrested by the Gestapo after an assassination attempt on Hitler in July, 1944. He was sent to Dachau, and was one of only three defendants to be acquitted at the Nuremberg Trials, over the objections of the Soviets, who wanted him executed. His curious career continued, when he worked as a paid consultant to Aristotle Onassis in the 1950s. Yet another Permindex board member, and according to documents obtained by Maurice Phillips, the active leader of Permindex, was Ferenc Nagy, who had briefly been the Prime Minister of Hungary. Phillips also unearthed a March 24, 1967 CIA memo, in which it is stated, "NAGY, Ferenc, (...) was a cleared contact of the International Organizations Division. His 201 file contains a number of references to his association with the World Trade Center." Nagy had asked the CIA if they'd be interested in using Permindex in some capacity. The Soviets would accuse Nagy and the CIA of being behind the 1956 uprising in Hungary. William Harvey, the CIA station chief in Rome, where both Permindex and Centro Mondiale Commerciale were located, has long been suspected of involvement in the assassination by researchers. Finally, Phillips found a letter from Major Louis Bloomfield, which stated that he and Nagy were in discussions with David Rockefeller to create New York City's World Trade Center based on the model of Permindex and the Centro Mondiale Commerciale. Nagy has been suspected by some researchers as being the still unidentified "Umbrella Man," who was seen in films and photos holding an umbrella over his head in Dealey Plaza, on the very sunny day of November 22, 1963.[41] Shaw described his work with Permindex in a September 1969 interview with *Penthouse* magazine, saying, "I didn't mind being on their board, although there was no money involved, but I would have to go to Rome annually for the board meetings and my way would be paid, so why not?" In the same interview, we learn from Shaw himself that he refused to take a lie-detector test when being questioned by Garrison's office. Garrison would allege that Shaw himself was the director of Permindex. Permindex, incidentally, opposed Algerian independence, something that Senator John F. Kennedy strongly supported.

Garrison was unable to convince the jury of Shaw's guilt as a JFK assassination conspirator, and they quickly acquitted him. The judge who presided over the Shaw trial, Edward A. Haggerty, Jr. would be arrested on December 17, 1969 along with sixteen others, in a vice raid at a motel "stag party." The Louisiana Supreme Court subsequently voted to remove Haggerty from office, citing "public misconduct off the bench . . . so seriously delinquent as to bring disgrace and discredit upon the judicial office." The Judicial commission investigated allegations against Haggerty that he had failed to perform duties, was habitually intemperate and had frequently appeared in public intoxicated, had physical issues that interfered with the performance of his duties, and had engaged in willful misconduct.[42] Unsurprisingly, Haggerty was found not guilty of all charges by a fellow judge (no jury). In an interview aired two years after his death in 1990, Haggerty would say, "I believe he [Shaw] was lying to the jury. Of course, the jury probably believed him. But I think Shaw put a good con job on the jury."

Jim Garrison was defeated for reelection, but he was ready by 1974 to resume his political career, and seemed to have a good chance in his bid to become a Louisiana State Supreme Court justice. However, two days before the election, on August 15, sixty-one-year-old Clay Shaw died. Following the inexorable tsunami of press coverage that followed, all of it sympathetic to the kindly businessman cast in the role of persecuted philanthropist, Garrison went down to defeat. In a subsequent interview with reporter Richard Boyle, Garrison expressed his skepticism about the convenient death of Shaw, and suggested that Boyle look into it. At one point, Garrison said, "I hear the coroner wants to have Clay Shaw's body exhumed." Boyle did indeed conduct an investigation. It was noted that New Orleans Parish Coroner Dr. Frank Minyard had remarked, only a few days after Shaw's death: "No police were called to Shaw's residence to ascertain if there was evidence of foul play. Instead, Shaw's personal physician played the part of coroner and police investigator and pronounced the man dead." There was, in fact, no official examination of Shaw's body. Minyard went on to ask, "How can we know for sure the man didn't commit suicide, wasn't given a mercy-killing shot, or wasn't murdered?" The coroner charged that Shaw "... had not been protected at his death, as required by law. ... All we're trying to do is prevent someone from dying at the discretion of someone else and not by that of the Good

Lord." A TV reporter who was interested in the murky circumstances around Shaw's death received a telephone call from a woman who refused to identify herself, claiming she'd seen something strange early in the morning of August 15. She reported witnessing an ambulance pull up in front of Shaw's house, at approximately 1 A.M., and then remove a dead body covered with a sheet on a stretcher. The body was carried into Shaw's house, whereupon the attendants got back into the ambulance and left. The official time of Shaw's death was listed as 12:40 A.M. Police were unable to locate the mystery witness. "If we come up with a lady who will testify to this, we will take legal steps to exhume the body," Minyard told reporters. Minyard was attacked in the press over his friendship with Garrison, and soon after, called off his investigation. When reporter Boyle contacted him, all he would say was "no comment."[43]

Former CIA officer Victor Marchetti would reveal that Richard Helms had instructed Agency personnel to do all they could to help out Shaw during his trial. Witness Betty Parrot told Garrison's office, in a March 31, 1967 interview, that a man named Bill Dalzell, who lived with her, was involved in an outfit called the Friends of Cuba, and that two of his fellow members were Sergio Arcacha Smith and FBI agent Regis Kennedy. She further revealed that "this group later moved from their office in the Balter Building and moved into an office in the International Trade Mart and then operated under the name of The Voice of Cuba or The Friends of Democratic Cuba." In a May 24, 1967 memo to Garrison, assistant D.A. William Martin wrote, "(DAVE BALDWIN) formerly of this City and a former newspaper reporter for the *New Orleans States Item*, was a covert member of the Central Intelligence Agency and operated in India during the years of 1950, 1951 and 1952. Subsequent to his service in India Mr. BALDWIN returned to this city and was employed by CLAY SHAW as Public Relations Director for the International Trade Mart from 1952 through 1955...It was told to me that, during his employment at the Trade Mart, DAVID BALDWIN succeeded in recruiting CLAY SHAW for CIA operations, or, conversely, that CLAY SHAW had already been recruited by the CIA by the time of BALDWIN's employment, and that his employment of BALDWIN was suggested or sponsored by the CIA ..."

Bill Davy discovered a 1968 report that was in Jim Garrison's files, which reveals that in the early 1960s, David Ferrie flew Charles A. Wight, an executive with Freeport Sulfur, a firm involved with mining nickel and cobalt in Cuba, and Clay Shaw to Cuba in a private plane owned by Freeport.[44] In what seems to have been quite an odd report for Shaw's defense team to have, both Dean Andrews and local reporter Richard Townley are recorded as saying, in an April 19, 1967 interview, that "Clay Shaw is supposed to have had an investment in some kind of firm owned by David Ferrie." Witness Jules Rico Kimble remembered accompanying Ferrie and Clay Shaw on a flight to Montreal, Canada. On the flight home, Shaw was accompanied by a man who appeared to be Mexican or Cuban.

Jules Rico Kimble is another fascinating character. He would later claim to be the mysterious "Raoul," whom James Earl Ray mentioned in reference to the Martin Luther King assassination. Kimble had a long record of mob activity and violence, often with political overtones. He was linked to Carlos Marcello and admitted to being involved in Mob activity in New Orleans, Montreal, and Memphis--three cities connected to James Earl Ray. He was interviewed in 1989, while serving a double life sentence at El Reno Prison. Kimble's claim that he flew with James Earl Ray to Montreal was recorded in the 1990 documentary "Who Killed Martin Luther King?" In the video, Jim Garrison states, "In the early part of our investigation into John Kennedy's murder, one of the most interesting individuals we encountered was Jules Rico Kimble. We learned from him about his relationship as a, you might say spear carrier for the CIA here in New Orleans. His relationship with David Ferrie and Clay Shaw who were considerably more than spear carriers, who were involved here in New Orleans, with the New Orleans end of the murder of John Kennedy and about Jules Rico Kimble's trip to Montreal--a town where he seemed to be knowledgeable, but we weren't able to get much more than that..." At another point in the video, Garrison says, "Every single statement that he gave us turned out to be true without exception. There was no dissembling. It was only in retrospect I can see from going through his whole file here. The only information that is not true is what had been planted in his mind back at that time at the end of his service for the CIA... where they have planted in his mind the idea that he was really working for the Ku Klux Klan or the White Citizens, which is kind of a standard operating procedure for intelligence agencies before they dismiss somebody, after they've performed things." Kimble himself declares, "Worked for the government, the CIA, for quite a few years, in the assassination.... of John F. Kennedy.... I had a contract there [Montreal], and I would visit up there. At that time, CIA was working Quebec.... I did a couple jobs up there." He drops a bombshell, claiming that he was borrowed from the CIA by the FBI and an agent took him to meet James

Earl Ray at the Atlanta Airport to fly him to Canada. When questioned onscreen, he admitted to being the elusive "Raoul."

An illuminating anecdote was shared by Warren Hinckle, editor of *Ramparts* magazine. It illustrates the obstacles Garrison was contending with. During the height of Garrison's investigation, he contacted Hinckle, whose magazine had been the foremost outlet for Warren Report critics in the mainstream media, and insisted they speak immediately. Quoting Hinckle, "Jim Garrison said, This is urgent. Can you take this in your mailroom? They'd never think to tap the mailroom Garrison began talking when I picked up the mailroom extension: This is risky, but I have little choice. It is imperative that I get this information to you now. Important new evidence has surfaced. Those Texas oilmen do not appear to be involved in President Kennedy's murder in the way we first thought. It was the Military-Industrial Complex that put up the money for the assassination – but as far as we can tell, the conspiracy was limited to the aerospace wing. I've got the names of three companies and their employees who were involved in setting up the President's murder. Do you have a pencil? I wrote down the names of the three defense contractors – Garrison identified them as Lockheed, Boeing, and General Dynamics – and the names of those executives in their employ whom the District Attorney said had been instrumental in the murder of Jack Kennedy ... I said that I had everything down, and Garrison said a hurried good-bye: "It's poor security procedure to use the phone, but the situation warrants the risk ... I wanted you to have this in case something happens ..."[45]

The Orleans Parish Grand Jury testimony related to Jim Garrison's investigation contains some interesting information. Kerry Thornley was one of Oswald's associates in the Marines, but he seemed to remember a lot more details about the future patsy than all the others. Often incriminating details, Thornley described several troubling instances of Oswald's rebellious behavior, and told the grand jury, "The first thought that came into my mind when I heard about the assassination was that he had done this kind of thing again ... my first reaction was that kind of thing always happened to Oswald." Thornley claimed that Oswald routinely referenced "Big Brother" and compared the Marine Corps to the "party leaders" of Orwell's *1984*. Thornley knew Oswald for only three months, and yet the official narrative of the future patsy's time in the Marines is built around his impressions. In many ways, Thornley was the Ruth Paine of Oswald's military service. In 1961, Thorney notably moved from California to New Orleans, which was the epicenter of the ground level conspiracy Jim Garrison focused on. At one point in his testimony, there is a throwaway mention of Thornley writing for *Ramparts* magazine, which as noted was almost alone among the print media in providing the critics of the Warren Report a publishing platform. Thornley's landlord in New Orleans, Jack Spencer, was friends with Clay Shaw, and Thornley admitted "I think I talked to him twice." One of Thornley's more quotable comments was, "The only difference between Oswald and me is he happened to be there with the gun at the right time and had the guts to do it ..." Thornley's nonfiction 1965 book *Oswald* defended the official assassination story. Thornley fought Garrison's subpoena to testify, and was eventually charged with perjury by the New Orleans D.A., but the charge was dropped by his successor in office, Harry Connick, Sr. Thornley was a decidedly "counterculture" figure, but like most of the Left, he despised the Kennedys.

Thornley was of great interest to Jim Garrison. As Garrison noted, "It is hard to avoid becoming curious about Kerry Thornley, whose extravagant testimony differed so enormously from all the other Marines who served with Oswald. Garrison pointed out that Thornley stayed in Washington for some six months before testifying to the Warren Commission, while working as an apartment building doorman in the northern Virginia suburbs. The D.A.'s office found that Thornley's doorman salary was less than his rent, giving rise to speculation that someone was backing him financially. Garrison openly insinuated that Thornley might well have been impersonating Oswald in the Bolton Ford Incident. Garrison actually questioned Thornley about this, and wrote that, "Thornley was unable to recall using Oswald's name or being at Bolton Ford." Thornley was very similar in size and appearance to Oswald. Thornley gave Garrison the intriguing information that he had indeed met Guy Banister, and they had discussed the book he was writing about the pre-assassination-era Oswald. Garrison found that Thornley had been living in New Orleans with John Spencer, only a few blocks away from Clay Shaw. As noted, Spencer and Shaw were friends who frequently visited each other. After the assassination, Thornley left New Orleans abruptly, leaving a message for Spencer that read, "I must leave. I am going to the Washington, D.C. area, probably Alexandria, Virginia." In a lengthy affidavit Thornley sent to Garrison, Oswald's former Marine buddy cavalierly mentioned how he and notorious mobster Johnny Roselli had become good friends after he left Washington, and moved back to California. Roselli would later wind up in an oil drum in the waters off the coast of

Florida, right before he was scheduled to testify before the House Select Committee on Assassinations. In 1992, Thornley confessed to being part of a conspiracy to kill JFK, during an appearance on the television show *A Current Affair*. Thornley declared, "I wanted him dead. I would have shot him myself." He didn't name any fellow co-conspirators. Thornley died in 1998, while working on a book with journalist Sondra London.

On the question of Oswald potentially having been impersonated, Lou Ivon of Garrison's staff explored the subject around which John Armstrong would later formulate his massive book *Harvey & Lee*. In a November 14, 1968 memo to Garrison, Ivon went over the curious discrepancies in Lee Harvey Oswald's height. Of special interest is the fact that Kerry Thornley described Oswald as being about 5'5", far shorter than anyone else ever did. It is reasonable speculation that this might have been related to the fact that Thornley strongly resembled Oswald, and was very close to the alleged assassin's average reported height, most often recorded between 5'9" and 5'11". Foreshadowing what we would see in the future work of Armstrong and Jack White, Ivon wrote, "So we have a 5'6" Oswald coming back to the U.S., going to Robert's house at Fort Worth, and growing 5 inches in time to be observed by John Fain 13 days later." Robert was Lee's older brother, and unlike his mother, firmly believed in Lee's guilt. Ivon concluded, "If you really want to know what I think, it is that Robert knew this returning defector was not really Lee..." Ivon also observed that Oswald gave the wrong place for his own birth – New Orleans, Texas, on two occasions, including that which appears in his Marine records. Looking at a Department of State memo found in Warren Commission Vol. XVIII, p. 143, Ivon notes that "The last paragraph of this letter contains an interesting statement. Rusk, the writer of the letter says, "It is assumed that there is no doubt that the person who has been in communication with the Embassy is the person who was issued a passport in the name of Lee Harvey Oswald." This memo was dated July 11, 1961, again demonstrating that the U.S. government was concerned with the actual identity of Oswald, years before the assassination of President Kennedy. Ivon speculated, "My guess is that the impersonation started in the Marines ... Bill Boxley said that the CIA has successfully put over impersonations so that even mothers are fooled."

Harold Weisberg, before he inexplicably turned against Garrison, was very interested in Kerry Thornley, and his resemblance to Oswald. In a letter published in the June 28-July 4 issue of *Open City*, Weisberg responded to previously published articles by both Thornley and researcher David Lifton. Touching upon Thornley's appearance, Weisberg commented, "How honest is your caption on the picture of the bearded Kerry Thornley? There are a number of photographs of him at the time of the assassination. Could you not have found a single one of them?" Weisberg comments on Thornley's myriad of curious connections, stating, "Now, the day after the assassination he was interviewed by the Secret Service. Two days later, the FBI. Two more days, and he went back to the FBI on his own. 'Libertarian' is the word with which he describes himself, this FBI-seeking Thornley, the same Thornley who pinned a bum 'Communist' rap on the murdered Oswald when his other Marine Corps buddies would not." Weisberg closes with an attack on Lifton, writing, "Dave is best known for the deep conviction that President Kennedy was assassinated from paper-mache trees in Dealey Plaza. More recently, he has been the associate of Wesley J. Liebeler, most active member of the Warren Commission staff, the man who wound up in charge of that part of the work of which Thornley was part." It is interesting that Weisberg, at this point still loyal to Garrison, was aware as early as 1968 about Lifton's strange association with Liebeler, who was an important part of Lifton's highly publicized book *Best Evidence*, published in 1980. Thornley's response to Weisberg which appeared in the July 12-18, 1968 issue of *Open City*, disclosed some fascinating information. Thornley criticizes the Federal Reserve, blasts our "imperialist foreign policy," expresses admiration for the genuinely principled Senator Robert A. Taft, and mentions "my good friend Dr. Murray N. Rothbard," whose work inspired Lew Rockwell (former chief of staff to Ron Paul), who has published many articles by co-author Donald Jeffries. Thornley goes on to blast the foreign and domestic policies of John F. Kennedy. Regarding the JFK assassination, Thornley admitted, "I celebrated, openly and in public." In the previously mentioned 1992 appearance on *A Current Affair*, Thornley said, regarding Jim Garrison, "You should not have gone after me for perjury. You should have gone after me for conspiracy to commit murder. I did not commit perjury. However, I was involved in a conspiracy to murder John F. Kennedy." Directly addressing the subject of impersonation, Thornley declared, "Jim Garrison thought that I was impersonating Oswald, or that I was coaching others to do so, so as to frame Oswald for the Kennedy assassination, so that the true assassins could escape. Garrison thought that I double-crossed Oswald, that I set Oswald up for the assassination. Which offended me enormously, I thought, I would gladly have killed Kennedy, I wouldn't have betrayed Oswald."

In a February 28, 2023 interview on the Conspirinormal podcast, Sondra London spoke about Kerry Thornley. She described the manner in which he'd written his book about Oswald *before* the assassination, doing it dramatically in public. She noted, "He sat out in the Café Napoleon in New Orleans, and ranted while he wrote. He ranted about wanting Kennedy assassinated." It boggles the mind to picture Thornley making what amounted to concrete threats against President Kennedy, without the FBI or law enforcement seeming the slightest bit interested. London called Thornley a "difficult person" and a "genius." She alleged that he was "very much involved in the conspiracy around the Kennedy assassination." She said she learned about "mind control" from Thornley. She went on to state that "Kerry Thornley participated in these brainwashing sessions with someone that he thinks was E. Howard Hunt." On her website, London has a video of Kerry Thornley's taped confession to being a part of a plot to kill JFK. Thornley oddly attributes being triggered to recall his role by Garrison's investigation, but this clearly conflicts with the combative attitude he displays towards Garrison in the letter quoted above, in 1968. He claimed to have had conversations about assassinating JFK with Slim Brooks, aka Jerry Milton Brooks, who was head of the Anti-Communist League of the Caribbean, and worked for Guy Banister, as well as legendary CIA agent E. Howard Hunt. Thornley stated that he met them both right around the time of the Bay of Pigs invasion.

Another potentially bombshell Orleans Parish witness was Jim Hicks. Jim Garrison started out the questioning by noting how nervous Hicks was, and assuring him they were not going to "try and trap you in any way," and "you are not a target of the office in any sense." Hicks, who was in Dealey Plaza at the time of the assassination, described how the Stemmons Freeway sign had been damaged during the shooting, and was removed within *thirty minutes,* by men "I assumed to be members of the Dallas police force." This corroborated Dealey Plaza groundskeeper Emmett Hudson's testimony before the Warren Commission. Immediately before the assassination, Hicks noticed two men in a suspicious car in the parking lot behind the Book Depository. He heard four shots, from at least two different directions, and saw a man standing on the trunk of the car, which backed up to the picket fence on the Grassy Knoll. This sounded very much like what Warren Commission witness S.M. Holland had reported. Like so many other witnesses, Hicks claimed to have been threatened, with phone calls advising him to "shut up or things will happen to your family." Hicks was beaten up by "two Negroes" in his hotel room and thrown through a window, during the period he was testifying before the grand jury. Hicks oddly told the press he didn't think the attack had anything to do with his testimony.[46] A photo taken of a man purported to be Hicks in Dealey Plaza showed something that resembled a radio protruding from his back pocket. This photo was first published in Gary Shaw and Larry Harris' wonderful, vastly underrated 1976 book, *Cover-Up: The Governmental Conspiracy to Conceal the Facts about the Public Execution of John Kennedy*. While there is nothing about this in his Parish testimony, Hicks supposedly admitted, first to researcher Jones Harris, and then to Jim Garrison, that he'd been the radio man for the assassins, according to researcher Richard E. Sprague (not to be confused with the HSCA's first chief counsel Richard A. Sprague). Sprague claimed that "Since the time of his admissions, Jim Hicks has been locked up in an Air Force Hospital for the insane located in Oklahoma."[47] Fletcher Prouty, in his important 1975 article "The Guns of Dallas," wrote, "The photo shows a two-way radio in the man's left hip pocket with a wire dangling down. This wire is an antenna. What did the Warren Commission say about this? Not a word. They did not see the pictures. This man is known. He is James Hicks, currently in an insane asylum."[48]

On January 4, 1968, a week before his Parish testimony, Hicks was interviewed by WMAL Radio in Washington, D.C. He told them, "I met people in Dallas that could possibly have something to do with it after the assassination. And things I saw at the assassination that lead me to believe there was more than one assassin. I told the Dallas police that I saw it, and I would be glad to tell them anything they wanted to know, if they wanted me, and they evidently didn't …" Hicks also claimed to have been introduced to Clay Bertrand, about four or five days after the assassination, at the Aldophus Hotel in Dallas. The physical description he provided matched Clay Shaw. Like many conspiracy-friendly witnesses, Hicks has been largely rejected by the dysfunctional research community. There are unsourced assertions on forums, stating that Hicks admitted he'd made the story up in a bar, while no one seems to believe that his physical assault was connected to his testimony. Instead, his story is passed off as a sad tale of someone with a drinking problem. That's a slight deviation from the normal revisionist line, which is to dismiss these witnesses as being mentally ill (although Hicks was, of course, reportedly in a mental health facility). There are even allegations (and again, with no source) that someone else made the claim about him having been the radio man in Dealey Plaza. Hicks bore a strong resemblance to the chunky man photographed in Mexico City and erroneously identified as Lee Harvey Oswald, whom he looked nothing like. One online source claimed that Hicks remained in the Air Force mental institution until 1988, and "A few days after his release, Hicks was murdered in Oklahoma." The footnote source for this is Richard E. Sprague's book *The Taking of America, 1-2-3*, which was first published in 1976. However, there is no reference to the death of Hicks in the book, which was written too early to report something like this, unless it was an updated edition. A website called "JFK Casualties" lists Jim Hicks among the countless deaths associated with the assassination, merely noting he was murdered in 1980.

A June 27, 1968 FBI memo from W.A. Branigan to William C. Sullivan references Hicks being committed to a mental hospital and declared "Hicks obviously was a publicity seeker who interjected himself into the Garrison probe in order to generate publicity for himself. It is not surprising that he has been found mentally ill and has been committed to a mental institution. Practically all of Garrison's witnesses have been mental cases, dope addicts, criminals with unsavory backgrounds and the like." *Doonesbury* comic strip writer Garry Trudeau, one-time darling of the Left who has been married to former NBC *Today* show host Jane Pauley since 1980, included Hicks' name in a strip ridiculing JFK assassination "conspiracy theorists." Harold Weisberg was dubious about Hicks' story, but at that point he had turned on Garrison and was clearly not objective on the subject. He ridiculed fellow critic Robert Groden for claiming, "with his customary lack of any source at all," that Hicks had been the victim of homicide.

Paige (she never gave her last name) from the Metropolitan Library System in Oklahoma, also worked diligently to find information about Hicks for the authors of this book. She clarified some things, but also raised more questions for which there appear to be no answers. In a September 20, 2021 email, she wrote, "It turns out that there are actually two James Hicks, which is behind at least some of the confusion. Karan Snodgrass was married to James Daniel Hicks at the time of the assassination, and they later divorced in the 1970s. James Daniel Hicks has since passed away, and there is an obituary and a couple of pictures of him on his findagrave page (link in the document). Karan appears to still be living in Texas, but remarried. Her current last name is Sills, and the listing I found for her listed her in Arlington. James Frederick Hicks is the one who was being interviewed as a witness. He was at some point living in Enid while being subpoenaed, but it looks like he may have moved during that time. He hit a string of bad luck, got divorced, and lost his job, according to articles published in local papers. It also looks like he had a bit of an arrest history.... There is a James F. Hicks who passed away in Oklahoma in 1988, but there is no information that I could find to tie him to this James ..." In a follow-up email two days later, Paige stated, "James F Hicks said in various news articles (included in the last document I sent you) that he was married but that his wife divorced him in 1968 after he was subpoenaed. The Assassination Archives and Research Center has a copy of his interview with Jim Garrison. In it he says that he was not married at the time of the assassination. So, he was married sometime between 1963 and 1968, but I cannot find any references to his wife's name. However, Karan was already married to the other James Daniel Hicks before the assassination."

So there were two Jim Hicks involved here, and one of them had a wife who worked in the Texas School Book Depository Building. Needless to say, it is confusing that two different men named Jim Hicks were connected in some way to the events in Dealey Plaza. It took a great deal of research, but we were able to establish that the Jim Hicks who spoke to Jim Garrison, and testified before the Orleans Grand Jury, was indeed murdered in July, 1988 by a "transient" named Lonnie Green. A partial obituary disclosed that Hicks had been in mental hospitals, as other reports had indicated, and been arrested for public drunkenness. He was described as having lived in recent years "in shelters, abandoned homes, and on the streets." Jim Hicks was just fifty-two years old when he was killed, but the actual circumstances of his murder aren't visible in the partial record.[49] There is also a death record for a James Wade Hicks, killed at just nineteen in a motorcycle accident in Oklahoma in 1986. It's certainly reasonable to speculate that this could be Jim Hicks' son.[50]

Karan Hicks worked for the South-Western Publishing Company in the Texas School Book Depository Building. While she was married to the other Jim Hicks, Karan Hicks is an interesting and neglected witness in her own right. In a March 20, 1964 FBI report, she testified to standing in front of the TSBD, with one of the closest vantage points of any witness, at the time of the assassination. She stated that the limousine was directly in front of her when the shots were fired. Evidently, she wasn't asked where she thought the shots were fired from, or anything else of relevance, which was unfortunately par for the course in this "investigation." Standing with her were fellow TSBD employees Gloria Calvery, whom researchers have paid more attention to over the years (she died in 1998 at fifty-six years of age), Carol Reed, and Karen Westbrook. Calvery is often used by adherents of the "Prayer Man" theory, which holds that an indistinct figure in the background of the TSBD doorway was actually Lee Harvey Oswald. This figure is not the one in the famed Altgens photograph, which is clearer and has been the source of so much controversy over the years. Karen Westbrook Stanton would give filmed oral testimony to the Sixth Floor Museum in Dallas in 2017. In her oral history, Stanton claimed that the furor around the Altgens photograph became "a joke" among her co-workers, since it was obvious to them that the figure was Billy Lovelady. She also described how she often saw Oswald sitting by himself in the break room, always reading what she termed "strange looking material, a few little paper pamphlet kind of things." She said that the profile of Oswald being promulgated to the public matched "exactly" her own impressions. Stanton consistently referred to Gloria Calvery as "Calvert," and didn't mention Karan Hicks when asked to identify the women watching the motorcade with her on Elm Street. The interviewer noted that Gloria Calvery's son "disagrees with you" regarding the identity of the woman standing next to her. Stanton, during her dismissal of the "conspiracy theorists" who she said had contacted her over the years, mentioned testifying before the Warren Commission. She did not; her name only appears in the record in that March 20, 1964 FBI report.

Yet another Orleans Parish witness neglected by researchers was Josephine Hug, who was a secretary in the International Trade Mart building. Her office adjoined Clay Shaw's, so she had a perfect view of those coming in and out of Shaw's office. Hug's desk was directly in front of Goldie Moore, Shaw's secretary. She answered, "Seems like to me she would," when asked if Moore would have known of Ferrie's presence in Shaw's office. Hug recognized Ferrie from his photograph in the newspapers. Hug noted colorfully how Dr. James Nix, with whom she'd discussed David Ferrie, had commented to her, "How could a man write a suicide note and then die from a cerebral hemorrhage?" She would come to clearly try and distance herself from previous statements about Ferrie being in Shaw's office, which she'd made to several witnesses, as well as having expressed fear for her safety to Jim Garrison's office, which included a discussion of the suspicious deaths associated with the assassination. At length, she flip-flopped and testified that she now believed that the man she'd seen had not been Ferrie. After saying she recognized him from newspaper pictures, she belatedly declared that she realized she was mistaken from looking at newspaper pictures. She was then shown a picture of Morris

Brownlee, David Ferrie's godson, and responded, "Well, I am not positive, but this looks like the man who came in Mr. Shaw's office with the attaché case." Brownlee would tell Gus Russo, author of the extremely misleading book *Live by the Sword: The Secret War Against Castro and the Death of JFK*, that Ferrie "has been taking the rap for Robert Kennedy, who was behind it all (the exile movement)." Richard Billings wrote that Garrison considered Brownlee one of his early suspects, who was now "cooperating with him." Brownlee is said here to have been "almost like brothers" with Ferrie, and to have worked along with him for Carlos Marcello and G. Wray Gill. The most interesting passage reads, "on November 22, 1963, it turns out Brownlee had been missing for a number of days." John George, a friend of journalist Hoke May, through whom Brownlee was brought to Garrison's attention, told the district attorney that Brownlee was directly involved in the assassination. George and Brownlee both told Garrison that certain papers belonging to Ferrie had been taken to Mexico, and they knew where they were. They promised to provide them to Garrison, but there is no further information about that in the record.[51] Goldie Moore, who had been Shaw's secretary for nineteen years, testified to the Orleans Parish grand jury, but provided no noteworthy information. She denied ever having seen David Ferrie.

Harry Connick, Sr., father of the famous actor and singer, ordered all of the Orleans Parish grand jury testimony to be destroyed, but fortunately the man he tasked with destroying them, Gary Raymond, instead hid them in his garage for over two decades, before turning them over to reporter Richard Angelico, who passed them on to the ARRB in 1995. An angry Connick, who was still District Attorney, convicted Raymond and Angelico of contempt of court, and demanded that the ARRB return the records. The ARRB eventually prevailed.

While she didn't testify before the HSCA and was not contacted by the ARRB, Ruth Paine did testify to the Orleans Parish grand jury. Interestingly, Ruth stated that she saw no signs of physical abuse from Lee, and that Marina had not complained to her about that. She didn't perceive him as violent. Like Buell Wesley Frazier, Oswald's co-worker who drove him to work on November 22, 1963, she described him as "a family man." Ruth was a card-carrying member of the ACLU, but oddly resented Lee asking her to try and contact an attorney for him. She also testified that, after he thanked her for being helpful to his family, "I did not appreciate his thanks at that point." It is revealed in Ruth's testimony that files pertaining to her sister Sylvia Hyde remained classified for unknown reasons. On the 1993 PBS *Frontline* disinfo piece on Oswald, Ruth would contradict her earlier testimony, and declare, "There's no doubt in my mind that he believed violence was the only effective tool." For whatever reason, former close friends Ruth and Marina only saw each other once—in 1964—following the events in Dallas.

Lee Harvey Oswald's best friend as a young teenager in New Orleans was Edward Voebel, mentioned earlier in connection with Jack Martin. He would tell the FBI and the Warren Commission that young Oswald had no interest in politics, at a time when the Warren Commission claimed he was already hankering to join the Communist Party, and called his supposed fascination with communism "a lot of baloney." He also recounted how his close friend didn't tell him when he moved; he simply went to Oswald's apartment and found him gone. Voebel took the famous photo of Oswald with a missing tooth, sitting in the back of a classroom, which was later published by *Life* magazine. Voebel was one of several witnesses researcher John Armstrong used to buttress his theory that there had not only been two Oswalds (*Harvey & Lee*), but two Marguerites. Voebel told the Warren Commission that the woman he'd seen represented as Oswald's mother in the media was far different than he recalled. "I didn't recognize her. She was a lot thinner…" According to the briefing materials of HSCA member Rep. Stewart McKinney, Voebel had also been a fellow cadet in the Civil Air Patrol with Oswald, where they both were seemingly in pilot David Ferrie's squadron. Voebel called Ferrie an emotional "oddball." Voebel would claim that Oswald and a "cadre of CAP cadets" were in Ferrie's apartment for a graduation party. According to a November 26, 1963 FBI teletype, "Voebel was unable to recall if Oswald attended meetings under command of Ferrie or with previous commander." Voebel told the FBI that he had "been frightened" by an individual who came to his home claiming to be a news reporter and "acted very suspicious." Voebel also received a "crank-type telephone call" during the course of their interview. As alluded to earlier, In May, 1971, Voebel abruptly became sick and was taken to the New Orleans Ochsner Clinic, allegedly because of "insecticide poisons." In an updated edition of their book *Coup d'etat in America: The CIA and the Assassination of John F. Kennedy,* authors Michael Canfield and A.J. Weberman attributed Voebel's death to a blood clot brought on by "a sudden attack of pneumonia." Weberman interviewed Voebel's mother Doris Baretenelli in 1993. She declared that the Ochsner clinic had told him, after he went there complaining of pains in his chest, "Go home, that it's just nervousness and indigestion." When he felt worse and went back, they admitted him to the hospital for pneumonia. After ten days in the hospital, his mother called him but Edward told her not to come visit him as he was feeling better and she could just see him at home the next day. Doris said, "They told him to go take a shower. And when he put his foot on the floor he was gone. It was a blood clot all along and they were treating him for the wrong thing."

Dr. Alton Ochsner was affiliated with the CIA's Information Council of the Americas. Voebel's death certificate inexplicably states that he died at Foundation Hospital in Metairie, Louisiana, when he had actually been admitted to the Ochsner Clinic. In 1978, Voebel's father Sidney, whom Doris informed Weberman had abandoned her and their three children when they were very young, told the HSCA that he felt his son had died under mysterious circumstances. Of course, it goes without saying that Voebel's testimony to the HSCA is unavailable to the public. When Edward Voebel was questioned the second time by the FBI, he told them that he'd just been notified by Bill Slatter of NBC that David Ferrie was a homosexual. That seems like an odd tidbit for a newsman to disclose to a low profile witness like Voebel. Slatter was an associate of William Stuckey, a columnist for the *New Orleans States-Item* and host of the NBC radio program "Latin Listening Post." Recall that Stuckey was the one who interviewed Oswald on radio, in a "debate" with Carlos Bringuier and Ed Butler. Weberman wrote that "William Stuckey knew HEMMING, STURGIS, BRINGUIER and OSWALD. Bill Slatter videotaped OSWALD for William Stuckey." Evidently, Stuckey was yet another odd death connected to this case. Weberman claimed that Stuckey's mother had stated, "The autopsy said he died of a wound, I never did know the details. It didn't say gunshot wound. They put him in Seaton Hospital, near San Francisco. When I called the Hospital they said he had a heart problem, but the autopsy showed a wound. So I'll never know what happened. He never did regain consciousness. He only lived five days." According to Weberman, "Seaton Hospital had no record of William Stuckey, nor did the San Mateo County Recorder's Office." Author and researcher Jim DiEugenio claims that Butler's contacts included Charles Cabell, the Deputy Director of the CIA fired along with Allen Dulles by JFK, after the Bay of Pigs, and spymaster Ed Lansdale, whom Fletcher Prouty claimed was photographed in Dealey Plaza.

Don Jeffries was able to speak with Ed Voebel's niece, Gwen Ann Segal, on July 3, 2023. During a long and pleasant conversation, it was learned that no one else in the family found Voebel's death to be suspicious. Gwen stated that they accept the conclusion that he died of a blood clot, as she explained that "they run in the family." Voebel's father appears to have been the only one to have asked questions about the death, but Gwen remarked that he had left his wife when the children were very young, and that "I wouldn't place any stock in anything he said." Shockingly, only minutes after the call ended, Gwen called Jeffries back and said she had spoken to her mom. "You were right – there *was* a conspiracy," she declared. Her mother had chosen not to tell her for very understandable reasons: "Everyone died who knew Lee Harvey Oswald." Teddi "Cookie" Segal, sister of Ed Voebel, told Jeffries, in a subsequent phone conversation, "We believe the CIA got him." However, she referred him to her twin sister, Doris "Sweetie Pie" Kunitz, who knew more about it.

Jeffries called Sweetie Pie. She told him that her brother "Butch," as they called him, had protected Oswald when he was being bullied at Beauregard Junior High School. Regarding him being interviewed on the night of the assassination, she wasn't aware of that, and in fact none of the family members Jeffries talked with had ever heard that. Sweetie Pie noted that Butch wasn't the type to contact the government, so this presented the intriguing probability that someone in the government learned about Voebel on the day of the assassination, and felt he was significant enough to contact him. Sweetie Pie explained that the entire family spent most of their waking moments in the family florist shop. After her brother suddenly became ill, she recalled that "they asked him if he had been around any insecticides." Naturally, he had been, given the time he spent in the florist shop, but this corroborated the other reports suggesting poisoning. Whenever someone from the government would question Voebel, they would take him outside of the flower shop, so no one else could hear. While they were at Beauregard, Oswald once showed Voebel a gun and asked him if it looked real, which Butch thought was odd. Sweetie Pie talked to him earlier on the day he died, and he was breathing heavy, but told her he was okay and would be home soon. She thought that Oswald had come to their home one time, but it was hard to recall, since they were so busy with the flower shop. "They all belonged to that air patrol, and they all died. What was the connection there?" Sweetie Pie asked. She maintained that "three or four" of Ferrie's fellow members of the Civil Air Patrol had died mysteriously. She'd actually been interviewed not long after her brother was buried, at the cemetery, by whom she couldn't remember, and stated then that she thought her brother was murdered. In school, she was a year behind Oswald and Butch, and remembered the future patsy as "a small little guy." Oswald listed Voebel as his only friend on a form he filled out for the school. Sweetie Pie found one photograph of her brother quite strange. "I came across a picture of my brother in a white suit with a face shield hood on, and I have no idea what that meant." She mentioned *Dr. Mary's Monkey* and felt it might be connected to it.

Sweetie Pie's memories of her brother defending Oswald from being bullied are in stark contrast to the recollections of another Beauregard student, John Neumeyer, who like the Voebel twin girls, was a grade behind Oswald. In a November 27, 1963 FBI report, Neumeyer recalled getting into a brief fight with Oswald, who had been "picking on" his brother. Neumeyer didn't remember much about Oswald, except that his nickname was "Yankee," and he "did not seem to get along with other students as he, NEUMEYER, had heard Oswald often became involved in fights." This kind of glaring inconsistency about young Oswald is what triggered John Armstrong's massive book *Harvey & Lee*. However, the contrasting testimony of the Voebel sisters and Neumeyer seems to suggest that the "two Oswalds" postulated by Armstrong were actually in the same school at the same time. Given that they both seemingly used the same name, this borders on the incomprehensible.

Jeffries talked to Steven Voebel, son of Edward, on July 4, 2023. He said it was "definitely a conspiracy." Steven wondered why his aunts hadn't gotten his father's body exhumed to check for poison. He was philosophical about things, declaring that "The government's the government. A cover up's a cover up." His said his mother never really believed in the "mystery" of his father's death. "She never bought into it." It was primarily the sisters, Cookie and Sweetie Pie, who questioned the death of their brother Butch. Later on July 4, Steven texted Jeffries, saying, "Mom said she doesn't know anything else he never talked to her about it and he was in a hospital for three or four days."

There were a series of interesting letters exchanged between Jim Garrison and L. Fletcher Prouty, whom Oliver Stone based his character "Mr. X," played by Donald Sutherland, on. In a November 4, 1985 letter to Prouty, Garrison recounted, "Nevertheless, after seven or eight complimentary rejections ('we found the material fascinating') from the established publishers, the probabilities of Company penetrations are high enough that it should have by now two of three copies of the partial (only) manuscript which I submitted. Saturday morning, for example, I received the results of an I.R.S. audit of my 1983 income tax telling me that I owe $4,000.00 more plus $790.00 interest for my C.P.A.'s deduction of my payments toward my judicial retirement because, says I.R.S., that retirement program is 'funded.'" Speaking of the notorious "tramps" that were photographed after the assassination, Garrison wrote, "As to the fact that the arresting men were not real officers, you are absolutely right. – rather than at port arms, as any city policeman would have learned to do on his first day of duty. Secondly, his trousers don't begin to fit and, while the Dallas police department may have a lot of sang-froid about the murder of a liberal President, it couldn't have been that careless about a police officer's uniform. Thirdly, the lead police officer is wearing in his right ear the same kind of plastic radio receiver that the man picking up the large (looks like a .45 caliber) bullet is wearing. This is the man next to Deputy Sheriff Buddy Walther, you may recall, who filed a report about the finding of the bullet, but not its caliber, and not long afterwards had a fatal accident." Researcher Mark Oakes verified with Walthers' widow that he had indeed told her and others that he found a bullet in the Dealey Plaza grass on the day of the assassination.

In a January 19, 1987 letter to Prouty, Garrison describes what has been happening with his manuscript, which would eventually become the book *On the Trail of the Assassins*. "I thought I'd better send you a copy of my letter to the publisher. I'm not really that upset about his being touted off the book at the eleventh hour inasmuch as I expected something like that early on when I first learned that he was required (apparently by his Board of Directors or whatever) to have the final manuscript 'cleared' by Anthony Summers, Peter Dale Scott or Sylvia Meagher. I knew the first two would tear it apart, for reasons I won't spell out here, but I thought I might have an outside chance with her. I was wrong." Garrison continued, "She did the job quite professionally, whether wittingly or unwittingly. According to the publisher's letter (1) at first demonstrated enthusiasm (which would suggest objectivity) (2) and, only with her afterthought, launched her torpedo (expressing how 'appalled' she was to find my 'misrepresentation' of Forest Sorrell's statement)." Meagher, who wrote one of the better books on the assassination, *Accessories After the Fact,* had turned on Garrison more quickly than Harold Weisberg had, to the point that, by 1987, Garrison could say that, "She shows no sign whatever of interest in the reasons for the assassination."

In another letter, which is undated in the record, Garrison asked Prouty: "Recently in going through some of my papers I came across the long distance calls made by David Ferrie which I had obtained (from his lawyer's office where he made them) and which the FBI had missed because they had only searched his apartment. For the first time I noted that he had made a number of calls in 1963 to the Washington, D.C. area. While 1963 is a ways back, it occurred to me that you might have a contact in the vicinity who would be able to convert the number called into the individual and address concerned. You may recall, from my book, the good fortune I had in following up on his September 24th call to Chicago, Illinois, leading to Lawrence V. Meyers who subsequently met with Ruby in Dallas. Just on the off chance that you might have access to someone who has a blue book or conversion book for 1963, I thought you might be interested in having a list of those calls made to the Washington area by Ferrie during that year." In a June 19, 1986 response, Prouty wrote, "Next your number from the Ferrie calls: ST-3-8905 rang some bells in memory. Right away. I found that Dick Bissell's phone number was 8807. That was an office in the CIA but physically located at 1818 H Street NW in Washington in the Matomic Building where the U-2 program was run. So I looked for a cluster of 8000 numbers. I came up with these: Al Cox (a very deep agent from Asia work) 8992 – a close associate of Ed Lansdale's, Drummond-8063, Donaldson (another deep agent) 8483, Gottke (whom I believe was with the U-2) 8689, Ben Kyker (another deep agent) 8193, Lukowsk-8764, Morehouse-8344, Marowicz-8055, Otoupalik (deep in what was called "Air Division") 8575 and 143-4243, Trimble-8487, Urie-8423. As a result of (b) above, I would say that the chances are good that the Ferrie calls were to someone in the DDP (Clandestine section) as that is close to Bissell's number and to people who worked for him."

These letters are full of interesting nuggets. Regarding George Lardner, Jr., Prouty stated, in a November 7, 1985 letter to Garrison: "Another thing, it has always interested me that the man with Ferrie the night he died was a *Washington Post* reporter, and that this same reporter was the last visitor with George de Mohrenschildt in Palm Beach. I had a strange telephone call from Brussels, Belgium, two days before George died. A reporter there had been having lunch with him when all of a sudden he got up, excused himself for a moment and disappeared. The call I got was to see if I could find out if he had come back to the States. He left everything he had with him in his Brussels hotel room and this reporter (Oltmans) picked it all up. He owed the hotel an unusually large bill." Prouty is confusing Lardner here with Edward Epstein, author of the early book about the Warren Commission, *Inquest,* who morphed into a predictable neocon type that essentially supported all the work he'd once critiqued.

Researcher Ted Gandolfo worked closely with Jim Garrison, and became one of the foremost critics of the HSCA. In the April 1992 issue of R.B. Cutler's *Grassy Knoll Gazette,* he stated, "Jim Garrison told me, during a taped interview, that the top HSCA's chief investigator, Clifford Fenton, went to acquire Garrison's evidence of direct CIA involvement in the JFK assassination. Received massive evidence/proof of same. Gave it to chief counsel Robert Blakey, who, in turn, completely suppressed… covered-up all of it… It appears nowhere in either the HSCA's final report nor in the 12 volumes of the committee's testimony and exhibits." Gandolfo would call Blakey a "legal hit man for organized crime," who had allowed the HSCA to be "captured by the FBI and CIA." He claimed that one elderly male witness "had broken down and was reduced to tears in the Committee's hearing room" after being severely abused by the HSCA. "A reason that the Committee questions witnesses behind closed doors is that the American people would not stand for their abusive questioning in public." Gandolfo charged. "Witnesses have been denied counsel of their choice by the committee and denied an opportunity to testify in-public." Gandolfo went on to declare, "This Select Committee has combined the worst of two eras. Like the Warren Commission of the 1960s, which permitted witnesses to testify in public if they insisted upon that right, the Select Committee adheres to its policy of secrecy. Unlike Joe McCarthy of the 1950's, the Committee does not permit witnesses to be represented by counsel of their choice. I now understand how Dr. Frankenstein felt when he looked up one day and saw the monster begin a rampage." Gandolfo alleged that Blakey had, "on February 4, 1976, associated himself with Moe Dalitz, one of the early activists with organized crime in America." Blakey performed unspecified services for the veteran mobster, and Gandolfo stated that he "refuses to disclose how much money he was paid." Blakey's attorney, interestingly enough, was Louis Nizer, who also represented Dalitz. Nizer was a celebrated leftist who worked with LBJ crony Jack Valenti to establish the ratings system for Motion Pictures. And, most revealingly, Nizer wrote a glowing Foreword to the Warren Report.

In February 1978, evidently the taped interview referenced previously, broadcaster/critic Ted Gandolfo spoke with Jim Garrison. During the conversation, Garrison alleged that committee investigators "have meetings in which they're specifically discussing the assassination. With Shaw and Ferrie present.... They have a fucking confession from one of the guys participating in the meetings.... On tape. Hours, dates, places, trips to Dallas in preparation." This individual, never identified (Garrison expresses great fear for his safety), is referred to by Gandolfo as "the person in the Banister office," to which Garrison responds, "Yeah." Garrison was concerned that "they just leave him available to be killed as the months pass and they don't take his deposition." Gandolfo would later tell an audience that this individual was Thomas Beckham, who as a youth came under the influence of Guy Banister and Jack Martin. Gandolfo said that Beckham had provided the HSCA's Clifford Fenton with maps of the Dealey Plaza firing zones, and sewer systems, and names of participants like Frank Sturgis, Richard Case Nagell, Jim Hicks, Jack Lawrence, and Harry Dean. Fenton submitted his report to Blakey, who assigned two men to take Beckham's testimony and "scared him to death," according to Gandolfo. After the assassination, Beckham became business partners with the previously mentioned Fred Lee Crisman, an intriguing crossover character from the UFO world. Garrison spoke for other critics when he told the HSCA that Crisman had been one of the three notorious "tramps" arrested in Dallas shortly after shots were fired. Garrison also claimed that Crisman was the first person Clay Shaw called after being charged. According to Joan Mellen, when she approached Beckham while researching her book about the Garrison case, *A Farewell to Justice,* he appeared to be especially afraid of Jack Martin, and asked her if he was still alive.

Gandolfo wrote a letter to President Reagan on October 18, 1984, in which he stated, "I am sending you this letter in the hope that a grave miscarriage of justice may yet be rectified. It involves the fact that very crucial evidence and information relating to the assassination of President John F. Kennedy has been, and definitely was, entirely suppressed and covered up by the House Select Committee on Assassinations in general and by their Chief Counsel G. Robert Blakey in particular.... On February 11, 1978, I had a long conversation with former New Orleans District Attorney, now Judge, Jim Garrison. During our conversation, which I tape recorded, he told me that the House Select Committee on Assassinations had sent a team of investigators, headed by Mr. Clifford Fenton, to Mr. Garrison's office to secure the evidence that Garrison had accumulated during his investigation of the JFK assassination in 1967 to 1969. Garrison told me that as a result of the Committee's investigators viewing and hearing this evidence, that they all were convinced of a massive conspiracy to murder JFK ..." As co-author Don Jeffries related in his book *Hidden History,* researcher David Lifton claimed that a top official in Reagan's administration had told him Reagan was obsessed with the JFK assassination.[52] If that is true, he nevertheless seems not to have acted at all on Gandolfo's information. Gandolfo appeared on the June 13, 1993 broadcast of Pacifica Radio's "Something Happening." This was exceedingly strange, given that "neocon" researcher Paul Hoch had run his obituary in his March 3, 1993 *Echoes of Conspiracy* journal. Gandolfo's widow confirmed his passing to *Probe* magazine. Regardless, on the program, Gandolfo alleged that Captain Will Fritz had secretly recorded all of Oswald's interrogation sessions, but suppressed them. He contended that "two assassination researchers" had come into possession of the tapes and would make them available at a major press conference on November 22, 1993. At that time, "Every tree in the forest will fall," Gandolfo stated. Robert Groden also referred to these hidden tapes as well on the program.[53] Like so much else in this case, these tantalizing references are the last word on the subject.

We reached out to Steve Jaffe, one of the last who worked with Jim Garrison on his investigation into the JFK assassination. In an April 13, 2023 email reply, Jaffe wrote, "I respond to anyone who mentions John Barbour's name. He's the leading authority on all things Garrison. And as it turns out, I seem to be the last living official staff investigator still living from Garrison's investigation of the assassination of President Kennedy. It's interesting to hear that someone who was a close friend of Dean Andrews would write a book about the late DA of New Orleans, Jim Garrison. I consider Garrison one of the most courageous people who ever studied this case, let alone officially investigated the assassination of President Kennedy in order to bring out the truth which was fought at the highest levels of politics and government and ended in a coup. I don't know how much you know about the case but if you watch John's films you will know the truth exists and he captured the essence of it on film in his brilliant documentaries. My work for Garrison and with Mark Lane took me on a very educational journey about the assassination and about the law. About power and the abuse of it. What I found, among other things, is that power corrupts and absolute power corrupts absolutely. JFK had many enemies when he came into the White House which were earned on a number of fronts. Kennedy's own courage (the topic of his award-winning book), earned him enemies in the government he would head up after his election. Sadly, his enemies became frustrated with the kind of idealism, vision and desire for peace that he espoused. However, at that level of politics and government, it's all hardball. They play for keeps and the losers are either dead or able to escape. No one commits that kind of murder of a head of state and leaves a signed memo on how they did it. I'm not sure how you could write a book where the truth is involved if Dean Andrews is at the heart of it though he did seem to have a good sense of humor. He knew that cooperating with Garrison might help to strengthen Garrison's case but he favored his personal survival over everything else. Andrews had knowledge of the relationship between Clay Shaw and Lee Oswald. He chose not to share it with Garrison under the heading of his patriotic duty. Can you blame him? Maybe not. Many people died just sharing what they knew in good faith and out of a sense of pride in their own integrity…" Jaffe went on to politely note that he had his own book coming out later that year, "which will scientifically provide proof of the conspiracy from a legal standpoint." On April 16, 2023, Jaffe replied again, writing, "I realized, as did Garrison, that Dean Andrews was afraid for his life. We knew more about him than he thought we did. You know, I'm sure, how it came out."

Endnotes

1   Davy, pp. 15-16

2   Ibid, p. 17

3   Donald Jeffries, *Hidden History: An Expose of Modern Crimes, Conspiracies, and Cover-Ups in American Politics,* New York, Skyhorse Publishing, 2016 paperback edition, p. 42

4   Ibid, p. 40

5   Campbell Interview with author James DiEugenio, September 3, 1994

6   Davy, p. 58

7   Ibid. p. 20

8   **Joseph P. Farrell,** *LBJ and the Conspiracy to Kill Kennedy: A Coalescence of Interests,* Adventures Unlimited Press, 2011, pp. 28-29

9   *Dallas Times Herald,* August 7, 1978

10   Jim Marrs, *The Rise of the Fourth Reich: The Secret Societies That Threaten to Take Over America,* New York, William Morrow (reprint), p. 225

11   May 23, 1961 memo from the Special Agent in Charge, Miami, to J. Edgar Hoover.

12   *The American-Statesman,* October 26, 1952

13   *Washington Star,* March 3, 1967

14   *Washington Daily News,* February 20, 1967

15   *The Dayton Herald,* February 17, 1943

16   *Times-Picayune,* November 21, 2013

17   *New Orleans States-Item,* April 25, 1967

18   Jim Garrison Interview with *Playboy* magazine, October 1967

19   The Education Forum, "Gordon Novel," January 4, 2005

20   Ibid, January 13, 2005

21   Ibid, June 9, 2008

22   Richard Billings' Journal, May 22-23, 1967

23   Novel vs. Garrison, May 7, 1969, p. 534

24   CIA Memo from Ray Rocca to Associate Director of Plans, May 12, 1967

25   NODA affidavit of Fred H. Leemans Sr., January 6, 1969

26   FBI Memo from Cartha DeLoach to Clyde Tolson, April 4, 1967

27   Jim Hougan, *Spooks,* New York, William Morrow & Company, 1978, pp. 270-271

28   Letter from Caroline Christenberry to Clay Shaw, March 9, 1969

29   Ibid

30   Gus Russo, *Live by the Sword: The Secret War Against Castro and the Death of JFK,* Baltimore, Bancroft Press, 1998, pp. 150-151

31   Davy, p. 9

32   Anthony Summers, *Conspiracy,* New York, McGraw-Hill, 1980, pp. 364-365

33   CIA Memo from Chief, Security Division, July 20, 1953

34   *New Orleans States-Item,* November 20, 1972

35   The Fourth Decade, March 1999

36   *The New York Review,* September 14, 1967

37   Davy, p. 72

38   *Kennedys and King,* September 10, 2022

39   *Executive Intelligence Review,* September 8, 1995

40   *The Gazette,* January 27, 2007

41   William Torbitt, *The Torbitt Document: Nomenclature of an Assassination Cabal,* Prevailing Winds, 1970, p. 37

42   *New York Times,* November 24, 1970

43   *True,* April 1975

44   Memorandum from Andrew Sciambra to Jim Garrison, October 9, 1968

45   Warren Hinckle, *If You Have a Lemon, Make Lemonade,* New York, Putnam, 1974, pp. 198-199

46   *New Orleans Times-Picayune,* January 12, 1969

47   Computers and Automation, The Assassination of President JFK: The application of computers to the photographic evidence, May 1970

48   *Gallery,* October 1975

49   *Tulsa World,* July 2, 1988

50   *The Oklahoman,* July 7, 1986

51   Richard Billings' New Orleans Journal, May 22-23, 1967

52   Jeffries, *Hidden History,* p. 119

53   *Probe,* August 1993

Dean Andrews Jr. with his attorney Sam Monk Zeldon leaving New Orleans criminal court building on March 22, 1967. AP wirephoto.

CHAPTER THREE

DEAN ANDREWS AND HIS FLUID RECOLLECTIONS

They ain't gonna find anything, because there's nothing there.
                                                                    —Dean Andrews, Jr.

D ean Andrews, Jr. would tell Jim Garrison that he knew David Ferrie in a March 2, 1967 interview. He also said he'd met Clay Bertrand once or twice, and described his voice in detail. He recounted how Bertrand had assured him, during Oswald's visit to his office, "I'll personally handle the fee." He noted that all the homosexuals who wanted him to represent him had Bertrand's number and would call him from his office.

An FBI report written on November 29, 1963, by the ubiquitous Regis Kennedy, noted that the doctors for Dean Andrews, Jr. were letting him go home from the Hotel Dieu Hospital that day. Andrews was said to soon be "strong enough to go to his office, where he will attempt to identify this individual whom he believed to be named Clay Bertrand." It was stated that Andrews had thus far been unable to identify Bertrand. In a December 3 FBI memo Andrews testified that Bertrand had said he'd call him back, but never did, and he wasn't given Bertrand's phone number. Andrews stated here that both Bertrand's name and his voice sounded familiar. Andrews for the first time alluded to how the call now seemed "like a dream" to him, but felt it had to have been real because of his call to his attorney Monk Zelden, who was the one to inform him that Oswald had just been shot live on television. Andrews also stated that he'd discussed the call with his secretary Eva Springer, and his investigator Sergeant R.M. Davis, and also his wife. Andrews had no recollection of contacting the FBI, but did remember being interviewed by both them and the Secret Service. While he could find no records relating to Clay Bertrand, "he has every reason to believe he has met Clay Bertrand before and the name seems to be familiar to him..." Andrews continued to dance a fine line, as the memo notes that he "repeated at the conclusion of the interview that this entire incident could have been dreamed by him in view of the physical condition [he was] in at the time. He stated however, that he believes he did receive a call from an individual that he recalls as CLAY BERTRAND and he feels he will be able to identify CLAY BERTRAND either from material that is in his [files] or recognize him. Mr. ANDREWS stated that he has a mental picture of CLAY BERTRAND as being approximately 6'1" to 6'2", brown hair, excellent appearance, well dressed and although a homosexual is not obvious and probably has a good job in the city." Interestingly, Andrews was puzzled as to how the caller had located him in the hospital, since his home phone was unlisted, and his office had been closed on November 22 and November 23.

In another FBI report written by Regis Kennedy, on December 6, just three days later, Andrews made more qualifications. The memo notes, "ANDREWS stated that he realizes the serious physical condition he was in while he was confined in the hospital and has verified from his physician that he was under extremely heavy sedation for the first four days he was in the hospital, that is from November 20 to November 24, 1963. ANDREWS advised he has talked with his secretary, EVA SPRINGER and his investigator, Sergeant R.M. DAVIS, United States Army, retired, and he determined that there are a number of variances in his independent recollection of incidents that happened, and incidents recalled by his employees." Springer reported that Andrews had called and told her he had been phoned by "Bertrand," and *was going* to represent Oswald in Dallas. Again, the memo notes the oddity that "Miss Springer terminated the conversation at this time by saying she would not go to Dallas with him." Kennedy goes on to write that "ANDREWS stated he has no recollection of this telephone conversation, cannot understand why he called his secretary and is unable to account for the name BERTRAND in this conversation. He particularly pointed out that he did not mention the first name to his secretary." Continuing in an obvious vein, we are told that "Mr. ANDREWS stated that Sergeant R.M. DAVIS has told him that DAVIS visited him, DEAN ANDREWS, on the afternoon of November 23, 1963 from approximately noon to 3:30 PM or 4:00 PM. During this period DAVIS told ANDREWS that he, ANDREWS, did not receive a call and mentioned nothing to him, DAVIS, about representing OSWALD." Davis recalled instead that Andrews had told him about the call from Bertrand and the request to represent Oswald on the following day, November 24, and "ANDREWS advised that he does not recall this conversation with Sergeant DAVIS and could not recall where he had picked up the name CLAY BERTRAND." Backpedaling further, "ANDREWS stated with regard to the alleged telephone call that he thought he received, it is now obvious to him that the basic details which he would have immediately determined, are not present in the conversation. That is, what authority did BERTRAND have to commit OSWALD as a client, who referred BERTRAND to him, who would handle the finances for the defense, when would he personally see BERTRAND, how could he get in touch with BERTRAND and further that he could locate no notes of this call in his hospital room." After stressing that his doctor told him he would have been physically unable to use the telephone, the memo closes with "ANDREWS advised that based on the discrepancy between his memory and facts as related to him by his employees and further, the fact that he cannot identify CLAY BERTRAND he can reach only one conclusion: that is that the call received by him while in Hotel Dieu Hospital under sedation, was a figment of his imagination."

Dean Andrews's Grand Jury testimony in Parish, New Orleans, on June 28, 1967, had him changing his tune considerably. He now maintained that the man whom he knew as Clay Bertrand, who regularly sent him clients (often homosexual), and who called him in the hospital asking him to represent Oswald was Gene Davis. Andrews said he was introduced to Davis as Clay Bertrand at a "fag wedding reception" in the 1950s. He claimed that "I talk to him almost every day." This obviously is a huge contrast to what he told the Warren Commission. Dean would eventually say that Clay Bertrand "never existed." Witness Elmer Renfroe called this fellow "Miss Davis" when talking to Garrison's office, and never heard the name Clay Bertrand associated with him. Davis would deny all these allegations in a sworn affidavit.

Harold Weisberg commented on the "heavy sedation" claim thusly: "Exhibit 2899 (26H356-6) is a careful, prejudicial and somewhat less than honest selection of the brief documents we quoted earlier. The first is the very short FBI report quoting Andrews's doctor as saying the lawyer was "under heavy sedation" and quite erroneously offering the opinion, already known the Commission staff to be false, that the doctor 'did not believe Mr. ANDREWS was capable of using the telephone.' As indicated previously, Andrews did, in fact, use it – repeatedly. Its selection rather than Andrews's own testimony that he was under heavy sedation served to attract attention to this invalid opinion. It is not accidental. It is an unfortunately accurate measure of the integrity of the investigation of the assassination of John F. Kennedy. The second of these short FBI reports is the one that says Andrews got 'nose drops and cough medicine' and 'Phenobarbital,' hardly the represented 'heavy sedation.'"

During the Clay Shaw trial, Andrews was asked if he'd received "a telephone call of an unusual matter" while in the Hotel Dieu Hospital, and replied, "Well, I received a telephone call." When asked "Would you kindly tell us from whom you received this telephone call," Andrews objected from the witness stand, declaring, "May it please the court, I have two objections to that question. One, the attorney-client privilege, and secondly, an answer to this question in relationship to the charge that is pending, presently pending that I haven't been tried on yet, might, may, might, tend, would or could connect me with the link of circumstances which would incriminate me." When asked by Shaw's defense attorney Irvin Dymond, "Was this call to your knowledge from the defendant Clay Shaw?" Andrews responded, "No." He denied knowing Shaw. Dymond asked him, "During the course of your conversation with Mr. Kennedy, did you furnish him with a fictitious name identifying the person from whom you had received the phone call while you were in Hotel Dieu?" Andrews replied, "I respectfully decline to answer that question for the reason that it may, might tend to link me up with the chain of circumstances that may result in being used as evidence against me in the pending charge." He denied that Shaw was Bertrand, and said in regards to David Ferrie, "I knew him slightly." Andrews would attribute Bertrand to being "a figment of imagination," and confessed to "carrying on a farce" in order to prevent "bring[ing] a lot of heat and trouble to someone who didn't deserve it."[1]

There were several witnesses to the connections between all these ground level figures. Al Clark told Garrison's office that Clara "Bootsie Gay," who worked for a painting suppliers company, claimed to have seen a "chart, that had belonged to Davie Ferrie that indicated an assassination plot," while at attorney G. Wray Gill's office. Clark claimed to have met Kerry Thornley, and also Clay Shaw. Edward James Whalen, a career criminal, claimed to have met Ferrie and Clay Shaw, where Shaw offered him a substantial sum to kill someone who "could put him in prison for a long time." He would find out the person whom Shaw wanted killed was Jim Garrison. Whalen also claimed to have seen Dean Andrews at another gathering at Shaw's place. Ferrie told Whalen that Shaw had given Oswald financial support. He heard Ferrie mention the names of Senator John Tower and Dante Morochini. Whalen wanted nothing to do with it.[2] Former Banister employee Joe Newbrough told Garrison's office that Ferrie was in Banister's office daily for several months. Attorney G. Wray Gill, according to Newbrough, once sent Ferrie (who started out as a clerk in Gill's office) to Washington, D.C. to discuss a case with a Supreme Court Justice. He'd also heard that Carlos Marcello financed Ferrie's filling station. Newbrough told author William Davy about Guy Banister wanting him to get Shaw on the phone, and then handing the phone to Ferrie, who went on to have a conversation with Shaw.[3]

REGIS KENNEDY

Regis Kennedy (no relation to the president) is among several witnesses connected to the events in Dallas in 1963 who died "before they could be fully questioned," according to online sources. Kennedy reportedly suffered a heart attack the day before he was scheduled to testify before a grand jury on confiscated home movies of the assassination. The unreleased files contain an untitled communication from the Justice Department, a memo from Regis Kennedy to the special agent in charge of the FBI's New Orleans field office on May 18, 1967.[4] Garrison subpoenaed Kennedy on May 6, 1967. In a newspaper article, Kennedy was referred to as an agent who "investigated New Orleans angles" of the assassination in November 1963. However, Kennedy did testify at Shaw's trial on February 17, 1969, so it's unclear when "before he could be fully questioned" was. In his testimony, Kennedy claimed to have retired in 1968, but the entry at Find a Grave for him says he retired in 1972. Kennedy died on August 8, 1978 (aged 59-60, because no exact birth date is listed). Does this mean the "before he could be fully questioned" reference was to potential HSCA testimony? Only his parents and spouse, no child, are listed. But he is listed as Regis Leo Kennedy, Sr., so there may be a junior. Dean Andrews III told us he was close friends with Kennedy's son in high school, so he had at least one child. In his Orleans Parish testimony, Kennedy admitted he spent about "20 hours" looking for Clay Bertrand in the French Quarter, and that an unknown number of fellow FBI agents were looking for him, too. Oddly, Garrison's assistant James Alcock never directly asked him if he found any evidence of a Clay Bertrand, but Kennedy said he hadn't on cross-examination by lead defense attorney Irvin Dymond. In another of the endless connections here, Bill Wegmann and Guy Johnson, two other lawyers working for Shaw, had previously done work for Guy Banister.

A.J. Weberman published the following on his website: "Edward S. Suggs reported: 'Regis Kennedy used to come around [544 Camp Street] and was friendly with people in Guy Banister's office. Regis also spent a lot of time north of Lake Pontchartrain by the Cuban training camps.' On May 17, 1967, S.A. Regis Kennedy appeared before the New Orleans Parish Grand Jury during the 'Jim Garrison Investigation.' He invoked executive privilege in response to several questions. [FBI 62-109060-5255 5.18.67] Regis Kennedy wrote: 'I was asked if I knew W. Guy Banister and I told him yes. He then asked if I ever visited Banister's office and the identity of anyone I observed there. I answered that I had been in Guy Banister's office, and that the only person I could recall observing when I was there was Edward Suggs and two women, whose names I could not recall. I was also asked of my knowledge of the relationship between Banister, Arcacha Smith and OSWALD. I answered that I did not know... I was asked if I knew Dean Andrews and I acknowledged that I did... During the questioning concerning Andrews I was asked by a member of the jury whether I had investigated Dean Andrews and I replied that my contacts with Dean Andrews were set forth in the Warren Commission report.' [FBI TO SAC from Regis Kennedy 5.18.67-5255] When the HSCA contacted Regis Kennedy he said: 'He doubted there was any connection between MARCELLO, Ferrie and Banister et al. to the assassination,' and referred the Committee to DeBRUEYS. A message from the New Orleans FBI Field Office to the Director regarding the testimony of DeBRUEYS and Regis Kennedy is still mostly withheld. [NARA FBI 124-10031-10275; FBI 62-109060 1st. NR 5175 dated 5.8.67].'

FBI agents Regis Kennedy and Warren de Brueys appear to have been closely connected to the ground level conspirators in New Orleans. A frustrated Jim Garrison told *Playboy* during an October, 1967 interview: "Regis Kennedy is one of the FBI agents who interrogated David Ferrie in November 1963, and I hoped to learn from him what information the Bureau had elicited from Ferrie. But on the instructions of our old friend Attorney General Ramsey Clark, Kennedy refused to answer the questions put to him by the grand jury on the grounds of executive privilege. Warren De Brueys is a former FBI agent based in New Orleans who also questioned Ferrie in 1963. Between 1961 and 1963, De Brueys was involved with anti-Castro exile activities in New Orleans and was seen frequently at meetings of the right-wing Cuban Democratic Revolutionary Front. I'd like to find out the exact nature of De Brueys' relationship with Lee Oswald. As long as Oswald was in New Orleans, so was De Brueys. When Oswald moved to Dallas, De Brueys followed him. After the assassination, De Brueys returned to New Orleans. This may all be coincidence, but I find it interesting that De Brueys refuses to cooperate with our office – significant and frustrating, because I feel he could shed considerable light on Oswald's ties to anti-Castro groups."

Jim Garrison was reported to be subpoenaing Allen Dulles to testify before the grand jury. In a newspaper article reporting this, it was mentioned that Dulles "ended his tenure as Director of the CIA in 1961," which was a shocking way of not noting that he'd been fired by JFK after the Bay of Pigs. And then, of course, went on to serve on the Warren Commission. The same article states that Max Gonzales, a New Orleans court clerk, had witnessed meetings at the New Orleans Airport between David Ferrie and Edgar Eugene Bradley. Bradley would be shielded from extradition to New Orleans, like so many others on Garrison's list of witnesses, by then-California Governor Ronald Reagan.[5]

Researcher A.J. Weberman interviewed one of David Ferrie's young companions on his curious post-assassination drive to Houston to go skating (the other being Melvin Coffey). On his website, Weberman recounted: "In August 1993 Alvin Beauboeuf was contacted by this researcher. He related that he first met David Ferrie in the Civil Air Patrol: 'Dave, at that particular time, was accused of a crime against nature with someone I knew. A real scuze-ball named Mike Crouchet. Ferrie asked me to be a character witness against him in court. It never went that far. After Dave lost his job with Eastern Airlines, the judge threw it out. It never went to trial. Dave was bisexual. No other Civil Air Patrol members came forward and said, 'He did it to me too.' I was a teenager back then. If I had any better sense, I would have never got mixed-up in it. My dad died when I was 13. Anytime I had a problem in school I went to Dave's house for some help. He had a blackboard there. He wouldn't quit until you understood what he was trying to teach you. There wasn't anything he didn't know about. He had a lot of radical beliefs. He was involved with the Cuban Revolutionary Front, Arcacha. They talked a lot. I never heard the conversations. Dave had worked in conjunction with Guy Banister when they were working on the CARLOS MARCELLO case. Banister was a private investigator making his living off attorneys.' Alvin Beauboeuf was asked to comment on the previously cited document: 'Damn, that never popped up before! Wow! I never knew anything about that. Suggs had put OSWALD and Ferrie together right after the assassination. He told New Orleans District Attorney Jim Garrison that OSWALD and Dave were great buddies. If OSWALD was in fact hanging around the Camp Street location Suggs would have seen him, or talked to him, or met him, because Suggs was around there himself all the time. That's how you got that tie. I remember the old son-of-a bitch. I think he died in 1966. I don't know if it was a natural death or not." Beauboeuf was obviously wrong about Martin dying in 1966, as he was plenty active during Garrison's investigation.

Continuing, Weberman notes: "According to Alvin Beauboeuf, the address 618 North Pierce, was that of Melvin Coffey. As for the blonde, white female, name unknown he said, 'Whoa, where did she come from? Hello, no man. If I'd had a blonde bitch in there I would have known all about it. I promise you there wasn't no bitch there. Dave and I had a swinging pad before I was married. We had girls goin' in and out of there like crazy. But on that trip there was just the three of us. I placed the call to Alexandria. Dave called and talked to G. Wray Gil, who told him someone had implicated him in this OSWALD thing. Dave was at the telephone at the rink. He was always on the phone with somebody. In 1966 Garrison offered me money and job to testify that I knew Clay Shaw. Perry Russo came out making a bundle. I never did meet Perry Russo and I practically lived in Ferrie's house. The trip to Texas had been planned two weeks in advance. It all rolled out. The trial finished up and we just went. Unless Dave had some unique way of engineering me into going there.' On Sunday, November 24, 1963, David Ferrie, Alvin Beauboeuf and Melvin Coffey drove back to New Orleans. They stopped at a service station with a television, and saw RUBY kill OSWALD. David Ferrie then made several pay phone calls. Layton Martens reported having received a call from David Ferrie at about 3:00 p.m. Layton Martens: "After Suggs had related that Ferrie had stated the President should be killed and had outlined plans to this effect, he talked with G. Wray Gil [who said] there was nothing to worry about." Layton Martens said that when he inquired if the call was local or long distance David Ferrie replied that it was none of his business. During the conversation David Ferrie stated the name of OSWALD 'did not ring a bell with him and that he did not know him... Layton Martens said he knows David Ferrie to be a great admirer of President Kennedy.'" Martens had a small non-speaking cameo as an FBI agent in Oliver Stone's *JFK*. He enjoyed a successful career as a television anchor, radio talk show host, actor, lecturer on jazz music, an instructor in real estate, and the founder of his own public relations firm. He died of heart failure at age fifty-seven in 2000.[6] Only a few months before he died "unexpectedly," in the words of researcher Daniel Meyer, who was friends with Martens, Meyer asked him if he thought Garrison "had something." Martens replied that Garrison was "full of shit" and "crazy." He said he was writing a book on the subject, which would "clear some things up."[7]

Again, from A.J. Weberman's website: "Layton Martens claimed that in 1968 United States Attorney General Ramsey Clark suggested that he leave Louisiana, and go to Washington, to avoid testifying on this point. Layton Martens: 'Garrison was the most patently evil individual I ever knew. He molested a young boy at the Athletic Club. Jack Anderson ran the story. The kid's uncle was a Monsignor in the Catholic Church. Now that the kid is grown up, he doesn't mind talking about it. I can't prove it, but bribery was involved in the Garrison investigation. He dug up some witnesses. David Ferrie was a good American, he was not a homosexual, he was not some kind of weird fanatic creep. Otherwise he would not have been working under the Attorney General. There were letters about this, but they are missing. His arrests for homosexuality were manufactured. There was a serious recanting, and the charges were dropped. David Ferrie and my mom were very close after her divorce, and the two were talking about marriage. David Ferrie was just your basic, good American, who was doing the right thing. He didn't work for CARLOS MARCELLO. He worked for G. Wray Gil. G. Wray Gil was in a law firm representing many people. Ferrie could have flown CARLOS MARCELLO back to the United States. I wasn't there. I know he found a way to work with the Administration to get CARLOS MARCELLO back into the country. Cause the Attorney General had boo-booed. You can't just kidnap people, even though he was late for a deportation hearing. Understand, everyone wants to write books that say, 'He knew CARLOS MARCELLO, he must have been in with the mafia.' RUBY probably knew CARLOS MARCELLO too. Who cares? I been ignoring all this crap for 30 years.' In 1962 Layton Martens explained to the New Orleans FBI that he had been arrested by the New Orleans Police because he was associated with the Cuban Revolutionary Front, some of whom were homosexuals." During Garrison's investigation, Martens would be arrested for attempted murder in the French Quarter.

Demonstrating again the long reach of those engaged in these high crimes, in 1978 the mother of Layton Martens, Margarita (or Marguerite—the spelling varies in accounts) Martens, was confined to Southern Baptist Hospital, diagnosed as schizophrenic. Quoting from the HSCA interview with her: "Subject denies writing a letter concerning an assassination plot and states that she wrote her priest a letter dealing with her father beating her. She met David Ferrie in 1961 and didn't associate with him in 1963. He was her son's leader in the Civil Air Patrol. She never met LEE HARVEY OSWALD. If she wrote a letter about an assassination plot, it was while under the influence of pills and after her son's arrest during the Garrison probe." [HSCA 5.17.78 Martens Int.]. Mrs. Martens had been confined to a mental institution previously, in 1963. In a May 22, 1968 memo from Gary Sanders, one of Garrison's investigators, to Lou Ivon, it is stated, "On August 16, 1963, MRS. MARTENS was committed to Charity Hospital Mental Ward, Later MRS, MARTENS was transferred to Mandeville Mental Hospital, MRS. MARTENS was committed by the court order of Judge Howard Taylor (325-1270). The doctor who diagnosed MRS. MARTENS was DR. W. C. SUPER of Charity Hospital... After reading the complete history of the MARTENS case (Court orders, commitment papers, etc.), I found that MRS. MARTENS was committed by her son LAYTON MARTENS, Some of the psychiatric observations seem to be hearsay on the part of LAYTON MARTENS—The attachment gives part of DR. SUPER's diagnosis as 'son said' and '(son) says.' Doctor's notes continue to describe MRS. MARTENS as withdrawn and suspicious with delusions of persecution. The record shows that MRS. MARTENS was released from Mandeville on 29 November 1965." None other than Jack Martin wrote a very official sounding memo to Garrison's Chief Investigator Lou Ivon, on April 3, 1968, in which he discussed Layton Martens, and his "willingness to cooperate with your office." Assistant D.A. Jim Alcock had a phone conversation with Mrs. Martens, during which she claimed she couldn't tell him anything about any of the people suspected in the case, because she'd thrown Ferrie out of her home in January 1962 and "I never would associate with him anymore." She clearly was versed on the subject of the assassination, declaring, "The way I understand it, that a man and a red-headed woman were seen running away from the scene after President Kennedy was killed."

Viewed in a more conspiratorial way, a copy of a letter written by Mrs. Martens, apparently to her priest (Father Toups), was obtained by Lieutenant Francis Fruge of the Louisiana State Police, who was a central figure in the tragic story of Rose Cheramie, who famously tried to warn authorities about Kennedy being assassinated beforehand. According to Fruge, Mrs. Martens stated that she'd heard Ferrie, Shaw, and Banister, talking about killing JFK in August 1963. Fruge alleged that she'd had some kind of relationship with David Ferrie. Fruge claimed to have learned that it was Guy Banister who had her committed to a psychiatric hospital before the assassination took place.

This brings to mind how attorney David Kroman claimed to have "solved" the JFK assassination, insisting Garrison "has most of it correct but not the whole story." He was subsequently found stricken in his car from an "epileptic seizure." From his hospital bed, he declared "the assassination is solved," and promised to reveal the name of the assassin within a few days. Kroman described how his car had been forced off the road in Bismarck, North Dakota. He claimed that a government attempt to revoke his bail was "an attempt to shut me up." This was in regards to his being charged with insurance fraud and conspiracy (UPI, undated story). In a March 27, 1967 FBI report, it is recounted that Kroman claimed to have been assaulted in 1966, in Tennessee, during which "papers" were stolen from him. This was allegedly the day after he interviewed "a Dallas, Texas cab driver who drove Oswald in his escape." Presumably, he means William Whaley, but Whaley was killed in a car accident on December 19, 1965. The report goes on to note, "The cab driver reportedly was killed the next day after Kroman's assault in Tennessee." A newspaper account lists the Tennessee attack as happening in early January, 1966, so the dates are pretty close.[8] The FBI report reveals that Kroman was being sent to the federal prison in Springfield, Missouri for "psychiatric examination." Steve Jaffe interviewed David's brother Stanley Kroman, and in a November 8, 1967 memo to Garrison noted that Kroman had been assaulted just as he was about to contact Garrison's office, and once he had recovered and was about to try to contact Garrison again, he was accosted again and wound up in the hospital. Stanley told Jaffe that "DAVE was now hiding in California after having been released from the mental institution. He said that he still has most of the documents and tape recordings which he had collected in the investigation of the assassination...." Jaffe subsequently spoke to David Kroman on the phone, who expressed reluctance to testify at the Shaw trial without "some confirmation that he would be safe in giving his information to this office." Kroman obviously had some credibility concerns, and seemed to believe that oilman H.L. Hunt was the primary mover behind the conspiracy. In a February 14, 1968 memo, Steve Jaffe reported that Kroman had interviewed William Whaley on December 12 or 13, 1965.

Interestingly, Kroman appears to have been a prisoner at the Medical Center in Springfield, Missouri at the same time as Richard Case Nagell. Nagell memorably fired shots into the ceiling of an El Paso, Texas bank on September 20, 1963, in a purposeful attempt to be arrested. Nagell claimed to have foreknowledge of the JFK assassination, and wanted to avoid becoming a patsy. Kroman recounted that Nagell had been visited by William Martin from Garrison's office. Nagell tried several times to talk to Kroman about the assassination. Nagell told him he never expected to be released alive. Nagell's information was dubious; he described three mannlicher-carcano rifles as being used in the assassination, and claimed to have actually been working as an agent for the Russians during his service with the CIA. He also claimed the conspiracy was originally supposed to include the assassination of both Lyndon Johnson and Robert Kennedy as well. Garrison himself would travel to New York to talk with Nagell for several hours. Nagell would die from a supposed heart attack on November 1, 1995, one day after he'd received a letter from the ARRB.

Endnotes

1   *St. Petersburg Times,* February 26, 1969
2   Memo from James Alcock to Jim Garrison, September 18, 1967
3   Davy, p. 94
4   *Politico,* February 4, 2016
5   *LA Free Press,* March 1, 1968
6   *New Orleans Times-Picayune,* March 25, 2000
7   London Education Forum, October 1, 2010
8   *Minneapolis Morning Tribune,* January 14, 1966

Left to right, Richard E. Jeffries, Jr., Dean Andrews III and Donald Jeffries.

The Dean Andrews family won a first prize in A Mardi Gras Day Costume Contest. Left to Right: Susan, Dean, Dorothy and Dean III.

Dean was the founder of the iconic New Orleans' Jaz

The Times-Picayu

Founder of the Jazz Fest

Metairie

On April 24 as I was watching Channel 12's "Informed Sources," one of the panelists mentioned that it was indeed attorney Dean Andrews, lawyer-musician, who was the founder of the first Jazz Fest.

Many readers will recall that Dean Andrews gained notoriety in the Clay Shaw-Jim Garrison-Kennedy assassination caper. Andrews was the only one found guilty in that high drama. A jury found him guilty of perjury, but his conviction was overturned by the Louisiana Supreme Court and he was never retried. He died an innocent man.

Anyone remembering Dean's appearance will recall his roly-poly figure, dark blue suit, open collar and his trademark — his shades.

Dean was a Damon Runyon character of the first magnitude. As a court jester, he would hold forth daily around the coffee stand of the courthouse he was in attendance. His quips about the law and politics were often topical and always humorous.

He nicknamed District Attorney Jim Garrison as the

Dean Andrews
The Sunglass Kid

— his experience in att law school.

The judges and lawye difficulty digesting their f cause of the laughter his and humor provoked. H noted quip was his defini the difference between o and subjective law. Althou is a subject that legal s have pondered and writte for years, Dean describe

CHAPTER FOUR

THE DEAN ANDREWS III INTERVIEWS

C o-author William Law interviewed Dean Andrews III for many hours during the course of researching this book. As noted, Don Jeffries had talked with him many times over the years, but during these interviews he went more in depth on the subject of his father and Garrison's investigation, and disclosed information he never had before. We have gone through the tape recordings, and tried to choose the most pertinent parts for inclusion in this book. What follows are the edited comments of the son of the New Orleans lawyer.

DEAN ANDREWS III: "I mean, I was only like 12, you know, when he was assassinated, and, but I was a little older, though, when the case broke in New Orleans.... I mean, everything I have, some things can be verified, but a lot of it can't be verified, you know. My father related things to me. He read a lot of books, you know, on the assassination, and after he would read the book, father would read a book twice, and then he'd go through a book and put an asterisk by anything he questioned or he didn't understand, and then he, you know, he, once he had a, he would show me passages and tell me to make my own conclusions.

"You know, he was ... really paranoid towards the end of his life because, you know, everybody else had been killed, and ... Carlos Marcello was dead. Carlos Marcello was the guy, the Dixie Mafia boss, who, you know, kept my father alive. I mean, they were friends, very good friends."

WILLIAM LAW: "Now, you've just said something very interesting to me, that, you know, because Carlos Marcello was a well-known subject in the field of, you know, the JFK assassination."

ANDREWS: "Oh, yeah, yeah, you know, sure. Uh, they picked him up as he walked out of, I forget the name of the restaurant. It's a famous restaurant for breakfast at Brennan's. It's famous for elaborate breakfast. You know, a place where, you know, 20 years ago, 30 years ago, I remember the last time we went there.... He came out of there, remember, he came out of there wearing a suit, in business shoes, and they dropped him off, you know, on the edge of a Guatemalan jungle, for God's sakes, you know. So, definitely Carlos Marcello, you know, had a grudge against Robert Kennedy... and John Kennedy, for sure."

LAW: "Well, you know, your dad, your dad is kind of like a central figure in this."

ANDREWS: "Well yeah, I mean, you know, they were all, like I told them.... Marcello and my dad did with each other from the 50s. My father was an architect of his defense that kept him in the country. Now, he didn't argue before the Supreme Court. He was a young lawyer, fresh out of law school. But he heard through the grapevine Marcello's lawyers were stuck, and they didn't know what to do. It looked like he was going to be deported back to Sicily. So my father called his lawyers and said, well, I'll figure it out.... You know, I never really got into it with him. But that's, anyway, he ultimately got, was allowed to stay in the country."

LAW: "So your father was actually a lawyer for Carlos Marcello at one point."

ANDREWS: "Well, he did some minor work for some, you know, minor people. But I mean, he wasn't his big lawyer ... they were more friends. You know, they had more of a personal relationship. He had a, I don't know the name of his main lawyer. I can't, God, I can't remember. He was a ... I know he was gay.... And of course, you know ... from time to time, you know, they did dirty work for... the CIA, the FBI, who knows."

LAW: "So your dad was quite a colorful character. What did you think about the... in the *JFK* film, when John Candy portrayed your dad?"

ANDREWS: "I thought, you know ... he didn't have anything, he didn't have ... they wanted to talk to my mother and they wanted to talk to me. But my mother, you know, they even offered money to me, you know. But, I mean, my mother didn't want to have anything to do with that case. I mean, for her it was a nightmare. And I would have talked to Oliver Stone and Candy, but my mother didn't want to. At that time ... my life hasn't gone that well. I mean, you know, I basically had all kinds of little jobs ... I finally ended up driving a cab, something that I could do without ... it's point A to point B, keep your cab clean, your person clean, leave the radio off unless they want music, don't talk to them unless they start a conversation."

LAW: "Did you ever know Perry Raymond Russo?"

ANDREWS: "No, I never did."

LAW: "He drove a cab."

ANDREWS: "I never met him, you know. I'm sure, I don't know if my father knew him or not. You know ... he was another cab driver. My father ... he did minor work, you know. Well, I mean, okay, this is the thing. Garrison, my father, who else? What were the guys? Regis Kennedy, the FBI guy, Clay Shaw. They knew each other through the war or law school. One of the two or both, you know. And to tell you the truth, I think they're all bisexual, including my father. You know, in those days, you had to have a beard. You know, you couldn't have a career in politics or anything unless you were married. So you had to get married. So that's why I'm saying, except Clay Shaw. Clay Shaw was out of the closet, you know. Everybody knew he was gay. But my father, Jim Garrison. And Garrison, you know, he liked boys. I mean, he was a real pervert. He got arrested twice.... And I know it's true because he made a pass at me at the New Orleans Athletic Club, which was an exclusive, you know, athletic club.... My father had a contract with some gay Mardi Gras, well, social clubs.... And back then, part of your dues would cover jail if you got popped on a moral charge. You know, my father, for the ones he had contracts with, would come in and fix things because he knew people.... He could make things go away, you know. I mean, back in those days, literally, working with Carlos, my father could get people out of prison. They'd say that they're going to another prison, and then they'd send somebody else, a schmuck, to the other prison, and the other guy would be free. By the time they found out about it, the real prisoner was gone."

LAW: "Well, tell me about life in New Orleans in the 1960s as a kid."

ANDREWS: "Well, you know, I was 12 when the assassination happened. Right before it happened, I had to rush back to town because my father had been shot up with cocaine in the hospital. He had congestive heart failure. Somebody went into Hotel Dew and shot him up with enough cocaine to kill two men or a little horse or something, and nobody knew who did it. Nobody saw anybody. Nobody knows nothing. Nobody saw anything."

LAW: "And why was that?"

ANDREWS: "I think me and my father definitely felt that, you know, dead men tell no tales. He was supposedly going to be on his deathbed. He wasn't going to make it. So I think they wanted to just take him out before, you know, you go meet your maker… people might let out, who knows what's going to come out of his mouth, you know."

LAW: "You think this had something to do with Kennedy's assassination?"

ANDREWS: "Yeah, yeah, yeah. Take a look. Kennedy's killed on what, the 22nd? Well, this was right before that. Maybe, you know, five days before that, he had congestive heart failure, and that's when he got, you know, he had that happen to him, and I had to rush back from my uncle's farm in Arkansas, outside of El Dorado, Arkansas…. And I knew that my father was very, very, very sick, and, you know, the undertone was like he wasn't going to make it. But it changed. Somehow he picked up, and Carlos, through the grapevine, let it be known that that wasn't necessary. He didn't want it to happen. And, you know, he did enough favors, and he knew the stories of what happened to these people … where the bodies were buried or incinerated, whatever the hell they do, you know."

LAW: "Well, I know that you were pretty young when all this happened, but did your dad ever talk to you about any of this? I mean, did you ever have a one-on-one conversation with dad about all the things that transpired?"

ANDREWS: "Let me see. I asked him about all this, and he would, you know, have cryptic answers like, well, that makes sense … that's pretty good thinking on your part. And by the time we had these conversations, you know, in the mid-'70s, he really was crazy … totally paranoid. I mean … he was so bad off that he wanted to, he didn't want to be alone. My mother went, he went everywhere with my mother, you know, so I knew he was messed up. He totally lost it. But throughout the years … he'd get phone calls, and people would come wanting to interview him, and, you know, weird stuff. Like, in the middle of the summer … around 1 o'clock in the afternoon, this guy comes with a photographer in an English morning suit, says he's from the *Bombay Times*, you know, my father almost had a stroke. He was so messed up. I don't know whether the guy was from the *Bombay Times* or not, but I was really in shape and young then, and I made the guys hit the bricks. I said, turn around and go, or I'm going to smash the camera, and then smash it right over your head, dude. Look at my father. Look at him. He's trembling."

LAW: "And this was in the 70s?"

ANDREWS: "Yeah. And my car was stolen. That night, my car was stolen."

LAW: "You think there was a connection?"

ANDREWS: "Never got it back."

LAW: "You think there was a connection to that?"

ANDREWS: "I do, but you can't prove it. I mean … it could have been just a coincidence, you know. You know, my father never told me anything … I mean, basically, he implied it. He would give me articles and read this paragraph. He'd go through books and, you know, read that. You know, draw your own conclusions… I mean, he was cryptic, so he never came out and said anything, basically. Other than, the big thing I remember was something about Clay Shaw and Clay Bertrand. He said, well, if you read the case, if you get the file on the grand jury, essentially what I got convicted for was describing Clay Shaw differently for three times in a row. Different descriptions, different ideas and everything. And he says I did it deliberately."

LAW: "This was your dad, right? "

ANDREWS: "You know, because I had to … I mean, I couldn't do it. You know, Jim Garrison warned me to come out and say Clay Shaw is Clay Bertrand. And, you know, that would get me killed. Especially after this happened. You've got to remember, this stuff happened before Garrison, you know. And before Garrison went public, he was talking, my father was talking on the phone and meetings, having meetings, you know, at his office. You know, personally, I think my father … wanted to find out what kind of stuff he had. I mean, I think my father was part of a disinformation campaign, to tell you the truth. But that's just me.… That's why I believe that he was telling me that Clay Shaw and Clay Bertrand was the same people. He was in the hospital recovering from the cocaine when he got a call from somebody about going to see Oswald. Oswald was in my father's office around the time of the Fair Play for Cuba, I believe. And supposedly the cover story was, or the story was that he was asking questions about immigration. For something about his wife was apparently in trouble, or they were in trouble, I don't know. Or maybe another friend of his was in trouble. And my father didn't have any files on it. The lady named Train was his secretary, his personal secretary. And they didn't have anything in the office. But why would they? I mean, they would be taken out. I mean, if you are a field man. My father periodically, like twice a year, went up to Washington. Sometimes he would take my mother with us. And we'd do nothing but hang around and go to museums while he was gone all day somewhere. You know, he couldn't talk about it, blah, blah, blah, blah, blah, you know. So he was always pretty secretive. You know, if you read anything about my father, if you Google Dean Andrews Jr., it's all stuff that he's crazy. You know, he made everything up, and he's … I've never seen anything positive about my father, okay? … But, you know … just from things that he said, and especially … Clay Shaw was … a member of these organizations. And he would be somebody, an intelligent man who also knew a lot of people. And so, my father had no reason to get himself convicted of perjury unless he wanted to protect Clay Shaw."

LAW: "And why do you think he would protect Clay Shaw?"

ANDREWS: "Because somehow they were involved. You know, I mean, Garrison was. … You know, that was the link … Garrison wanted to, I guess he wanted to have leverage, you know, on Shaw. And if he had somebody that was going to… You know, he wanted to question him about the phone call, you know, 'who are you?' Well … I mean, he was not, he wasn't a flaming gay guy. He was gay, probably, everybody probably knew he was gay. I mean … when I say he was out … it's not out like it is today out. It's just that everything was on the down low, you know. And he, you know, associated with his personal life was, you know, typical older gay guy who liked younger men."

(*In a subsequent interview, Dean Andrews III talked some more. There was pride in his voice when he recalled that "the lawyers association loved to call him my father and get him to talk at the association dinners because you would just, you know, have people choking on their food laughing, you know."*)

LAW: "He just seems like a funny guy with a great sense of humor."

ANDREWS: "Yeah, he did, he was, but listen, when he was home he wasn't like that, okay? At home, you know, he wore a different hat, you know, and so I just found out about that as, later, as I got to be, you know, met people, various people that said they knew him… and it would relate to some sort of story. I mean, you know, he was, he wasn't home much, he wasn't home much growing up."

LAW: "Did you ever see him in the courtroom?"

ANDREWS: "Oh yeah."

LAW: "What was he like in the courtroom?"

ANDREWS: "Funny. The judges laughed. I mean, a lot of judges liked him. They either liked him or despised him. I mean, you know, you either went with his humor and his sarcasm, or you didn't.... And he loved to tell stories. For instance, when we got together at family parties, Christmas, you know, New Year's, Easter, my father didn't want to hang around with the adults, you know. He took all the kids to the movies, because he didn't like sitting around. I guess he thought they were squares, and he didn't want to waste his time, you know. My father loved jazz. He loved to go to the clubs, you know, and listen. He knew all the best musicians, you know, all the black musicians in town. And that's why he wanted to do a jazz thing, you know.... Well, I wish Garrison wouldn't have ... ever did what he did. You know, on one hand, he tried. I mean, you know, he's the only public official that ever tried to ... do a non-biased investigation. But ... he was doomed from the start. Part of him probably knew it, but I guess he felt that, or maybe not. He had a pretty big ego. I mean, you know, he was loved by the people."

LAW: "Did you know him? Did you ever meet him?"

ANDREWS: "Well, let me tell you something. For a while, he shut down all the clubs and all the b-girls, in other words, the bar girls. There'd be a bunch of them, you know, and then, you know, you'd go up to them and they'd come up to you. And, 'you want to buy me a drink?' And, sure, well, they ordered gin or vodka ... I mean, they'd drain the money out of guys' pockets, you know. And he shut that down. He shut down the prostitution in the French Quarter. Again, you know, that's messing with Marcello, you know.... He did things that nobody had ever done before in New Orleans, cleaned it up. That's why even after his case blew up in the space, he was elected judge."

(Dean went on to talk about his mother):

ANDREWS: "My mom now is in a nursing home, a Catholic nursing home, you know? She's 94 years old. She's still kicking."

LAW: "Is she still cognizant?"

ANDREWS: "I mean, her short-term memory isn't good anymore. Her long-term memory's intact, but she'd never talk about Garrison."

LAW: "Is that because it scared her? "

ANDREWS: "Well, no. She just didn't believe it. My mother believed that my father, you know, spun a story. Many people believe that he spun a story. I'm not objective. And why I don't believe it is because, you know, why would he commit perjury unless he felt that he had to, to protect himself and his family? I mean, why was he going up to Washington? What about the Bay of Pigs thing? I was there. He dragged me along."

LAW: "Well, tell me about that."

ANDREWS: "Well, whenever that time of history were, they were doing it, I believe. The only thing I went with them on Louisiana, it was across the lake and another parish over there in a state park that was, you know, not heavily used. I mean, back then, across the lake was like country, you see? It's all developed now, but back then, you know, I mean, people went hunting in state parks, you know, over there.... Nobody lived over there. Everybody lived in the city or Metairie, the first suburb, and that's where they had these things. And the guys were in military garb, and they were, you know, marching and somewhere else. They didn't have loaded weapons, you know. They were just being taught, you know, how to handle a gun and how to, you know, hand-to-hand combat things, marching and they were marching around and ... trying to shape up these freedom fighters, you know. And, of course, the official thing on, you know, is that ... there was no training of freedom fighters on American soil. Well, that's a lie. Like everything else, I mean ... I had a guy, a retired Navy man who was in statistics, you know, about the number of people that died, and he said that they always undercount the death ... I mean ... they admit to 500,000. It could have been 800,000. It could have been a million.... They can't take pictures. They can't be there. It's all done in secret.... And, you know, I mean, there's things that you get killed if you go into it.... How come nobody, how come the press didn't grab onto that like a bulldog? Well, they have their agenda, don't they?"

LAW: "Yes, they do. So what was it like for a kid?"

ANDREWS: "Well, my parents grew up in the south. They came from Arkansas.... Yeah, so, I mean, you know, that stuff happened and it was just devastating for us ... for my mother, for me. I lost friends. You know, he dropped out of the, you know. Right, out of the social circles. Country club, well, I mean, the athletic club. He never, I mean, he didn't withdraw, but he never went for years, and then he finally officially withdrew. I mean, he's paid his dues for years, but I mean, maybe he thought some way out of it, but I mean, and he did, you know ... he did get unconvicted, finally, by Louisiana Supreme Court. I don't know, five years later, six years later, seven years later, but the damage was done. It must have cost him a fortune financially."

LAW: "And he went to jail."

ANDREWS: "You know, let me tell you, he did go to jail, but it was like he had to go report to prison at eight o'clock at night, and then they'd let him out every day in the morning so he could work."

LAW: "And how long did that go on for?"

ANDREWS: "It went on for, I don't know, at least a year, 18 months, you know, before it got knocked down. Maybe it went on longer, you know, I mean, but I know that that's what was going on, definitely. So he did serve some time, you know, and you know, another thing, he wasn't angry with Garrison. He just did what he had to do, you know, everybody has their little part to play."

LAW: "Did he remain friends with Garrison?"

ANDREWS: "I don't know if they socialized or anything, but he had no bad feelings towards the guy. Whether they, you know, talked on the phone or anything after that, I don't know … I can't say … The fact that he wasn't mad at him, I didn't understand. I said, 'why, why, why, why? I mean, I don't understand. Why aren't you mad at him? He ruined everything for us, you know?' He wasn't mad at him, you know? The problem is, to me, the whole thing, if you're gonna … live in two different worlds, you shouldn't get married, you know? I mean, what was the marriage? Was it just cover? You know, I mean … all kinds of things went through my mind as I got older, you know, so I don't know..."

(Dean recounted how he got into a lot of trouble as a kid, and was eventually expelled from high school. Regarding William's question about being the son of a "prominent attorney," Dean corrected him, saying, "I mean, he knew a lot of people and he did things, but he wasn't in society as if by prominent you mean part of the Establishment. No, no, he was always on the fringe. I mean, he was a member of the New Orleans Athletic Club, and he knew a lot of people at all levels, but, I mean, he wasn't at the top level or anything.")

LAW: "Would you say that the involvement in the JFK matter tainted him for the rest of his life?"

ANDREWS: "Of course. Yeah, it ultimately drove him crazy. I mean, he, I have a little brother. He's 16 years younger than me. He's a heroin addict.

He's been doing heroin since he's 20 years old. He would come home from work and start looking for the microphones and he'd trash all the rooms, including his kids' rooms. Or he'd lock my brother out of the house and, you know, accuse my brother of being in on a conspiracy to kill him. I mean, you know, he went nuts, man. I wasn't there. I was away in college. My mother didn't know all the secrets. There were all kinds of secrets that I probably didn't know about. My mother didn't want to disturb me in college. I mean, I wasn't going to any great place. I went to Northwestern State in northwestern Louisiana. I followed a girl up there.... My father pulled strings to get me into law school ... but I dropped out ... I was a substitute teacher for a couple of years, just thinking about being a teacher, but the schools in New Orleans, they were so bad. I mean, they sent me to a lot of the really bad schools, you know, all black schools.... Well, I mean, like, you'd see people drinking beer. I had people screwing in the school ... I walked into, you know, they were playing, they had two dice games going on and a card game.... And then I ended up driving a cab. I just ended up driving a cab. I just ended up driving a cab because I could hold that job, you know, and it was simple as that. And I liked working at night ... I was married briefly, but that didn't work out. You know, I mean ... I didn't want to get married. She wanted to get married. I said, 'I'm not the type. I'm just in really good shape, you know, and I look real good. I'll probably end up being real fat like my father,' which wasn't true because I'm way fatter than my father ever got.... I was working for my father part-time. He had about seven laundromats and, you know, working around just helping him with whatever had to be done over at these places ... I got robbed twice, shot in the back once. But I still drove the cab. I liked the nightlife ... I liked all the, what I call the zombies and the vampires and the werewolves."

(I knew Dean had been in poor health for years. My brother and I visited him during one of his frequent stays in a rehab center. Describing his present physical condition, Dean told William, "I'm around 360. And I'm in poor health, man. I mean, I take 17 pills. I take two insulin shots, two different insulin shots. I take another shot once a week. I mean, it's not good. I mean, I'm in bad shape ... I have had congestive heart failure twice. I have real bad diabetes.... My legs below my knee are brown, you know, so. Between the weight, the heart, and the circulation, you know, I'm just, I don't know how I'm alive." Returning to the subject of his father, Dean related, "You know, my father spoke in riddles, you see.... You know, like, trying to just protect me. And so, I don't know. I mean, I just hope he, you know, I hope he, I don't know, I hope he found

some peace. He seemed like, you know, he was getting better when he died. He had a massive stroke, finally, and died.")

LAW: When did, what year did he pass?

ANDREWS: "He died on April 15, 1981. Eighty-one. Fifty-nine. Fifty-nine years old. So, he was relatively young when this stuff with JFK was going on. Yeah, but he'd had a lot of heart problems. He'd had congestive heart failure, you know, five or six, seven times, you know. So, you never know, you never know what's going to happen. I'm bad off right now."

(What one notices when talking with Dean is how often he lapses into quasi-Beatnik lingo himself, in the style of his father. Here's an example: "My really rich cousin took me, you know, to a predicate institute. Very, very expensive. And, you know, they cook with no oil, no butter, no sugar, no salt. And it's good food … I mean, we're talking about people that are, you know, three-digit multimillionaires go there. My cousin wasn't that rich, but she likes the hobnob with the rich, you know. It's a nice gig if you can get it. She ran with that crowd when she was young. You know, she'd go to spend a lot of time in France and the Caribbean, you know, and just go to parties, really. That's all she did for about 30 years. I wish I could be her. Would never get on a motorboat because a motorboat is evil. It's, you know, it's just middle-class crap. You know, it pollutes the water. Sail, you know, big sailboats, that's the ticket…. That's what the beautiful people do, you know. They have big sailboats. So, you know, she'd hang out with, like, the editor of French Vogue and people like that, you know. Yeah, she got some pictures of her in real designer Chanel outfits and YSL, YSL, whatever, all these guys. She was living the life. And then her sugar daddy died, and he gave her things, but they had loopholes, so his son took most of it back.")

William interviewed Dean again a few weeks later.

LAW: So, okay, what I've got written here is, Jim Garrison begins to investigate the goings-on in New Orleans. What transpired when your father was approached by Garrison in regards to the events there?

ANDREWS: "Well, you know, I 'came aware of it because he would call the house. I mean, you know, he had a couple of meetings with the guy. I found out, you know, I asked, he started calling the house. I said, 'what's Garrison calling the house about?' Because Garrison, you know, I didn't like Garrison. You know, I told you, Jack, he was a child molester. And at the NOAC, you know, my father would swim and then go play handball.

Play handball, and then we'd go swimming. I mean, you know, he used to knock that ball around with the lawyer friend of his, Monk Zeldin – and he represented my father. My father fired [him] because he wanted him just to plead guilty."

LAW: "Monk Zeldin wanted him to plead guilty?"

ANDREWS: "Oh, yeah. Oh, yeah."

LAW: "What else didn't you like about it? I mean, I know the obvious reason…"

ANDREWS: "Well, Garrison, well, I was, okay, so you go to the roof, and there's an outdoor running track, you know, on top of the roof. And there's an outdoor handball court, and there's some benches, and you can watch them play. People don't, people use that, you know, when the weather's good, you know, in New Orleans, it's a brief period. They're desperate, and the other rooms are booked. A guy comes up there, and, you know, he sits right next to me and shit. And so I thought that was weird for an adult to do that. And then he goes, 'how you doing?' you know, and puts his hand on my thigh. I just jumped up and, you know, ran out of there. My father, you know, I called my dad about it and said, well, he found out, he thought it might be Garrison, real tall guy, you know. And he just said, 'we're going to sit here and see if he's, because there's only one way out, you know.' And so I said, 'that's him right there,' you know, after a while. And my father said, 'Garrison?' He said, 'you sure that's the man?' I said, 'yeah.' He goes, 'okay, don't worry about it.' He's, you know, 'he was just, you know, he was bored, and he just, you know, probably just wanted to talk or something.' He gave me some crazy excuse. As a child, I didn't think anything of it. I thought it was, I said, 'yeah, I think it's weird to have a hand on a leg.' He goes, 'well, just don't think about it.' You know, I think my father didn't know what to tell me."

LAW: "Was that the first time you'd met Garrison?"

ANDREWS: "I can't recall. I mean, I know I'll never forget him since then. I mean, it was years. The only time I spoke to him, yeah, this was when I was little, you know. I was a boy, you know. I was like seven- or eight-years-old. The next thing you know, he's calling in '66 or '67 on a regular basis. And, you know, I'm going to tell you the truth, I forgot about it until I read the paper about him being arrested for child molestation."

LAW: "So tell me about the goings-on between—as much as you can remember – about the goings-on between you and your father when he was involved, getting started in the Garrison investigation."

ANDREWS: "Oh, well, he just said that Garrison was having an investigation and that he was talking to him about it because, you know, he knew some of the people that he was interested in."

LAW: "Like who?"

ANDREWS: "I didn't think anything of it. I thought, oh, God, I wonder if it's Carlos Marcello, you know."

LAW: "Did your dad ever tell you who he was interested in talking to your dad about?"

ANDREWS: "No, he never did. You know, all that come out when, you know, the stuff about the five guys in his office, gay guys in his office. See, I believe that because, again, you know, he was on the payroll to represent guys when they got in trouble, you know. And if he wasn't too bad of a defense, you know, he could get them off. I mean, you know, all he could say is, I knew one of them. Like, I knew one of them, you know. And I think that might have been somebody close to Clay Shaw. I don't think Clay Shaw would be seen in public with this ragtag, you know, I mean … one thing to party with him, but that's just my impression, you know. And so, you know, he just said that he's talking, you know, Garrison is thinking of indicting some criminals … and I can't really talk to you about it and don't worry about it. I mean, I know him for many years. And I don't know what my father could have done, you know … I mean, if he would have blown off Garrison that would have made him more curious, you know."

LAW: "So why do you think your father cooperated with Garrison?"

ANDREWS: "Yeah, I mean, the thing about being in Hotel Deux and having the, you know, it would have amounted to an assassination attempt, you know. I mean, somebody gives you all that cocaine and then nobody knows anything about it."

LAW: "Right, well, we're going to get to that one."

ANDREWS: "Well, that's all I can tell you about who he was talking to. He never said anything back then, you know. … You know, Jack … with my interactions with Garrison, he'd say, how you doing in school and blah, blah, blah. And, hey, are you playing sports? You know, just things you'd ask a kid because, you know, sometimes my father wasn't there and the pervert in him probably just wanted to talk.... You know, he called after 8 o'clock and my father was usually home by 8 o'clock. He'd make my mom mad because he'd missed supper, you know, and she'd have to keep..."

LAW: "Did he spend hours and hours at any given session talking to Garrison?"

ANDREWS: "Oh, I don't know how long they talked, you know. I doubt my father talked to him at home for more than an hour. You know, I just can't imagine him hanging on the phone more than that ... but they did have meetings. They did meet."

LAW: "In his office or did he ever..."

ANDREWS: "You know, informally. Informally. I mean, he never was sworn in or anything, you know."

LAW: "Do you know where the meetings mostly took place?"

ANDREWS: "One time they met at the NOSC because they were both members, you see."

LAW: "That's the health club?"

ANDREWS: "Yeah, and they might have played handball or they might have played pool or something. Or they might have just sat down, you know. If there's a reading room or there's rooms you can go to be quiet and get alone and talk, you know. Versus in the pool. They had a whole lot of massage tables that were very comfortable and chairs and tables. Or they could have been to the steam room. My father was big on the steam room. He dragged me in there sometimes. I hated it because it was just hot, you know. All these old men in sheets, you know. You're a little kid. You just go, oh, my God. Oh, my God, it was a nightmare."

LAW: "Well, now, your father and Garrison knew each other going back to law school. So as far as you know, did they hang out a lot together? I mean, were they friends?"

ANDREWS: "I don't know anything about that. I mean, they knew each other from school. And all I know is that a friend of my father's at his funeral was talking to me. You know, he talked about how he was a brave guy during the war. And that he, you know, that him and Garrison knew each other from law school. And that, you know, the story goes through the grapevine that the reason why he had a hard on for Clay Shaw, [in] part was because Clay Shaw took his sugar daddy away from him. That's what's being said. Who knows?"

LAW: "What do you mean by that statement, he took his sugar daddy away from him?"

ANDREWS: "Well, his sugar daddy, somebody who's going out with, and, you know, I guess Clay Shaw seduced him away. I mean, apparently everybody was, you know, having a secret life. That's the whole thing about, you know, professions in those days. You had to have a cover. You know, you had to be married if you're going to go into an elective office. And then you had to have your codename. You know, you didn't go by your real name. You know, your membership in an organization was your codename, like 'Clem Bertrand,' you know. So it wasn't just, it wasn't Shaw that used an alias. It was a lot of people at that point.... There's no ... you know, you got all these gay guys coming into the scene at parties, but obviously you never socialize with them publicly.... And, you know, I don't understand why Oswald would go with a bunch of guys. That's the part that I don't understand ... I mean, my father was in this, unfortunately, some kind of way. I mean, he never talked about his sex life. I mean ... birds of a feather, you know ... I mean, that's just my suspicion, especially with the Mafia boss. They spend so much time alone together, you know."

LAW: "You mean him and Carlos Marcello?"

ANDREWS: "Yeah."

LAW: "Okay, well then, let's go to that for a minute. So your father was very close to Marcello, the alleged Don of New Orleans. So what was their relationship like, and do you have any memories of meeting Carlos?"

ANDREWS: "Yeah, I met Carlos. My father was in the hospital and Carlos was in the hospital. And Carlos got there a couple of days, a day or two before my father left. So we walked down the hall and I met the guy, and he's real short. I mean, Carlos Marcello, I mean, he could have been no more than 5'6", you know. And he had a very gentle voice. He didn't talk loud, didn't shake his hand. It was like a limp handshake, you know. And so after we got back, you know, he was pleasant. He said, 'how you doing, boy? You making some grades?' Blah, blah, blah, you know. I think at that time I was really young.... And let's see, so basically what I know about them is that before, one time we went to dinner at, what's the name, Benicia's. You know, it was owned by, you know, a made guy. I can't remember his name.... And they had an upper tier, which was for private parties. And, you know, on one table there was Carlos Marcello and two of his henchmen and my dad. And then there was another table further away, all this top brass of the New Orleans Police Department, you know. And my father would have papers and envelopes, you know, in the newspaper. And, you know he'd go over there and talk for a while and come back.... And obviously there was some sort of payola going on. But I didn't ask him any questions, you know. When my father died.... And Garrison sent, I mean, he sent over a big, huge amounts of flowers and a wreath and everything. You know, he couldn't go to the funeral. I mean, I guess he could have. But I remember he told my mom that, you know, 'everywhere I go, you know, it's a big deal, and I don't want to interrupt the grieving period.'"

(Regarding Carlos Marcello, I had heard Dean comment many times on his weak handshake and soft, timid voice. Touching on this, he told William, "I said, Dad, he had such a weak handshake, and he talked so low. I could barely hear him. He says, 'well, that's a lesson in power, son. You know, when you're that powerful, you don't have to talk loud. You listen, you know. And he doesn't have to flex his, give you a hard shake, you know, to prove anything. He's got nothing to prove, you know. He's got his little thing going on, and if you're going to talk to him, you got to talk to him on his terms, which is he speaks low.' And then he said, 'you got to remember, this guy, you know, you never know when he has a tap, you know.'" Turning introspective, Dean wondered, regarding his father, "So everything is a mystery. You know, man. I mean, did he make it all up? That's what my mother thinks. But I don't think that. My mother had to process this somehow.... Because I remember going to the, you know, to the detention center.... So, you know, they had those exercises for the Bay of Pigs. You know, I remember seeing those soldiers.")

LAW: "Well, let me ask this question. When you were young, you visited the training camps that were involved with the Anacostia people."

ANDREWS: "Yeah, and the one that I remember the most is right across the lake, you know, somewhere across the lake that wasn't too far, you know, some state park. And it wasn't, you know, I didn't see very many people there.... I mean, these guys were marching ... they had some men that were practicing. You could hear the guns pop off in the distance. But they could have been, you know, I don't know. Back in those days, man, I mean, that was wild.... And you know, a lot of woods and stuff going on where you could blend in. And I took a ride with him somewhere up in Mississippi. I don't remember where. I know we went to Mississippi and it was the same thing going on. My father would drag me places with him, but I had no choice."

LAW: "How did he explain where you were going?"

ANDREWS: "I mean, he didn't just say 'we're going to go to the training camps, kid.' No, he said 'we're going to meet a friend and have lunch and then we're going to, you know, do a little hiking and we might do some fishing.' And we did. We did some fishing. And, you know, it was a lake."

LAW: "How old were you when he would take you to these camps?"

ANDREWS: "Bay of Pigs was ... Kennedy was in office. It was right after he took office, so it would have been '61. '61, '62... Well, if it was '61, I was 10. So '62, I was 11, you know. You got to remember that I didn't want to go ... I mean, there weren't kids there, just a bunch of adults."

LAW: "How did the guys treat you?"

ANDREWS: "He just said that, you know, they knew he brought his kids sometimes and there's nothing he can do about it. And that wasn't with them. I mean, I would go off and look around and just, you know, try to get away from the adults. I mean, this was like torture for me.... This was in the summertime. And in New Orleans ... the summer is there by May. You know, it's already over 90 degrees and insects and, you know, bugs and ... mosquitoes. And, like, I want to go home and sit in front of a television and watch Roy Rogers."

LAW: "Was it a big crowd of guys?"

ANDREWS: "I would say it was, I mean, not hundreds. I mean, it could have been, you know, hundreds. You know, a hundred guys, tops, that I was aware of. They were like an army. They were, you know, little cadres, I guess, little cadres of men. You know, you don't draw too much of a crowd ... I guess."

LAW: "I know I'm being unfair in asking you to remember this stuff because you're, like, 10 years old. But do you remember, like, if they were really taking it serious?"

ANDREWS: "Oh, yeah, oh, definitely. Yeah ... they had definite ... commanders and officers and, you know, they were training these guys to try to soldier them up. I mean, you know, it was like a chain of command and 'yes sir' and 'no sir' and all that crap. So this wasn't just a ragtag bunch of guys. These guys, they dressed appropriately for it. Well, they were relatively young people, you know. I mean, I'd say they looked old to me, but probably they were in their 20s or early 30s, most of them. Some of them looked like they could have been older than that. But, I mean, how

135

old was my father? He was born in '22. So he'd be 40 years old, '62. So, I mean, you know, so they had guys my father's age, you know, the officer types. They wore military fatigues, but they didn't have insignias on them or anything.… And I can't say that I saw them marching, you know, with rifles or anything."

LAW: "Did you ever see the weapons? Did they have guns, grenades, that kind of thing?"

ANDREWS: "I never did. Like I told you, you know, I heard some gunfire, and it was rhythmic, so I just thought somebody was practicing. You know, in other words, in those days, you'd go to the woods and teach your son how to shoot, you know, and stuff like that. So it was common to hear gunfire, you know, relatively close, but I wasn't around it, you know. I mean, that's all I remember about it, was having to go, guys in green fatigues, you know, my father talking to, like, I guess it was, like, the head honcho, whoever the guy was. My father spoke a little Spanish, so they'd go back and forth between Spanish and English."

LAW: "Most of these guys were Spanish fellas, right?"

ANDREWS: "Well, I don't know if they were Hispanic-looking to me. I mean, I don't know whether they were Spanish or Honduran or Cuban, I assume. But mostly darker-skinned guys. They had ties to Cuba, you know."

LAW: "Your father seems like a very bright and could be a very serious individual when it came to his…"

ANDREWS: "When he could, when he wanted to be. In his profession, but he also has, it seems to me, a side to him that is, forgive the word, hedonistic and.… He loved characters, you know. He was a character, and he liked people that were, you know, had some stick going on. I remember I went to his office, and he was playing chess with a Hell's Angel from Taos. I couldn't believe it.… He got home and said, 'Dad, what was that all about?' 'What's that?' 'He looked like a biker, you know, or something.' He goes, 'yeah, he was a biker. Didn't you see the back of his jacket?' I said, 'I know,' but I don't think I knew what a Hell's Angel was in those days. This was, you know, I was like around 13 or 14 when this happened.… So he had all kinds of friends."

LAW: "How did he act around you as a kid, or did you see him being like that without him noticing? If he went to Mardi Gras and you went to Mardi Gras, would he let that side of himself come out?"

ANDREWS: "A little bit, you know. But he was like restrained around us, you know, me and my sister, who was five years younger than me. So she has no memory at all, she says, of the Garrison and all the JFK stuff. She was 10, you know. I was like 15, so she didn't know anything. She never knew anything until years later. But you can tell when he's telling the story, you know, he'd wax. He would speak in the vernacular, depending on the story, who the story's coming from. Again, he was involved in the civil rights music business. You know, with educated black people, he'd speak educated. Most of the musicians, black jazz musicians, maybe in those days, didn't even finish high school. If they went to high school, they started working maybe after they got to grammar school.... My father wrote some short stories in the vernacular. The only thing I can compare it to is Confederacy of Dunces.... It won the Pulitzer Prize in 1978 for nonfiction. It's a hilarious book. It was all in the vernacular.... My sister supposedly has a couple of these old short stories."

(Dean continued to provide colorful anecdotes, including how his father took him and his little sister to see the Beatles in at City Park Stadium in New Orleans in 1964, during their first American tour. As Dean recounted, "But after 4 songs, which I couldn't hear, 4 or 5 songs, 6 tops, they shut down the concert. Because the girls were hanging on the Beatles, you know, on their legs and their feet. And the Beatles were, like, trapped. And I had these girls behind me that were screaming, screaming. I turned around. I said, 'do you mind? Some people are trying to listen.' And the girl put her hand on her hip and shook her finger in my face and said, 'this isn't for you. This is for girls.' 'Oh, shit, I'm a fan, you know.'")

LAW: "What did your dad say? Did he like it?"

ANDREWS: "No, he just laughed. He just laughed.... Okay, so they had a girl that ran up to the top of the stadium, and she was going to jump onto the Beatles' car. They each were in a limousine. And I said, Dad, that girl just said she was going to run up there and jump off. And so my father turned around, and she was going up there. And by the time my father got her, she had one leg over the banner, whatever you want to call it, the fence at the top of the stadium, whatever you want to call that. And he had to hold her. She was so worked up."

LAW: "Your dad did that?"

ANDREWS: "Yeah, he said, 'look how far. You might get killed.'"

LAW: "And did that calm her down?"

ANDREWS: "My father held on to her until the four limousines passed. Each Beatle was in their own limousine.... And then my father let the girl go. And she said, 'I'm going to go tell the police. He tried to kidnap me.' And my father said, 'go.' I mean, you know, I had an idea of what any father would do. Anybody with children wouldn't just sit around and say, oh, yeah, hey, this girl's going to commit suicide. Let's watch. And so he did his thing. And, you know, it was like that was startling. I said, 'man, Dad, I mean, whoa, that was, you know, pretty brave.' I mean, it had to be done. I mean ... I remember [him] saying 'I don't think about bravery so much as you have a responsibility as an adult to stop kids from harming themselves if you can...' He was a young guy then, you know, '64. He was 42. That's where he started having these heart attacks and stuff. My father had two heart attacks. And then he had congestive heart failure. But I got that. That's what I got now.... That's why he died. Although he died of a massive stroke. And my mother said he would hate this because he died on tax day, April 15th, you know. And, you know, it's just my father hated paying taxes like a lot of men, you know."

LAW: "So he felt comfortable enough with Marcello to be doing whatever he was doing? I mean, did they have some sort of physical relationship?"

ANDREWS: "I don't know. I don't want to know. But I mean, if that would fit in, why not Marcello too? Everybody else was bisexual in this crowd, you know. Why not throw in the Mafia boss? That would be, you know, you'd get killed. If they found out that the Mafia boss liked to suck cock, I mean, you know, that would be the end of him being a leader."

LAW: "This involves Clay Shaw. The Clay Shaw, Clay Bertrand. What are your thoughts on this point of contention so essential to the case?"

ANDREWS: "Well, I think that Clay Shaw was Clay Bertrand. My father, after he got almost assassinated, he wasn't going to tell anybody. That's what I think happened. Him and Garrison were talking. He might have told Garrison unofficially on the down low, no recordings, no nothing, face-to-face in the steam room at the New Orleans Athletic Club or something like that. And when he came down to testify, my father wasn't going to testify to anything, because he almost killed him. And if it wasn't for Carlos Marcello, he would have been killed."

LAW: "So you think Carlos protected your dad?"

ANDREWS: "I do, I do. I don't know anybody else who would have the juice. Since when do they try to kill somebody, and then they go, oh well, it didn't work out, let's forget about it. They go back and they do it."

(Turning again to his father, Dean said, "Well, the effect on him was bad.... Looking back on it, I can tell he was under tremendous stress. As a child, I just believed what he said. He says, well, this is going to blow over. Don't worry about it. But he had lots of stress on him looking back, and that's what brought him down. He couldn't shake the fact that he felt sooner or later that they were going to get him... So, you know, he took it to his grave. That's all I can tell you. My impression is that it was Clay Shaw that he would read all that stuff, and he'd say, read this and read that. And, you know, he said, you know, I said, you know, 'Dad, what about Clay Shaw and Clem Bertrand?' And he just said, 'well, you know, son, blah, blah, you know, that's a mystery....' I feel that my father, you know, after he was, after the assassination attempt, he wasn't going to say anything, except I don't know.... I mean, obviously, I mean, there were no heroes in this bunch.... They shot you up with enough cocaine to kill a horse, and somehow you survived. And, you know, the Mafia boss keeps you out of jail, keeps you out of being killed. It had to be somebody. Somebody put the kibosh on it, and I think it's Carlos, because I asked my dad about it. I said, 'Dad, how come you think they never came after you again?' And he said, 'well, friends in high places, you know, make sure it wasn't going to happen.' But, I don't know. To this day, I think he might have been killed. He was alone in the house, and they know how to cause strokes and heart attacks, and all of a sudden, boom, he's all alone in the house. Something happens. Poor guy. All he could do was drag himself outside and sit underneath a tree. He died in his underwear, in an undershirt, underneath a tree, in front of the house. You know, just trying to, I don't know, rather than call 911 for some reason, but you know who died like that? His father. That's the way his father died. I believe his father was in the military, hospital being for people with mental problems, playing softball. And all of a sudden, his father felt real bad. He looked up and just sat underneath the shade and prayed he never got up.... So, I think my father was recreating his father's death. I don't know. Who knows? He might have just panicked, you know?")

LAW: "How about your dad had an impressive résumé from his service in the Armed Forces. Can you tell me what you know about that era in his life?"

ANDREWS: "He was in the Navy. We have pictures of him in some island on Japan, and he was involved. Okay, he joined in 19 – he was born in '22. He joined when he was 20, so I think – no, no. I think he joined in – he went to Tulane on a football scholarship. His freshman year, he blew his knee out. So towards the end of '41, I think before Pearl Harbor, he joined the Navy. Or maybe it was after Pearl Harbor, and they had a program where they needed volunteers to go over to England and help drop bombs with those big B-17s. Of course, it wasn't official. They didn't wear American colors. It was like a thing, like if anything happens, you're on your own. The mission doesn't exist, because they had to blow up a lot of those factories. They had such an efficient military-industrial complex... He finally got wounded, but it wasn't much of a wound because he got a check for $20 for the rest of his life.... So it couldn't be much of a wound, but that's how he got out of that and somehow got into the intelligence somehow, some kind of way."

LAW: "Well, now, I understand your dad was a war hero. Do you know much about that story?"

ANDREWS: "Well, I don't know if he was a war hero. I mean, what he did was kind of heroic in the playing, but I can't recall a story like, well, he's manned a machine gun nest. My father never would tell me very much, so I don't know.... He didn't want to talk about it ... I think he wasn't cut out for cloak and dagger because he kept on having heart attacks, congestive heart failure. I think his stuff was because of figuring out a good defense for Carlos Marcello, he got hooked up with being a go-between, a field guy. As a result, he and Carlos became friends. My father saved him from getting deported, and they became friends rather than business associates. In other words, he was no official.... He might have discussed certain things.... My father was just like, he went to class in law school, but mainly he just played poker in the bottom of the law library. He paid a lot of attention. He paid attention in class, and he read his assignments, but he didn't study that much. He probably barely got out, probably."

LAW: "Do you think your dad was smart?"

ANDREWS: "I mean, he's the only guy I know that could sleep, watch television, and read a book at the same time. He'd be dozing and periodically go from the book to the television and snore for a while. The cycle would go on and on … I would ask him, 'okay, well, what happened five minutes ago in the movie?' Then I'd take a page. Let's say he was on page 180. I'd go back to page 160, and I'd give him a little prompting. I said, 'well, how did that get resolved?' Most of the time, he would remember what it was. So I figured, well, okay. So he had a good, clear, critical thinking mind … I mean, I never heard my father swear."

(Dean recounted how his father and his much younger brother would both recite classical poetry to girls as a pickup tactic, and how smart and successful the brother was. "He married a girl who was associated with the Mafia family…. And, you know, they got most of the concrete contracts in Jefferson Parish.")

LAW: "In his war service, your father's war service, do you think that it caused him to be noticed by any of the intelligence community?"

ANDREWS: "Well, yeah, that's how it started because, I mean, he was stationed in Los Alamos and White Sands, New Mexico. Those were highly secret locations for the bombs, the atom bomb and the hydrogen bomb. That's where he did the intelligence stuff originally, and I think he got switched to the Carlos Marcello, you know, which would maybe put him more with the FBI. Who knows? I mean, he was so secretive about all that stuff. All I know is, like I told you before, he'd go to Washington periodically and be there for a couple of days and come back, so he was reporting to somebody about something, you know…. It probably stopped when the Kennedy thing started off because, you know, I don't know. The whole thing for him was, he said he could handle it, but, you know, he had a hard time recovering, you know. His practice diminished because of mental problems, I guess. I only have one father … had a girlfriend from Nicaragua that he met in Tulane and she got pregnant and her family were real, you know, big shots in Nicaragua. She said, 'you can't marry a gringo. You either drop the gringo or Jack's going to stop coming.' But because of the Catholic Church, there was no such thing as she had the baby and gave it to my father. And so that's what my father was looking for, a wife to take care of this kid. Me. My mother denies it. But I asked my uncle about it and he got all shook up when I asked him about it. Like his eyes popped out of his head. He goes, where did you hear that at? So his body language and the tone of his voice, kind of like, you know, I said, 'it seems like, you know, the way you reacted, it would be true.' He goes, 'oh, no, it wasn't true….' So, and my mother's father, sometime, you know, he'd call me over and, you know, pat me on the head and give me five dollars a bit. He goes, 'oh, you poor boy, here, take five.' So I always wondered what that was about. What do you mean poor boy? So I think it might be true, you know.... But the mental illness in the family is very strong on my father's side,... So, and then my uncle, my uncle, that's how he joined the Navy. He went running around Tulane naked. Yeah, man, he's an original streaker. And so he had to go into the Navy to get ... you can join the Navy or go to jail, son. So, you know, my father ... as far as I know, I don't.... You know, I mean, late in life when I was in college is when I knew that something had gone wrong with him."

LAW: "Well, so tell me about that."

ANDREWS: "So there's a lot of pressure going on like that, you know.... All I know is as he got older, you know, the people kept on calling him and knocking on the door and eventually began to get spooked by it. In the back of his mind, he always thought, he just thought somebody was trying to kill him again."

LAW: "Well, before we get too deep into that, let me ask you this. What was the background between the relationship between your father and Jim Garrison? Do you know how that got started?"

ANDREWS: "Well, like I said, Jim Garrison is, well, was bisexual. Clay Shaw was, you know, out of the closet. My father was friends with these guys. I mean, I don't have no proof, but, you know, I just figured he might be the same way, you know? I mean, it's hard to be objective when it's your father. You know, you don't want to believe something like that, but then again, he did have those contracts with the gay community."

LAW: "Did he ever talk to you about any of that stuff?"

ANDREWS: "No, no, but he had pictures of these gay balls, and my mother hated them, you know? But he wouldn't let her throw them away, and I didn't know they weren't women, you know? I mean, because, I mean, they're in dresses and made up and everything, you know? I didn't know that they weren't guys ... until I was really older, and I'd look at the picture and go, wait a minute, something's wrong here ... when they were younger and not married, again, he was involved with these organizations because he was the lawyer that was under contract to get people out of jail when they were arrested and to get the charges either dropped or knocked down, you know? ... Oh, my father's law partner. He took on this young guy, and he was, again, you know, he was smart, but he was real shy, and so my father originally used him for research and then, you know, taught him how to be a trial lawyer, you know, step by step, and he told me that.... That Jim Garrison, he had a hatred of Clay Shaw because Clay Shaw, quote, stole his sugar daddy. In other words, he had a rich boyfriend, but Clay Shaw seduced him from Jim Garrison."

LAW: "How can you prove something like that?"

ANDREWS: "Uh, like I told you, he got arrested for trying to do things with boys, and that was in *Figaro Magazine*. It was published in the Townspeak Union. We're talking about '67, '68...

LAW: "But your father's law partner told you this..."

ANDREWS: "Yeah, a guy named Mike Barry. I suppose.... He's deceased."

(*Regarding his parents, Dean said, "They almost got divorced, but they asked the children for permission.... So we said, 'no, we don't like the idea of getting a divorce.' What else are you going to say? What do you think a twelve-year-old's going to say? 'Great idea, Dad. You like that young shit, huh?' I mean, you know, what do you expect me to say? 'No, I don't like the idea.'"*)

LAW: "Anything else that you can think of between, you know, the background of the relationship for your father and Jim Garrison?"

ANDREWS: "The NOAC, like I told you, they both were a member of the New Orleans Athletic Club. You know, I don't recall him playing handball with my father. I think they mainly ran into each other in, you know, the steam room. You know, there's a room where you could get massage and steam. It was these big old dudes, man, break your neck. You know, I couldn't take it. One time I asked my father to get a massage, and to me these guys were violent, you know what I mean? I mean, I was a little kid, and he just, I guess, only knew how to do it one way. It hurt me. I was sore for three or four days. So maybe they would talk in there, you know ... I mean, he got elected because he promised to clean up the French Quarter with prostitution and gambling and this and that, you know, and the crime. And, you know, that was a dangerous thing to do because Carlos Marcello owned much of the property in the French Quarter, especially on Bourbon Street. He might not technically own it, but, you know, it would be a dummy named somebody who he could control, you know. Because, I mean, he was convicted of felony charges when he was younger, so he was selling pot. And so I don't think he could own a bar room. And so they had proxy owners. Yeah, like Jack Ruby was a proxy, you know. He didn't really own the club. He was, you know, on paper he owned it, but he was just basically a manager, you know."

LAW: "Did you ever hear your dad talk about anything like that?"

ANDREWS: "Well, he had friends like that. I mean, one time he had to go down and see these guys at work, and he took me with him, you know. So I got to see my first strip show when I was, like, around 16, you know. 'Hey, hey, hey,' he goes, 'pay attention. You might learn something, kid, you know....' You know, I didn't know where we were going, but we were at Bourbon Street, and we're on Bourbon Street, and what was the name of that place? "Satin Dolls," something like that. I don't know if it exists anymore. And so my father, you know, we sat at the bar, and I got a Coke, and my father, the only thing, he quit drinking when I was born, but he'd have a creme de menthe, you know, it's a liqueur, and he'd have maybe one of those. And then they went back in the office, and I'm sitting up there, and these girls are acting like I'm a grown man, you know, so I was, like, terrified.... You know, the bar girl said, 'say, buy me a drink,' and so they'd order gin or vodka in a shot glass, and they'd just drink it ... my father, when I was like around 18, during Mardi Gras, I was sitting in one of the offices, you know, because I could get a good seat of, it wasn't that big of an office. I mean, you had three offices in the secretarial area and a small law library. And they had these two young girls in there, and in those days, you could open the windows, you know. And they opened the windows and bent over, leaning out, and one of them didn't have any underwear on, you know. So I didn't know what to do. This time, I was only like around 15. And the girl said, 'You see anything you like?' I said, 'What? What?' I was too scared. She goes, 'Are you gay?' I said, 'No, but I'm not used to seeing girls naked, okay?'"

LAW: "One of his secretaries?"

ANDREWS: "Well, I think he, no, they were just hookers, young hookers, around eighteen-years-old. I don't know where he knew them from. I imagine they worked for somebody who knew, who knew, met him through somebody who worked for him, because, you know, like I said, he had these contracts, and he was, you know. So he could get, maybe he had one with the girls, too, or I don't know. Maybe he used their services."

LAW: "From looking at, you know, the small film clips I've had or seen of your dad, and from the impression you get from the *JFK* movie, your dad was quite a gregarious person."

ANDREWS: "Oh, yeah, he could speak the King's English when he had to, but he was much more comfortable, you know, with the criminals. I mean, it's just flat out. He just ... or poor people. He just had a, you know, a social justice crusader streak in him that was pretty big. And I don't know what it was, he loved jazz so much, and, you know, most of the jazz musicians were poor black guys. Even though they were famous for being great, they weren't making a lot of money.... I can give you an example, there's a man named Danny Barker, he played with Xavier Cugat's band in New York. And my father got him to come back to play at the Jazz Fest, because he also had a sideline of him and a banjo, and he was telling stories, you know, like story songs, and so he wanted that ethnic input from the Jazz Fest. The only one, the first Jazz Fest was 1965, produced by my father. He had a big case, and he used the money to produce it himself, which really pissed my mother off, because all that, he broke even, but that didn't mean anything to my mother, you know, his X number of thousands of dollars, you know, were down the drain. And my dad, you know, he bought plots for people, like, you see what I had, this one time they had this Chinese family, he was helping with immigration, then the grandpa died suddenly, they got to be buried the next day, you know, they had a restaurant, but they were just eeking out a living, and so my father bought the plot, he'd do stuff like that, you know, things that most people wouldn't do, you know, it irritated my mother."

LAW: "So he was a good-hearted guy."

ANDREWS: "Yeah, he was, I think he, you know, he had to have, he had to, that kind of probably settled him down from whatever else he was into, you know."

LAW: "So your dad had that side to him, but he also had what we would term as a darker side."

ANDREWS: "Well, yeah, I mean, you know, like I say, I don't know what he was really up to other than he went to report to somebody in D.C. I mean, he was.... My father, you know, was gone a lot.... He was a social creature."

LAW: "Well, let's get back on the JFK track for a sec. It's said, I don't know if this is true, but it's said that Oswald was a client of your dad's. Do you know if that was in fact true?"

ANDREWS: "I never saw the guy. I'm just going by what he said. What he said was the guy came in, he had an issue about his wife's status in the country. That was what he said the original thing was about. But then again, he came in with a group of other people, so it wasn't like him and his wife, or at least one time he came in with a group of people. I get the impression that he was in the office more than one time. And the other guys were like Hispanics, and that makes sense because of the Bay of Pigs stuff and all that. Somehow Oswald might have been involved in that. Who knows? Oswald definitely went to parties with Clay Shaw."

LAW: "But your dad basically affirmed that it was Oswald that visited his office."

ANDREWS: "Yeah, but he couldn't prove it because there was no record. But I don't think my father would take a record. In other words, if, again, it's all if, if, if. In other words, if they were involved in something, why would he have a file? He could have a secret file but not come up with anything for the government because the pretext might have been his wife's immigration status, but they could have been talking about stuff involving God knows what, training for the Bay of Pigs."

LAW: "Did your dad ever express an opinion on Kennedy one way or the other?"

ANDREWS: "Well, my father was a lifelong Democrat, so I know he voted for Kennedy. He said he did, but, I mean, he didn't really talk that much about it to me. His mother was a lifelong Republican, so she was really irritated that some of her children would vote for a Democrat. She was a businesswoman."

LAW: "Now, you know, after JFK was killed, as the story goes, your dad was called by a Clay Bertrand to offer legal representation in Dallas for Oswald."

ANDREWS: "He was in the hospital. That's when they gave him all that cocaine."

LAW: "Well, we're going to get there. So, can you…. Do you have an explanation as to what led him to be chosen for that, to represent Oswald?"

ANDREWS: "Well, it was Clay Bertrand with Clay Shaw. And towards the end of his life, you know, he implied heavily. He didn't want to come out and exactly say anything. But, you know, he said, 'Clay Shaw, Clem Bertrand. You know, I knew them both well. And, you know, they were basically one time, you know, he kind of let it slip that they were the same guy. But, I mean, who knows? His mental health wasn't very good by that time."

LAW: "Well, tell me, if you can remember, tell me how he expressed it to you the time that he slipped and admitted that they were both the same guy."

ANDREWS: "I would ask him from time to time. I said, 'Dad, the reason you got convicted of perjury is because you gave all these different descriptions of Clem Bertrand.' And, you know, he kept on saying that he wasn't Clay Shaw. And, you know, 'why did Garrison, why did you get prosecuted and nobody else did? It seems like Garrison had a strong belief that you're lying. So, you know, what's the deal?' And he basically just, you know, but he was, his mental illness was real bad then. And he goes, 'well, you know, sometimes Clay Shaw used an alias, which, you know, might have been Clay Bertrand.' I mean, you know, it's all just a bunch of crap, really, you know. I mean, you can't use it. But, I mean, he did kind of say it. That's what I mean. So, I said, 'Dad,' I said, 'well, why would you, you know?' But once they tried to kill him, okay, look at the situation he's in. Even if, you know, he's, you know, his job was to give disinformation to Garrison. You know, he works in a two-way street. I mean, as if my father's going to really come out and tell Garrison anything, you know, of substance. Because that's probably, you know, he knew that my dad was involved in stuff. And so, he, you know, he evidently thought very strongly that he could identify him. And my father would. And he gave three different, if you read the transcript of the, or part of the transcript from the grand jury. My understanding is that he gave three different descriptions of Clem Bertrand, that all contradicted each other. And there might be other substance of things, but he did get convicted of perjury, specifically about, you know, Clem Bertrand."

LAW: "So, after Garrison did this to your dad, they'd been friends. Did that noticeably change their, i.e., their friendship?"

ANDREWS: "Well, I mean, once this thing went public, he never called my father at home anymore. And that's the weird thing. My father wasn't angry…. He goes, 'no, you know, he just had to do what he had to do.' I said (well, I mean, it's a real stoic position), 'you know, he just had to ruin our lives, and he had to do it. I mean, why would he do that, you know, unless he had a good reason?' So, periodically I'd ask him about it. And one time, that's what he said, you know. I mean, that I seem to recall, you

147

know, that there was an alias he used. But people use all kind of aliases, you know…. It just destroyed him mentally. He held on for a long time, but it just. You know, he's always waiting for somebody. You know, he thought these people, they could have, I don't know. Were they trying to kill him? Were they trying to scare him? Were they just checking, gauging him? For whatever reason, he got it built up in his head. And by that time, let's see, when was this? He stopped working and just got a small security check and was living off of past earnings…. He died in '81, and this was around '75, '74. I was away in college. I didn't know that he quit working. But once I, you know, and he put up a good front, but I was only there for Christmas. But once I moved back to New Orleans, you know, I could see that he was just not there anymore. He didn't want to be alone."

LAW: "So let's talk about how your dad wound up in, what is it, the Hotel Dieu?

ANDREWS: "Well, I believe it was congestive heart failure."

LAW: "This is the first time when they, when they, is this the first time when he went and that's when somebody gave him the cocaine?"

ANDREWS: "It was after, this was right around the time of the assassination. Two days before the assassination. He goes in there. It doesn't look good. I don't know whether he's going to pull out or not, and then somebody goes in there to make, you know, try to knock him off. Because, you know, they don't want any deathbed confessions."

LAW: "Right, so, but you think he actually did have heart problems at that point?"

ANDREWS: "Oh, yeah."

LAW: "And so while he's in there, this is when somebody gives him a big batch of cocaine. Have I got that right?"

ANDREWS: "Right, because they used cocaine in the hospitals in those days in Louisiana. He was shot up with pharmaceutical cocaine, enough to kill a horse, that's what I was told. I always remember, as I told you, if I didn't tell you, I was in El Dorado, Arkansas, visiting my cousins."

LAW: "And so how did you find out that he had been shot up with a bunch of cocaine? Who said that?"

ANDREWS: "They called up there and said, 'send Dean home because his father's very ill,' you know. And, you know, one of the older cousins said, 'look, this is really serious. They don't know whether your dad's going to make it or not.' So I went down there, and it turns out that I couldn't go see him anyway because I was too little... And then he pulled through."

LAW: "How does a guy go in for heart failure and live through a cocaine injection?"

ANDREWS: "Well, that's what happened. I mean, you know, I don't know what else to tell you. That's what I was told. It turns out that there was an accident, but on his chart it was said allergic to cocaine. Don't you understand? On his chart, allergic to cocaine, and nobody knows anything. 'No, we don't know anything about it.' We don't know who did it, how they got in, where it was from. 'You know, we're not missing any cocaine.' Yeah, that's the whole bit right there. And so, you know, I mean, they knew my father was a romantic type, and maybe they were afraid he was going to have second thoughts. I mean, there's a reason why Garrison started this thing about, you know, a big part of it was in New Orleans, you know, because it probably was."

LAW: "And so after he came out of the hospital, did he have any kind of, you know, somebody tries to kill you, it's got to change your, I don't know, change your personality?"

ANDREWS: "Well, again, you got to remember that I was 12 years old at the time, and he didn't act like, you know, his thing was, well, to me at that time, he said there was a big mistake at the hospital. They gave you the wrong medicine and too much of a dose.... The nurse isn't liable, the doctor's not liable, the hospital's not liable."

LAW: "Did your dad in later years express any opinion on that to you? Because you asked him questions about this, did that ever come up?"

ANDREWS: "Yes, it did come up. I mean, you know, once or twice I said, 'Dad, I mean, it seems to me that somebody was trying to kill you. You said that it was just an accident, but it was an accident right before Kennedy got killed. I mean, you know, you knew Clay Shaw, you knew David Ferrie. You know, Carlos Marcello hated the Kennedys because they picked him up off the street and dropped him off in a village in the Guatemalan jungle in a suit....' So he said all this, you know, he never would admit that it was an assassination attempt, you see. He was always very guarded and protective, you know, but it weighed on him.... I don't think it's something he made up. But my mother, you know, she didn't like to talk about it at all. So that would be a perfect answer to shut people up for her, you know.... I think it's too many coincidences, you know. I mean, any logical person could look at this and go, hey, there's something going on here."

(Dean went on to describe some alarming but all too common family dysfunction. He suffered from medical and weight issues, and was now confined to a wheelchair. He told William, "I'm really depressed, dude. I mean, you know, I just.... Everything is, you know, getting out of bed is a major ordeal. I don't know what else to tell you." He then noted, "It's following us around forever, you know. I mean, even up here. I go to Virginia and I meet Don's brother in a treatment program. And Don.... Because, 'wait a minute, Dean Andrews, he's from New Orleans. He's got to be related to the lawyer.' That's how I met Don. I mean, so that's like coincidence. I meet his brother in a treatment program. We become friends and then Don, you know, jumps on the name and.... Don tried.... We tried to get my mother talking about it at Don's house one night. We were over for dinner, but my mom... 'No, no, no, no.'")

LAW: "Just wasn't going to do it, huh?"

ANDREWS: "No, man, she's not biting on anything. For her, it's just a big mess. It altered her life in a negative way."

(The next interview was the fourth between William and Dean. Dean talked about how the heat affected him, because of his weight, and how his air conditioning wasn't working. "My blower motor, I don't know when they're going to ever fix something. It's been, like, broke for, like, two months, you know. There's nothing I can do." Dean related. "You know, if you have a Section 8 apartment, they know you don't have any money and you've got nowhere to go, so you've just got to wait for them to do it whenever they feel like doing it, you know.... I mean, I can't last a summer. They have to get it fixed before summertime." Dean remembered how his father wouldn't even let him change a tire, saying, "He never enjoyed physical labor. He enjoyed swimming, he enjoyed playing handball, enjoyed playing the clarinet.... I don't think my dad, until he got really older, was more than 40 pounds overweight... I mean, he wasn't really fat like me.... Even if he was carrying 50 pounds, he could still handle it, you know?")

LAW: "When he would talk to you when you were a kid, we see him as this kind of jive-talking guy, you know?"

ANDREWS: "He wasn't like that at home. He was like that outside of the home....That was just kind of a character. He caroused with black musicians. He loved jazz, and so he had clients.... He would rather be with the common people. In other words, you know, the less educated people of the region.... Salt of the earth type of thing."

LAW: "So the effect on you of the whole thing that happened in '63, it started to affect your family and you right away then."

ANDREWS: "Well, not right away because, I mean, it didn't pop up until '67. So you really didn't.... Garrison's thing didn't start, you know, as far as I can see, over the phone in '66, and then I think it got blown into the paper in '67, right? So it didn't change things automatically for me, but, I mean, it did, you know, after the, ... I don't know if that was in '67 or '68, I'm not sure."

LAW: "Right. So, okay, let's go to '63 then. Just to keep it in line here, I've got some questions that deal with these particular things. So let me go to this. So, okay, JFK's killed, and then your dad was called by a Clay Bertrand to offer legal representation in Dallas for Oswald.

ANDREWS: "Yeah, but he was in the hospital."

LAW: "Okay, but, so it says.... Can you offer an explanation as to what led this ... led him to being chosen for this?"

ANDREWS: "Well, it goes back to those contracts with the court of law, with the social organizations, the gay social organizations, okay? They had lawyers. You know, part of your scene was having, like, a lawyer, like my father, who would get them out of jams. You know, the average jams.... That's how the Clay Bertrand thing would come up, one of the aliases. Like, everybody had an alias, right? ... This was a thing in the underground homosexual thing, so to speak ... Clay Shaw, you know, used a number of aliases. A lot of people used a number of aliases, one of which was Clem Bertrand. Okay? And, uh ... Clay Shaw knew.... You know, had partied with Lee Harvey Oswald and some other people. Oswald apparently was bisexual, so..."

LAW: "So, I know we've covered some of this, but I'm trying to get as much of this as you can remember. So, did your dad allude to this at any point in his life?"

ANDREWS: "Oh, about Clay Shaw?"

LAW: "Yeah, did he allude to that?"

LAW: "I mean, years afterward, did he allude to it at all?"

ANDREWS: "Yeah, I mean…. The whole thing about him was…. You know, you know that Clay Shaw is Clem Bertrand, and I want you to say it in court. And if my father was going to do that, he definitely changed his mind after they almost killed him with the cocaine, you know? He never said that he was going to cooperate. I'm assuming, since they knew each other, number one, my father probably said, this is off-the-record, and then Garrison changed his mind that it was too big to be off-the-record, you know? And then somebody, my father almost got killed, and so he wasn't going to get involved in anything except disinformation, you know? … I feel that he was like a double agent. In other words, he was giving Garrison some stuff, but then really collecting more to let the Feds know what he was about, so they could be one step ahead of him, you know? That's how I see it."

LAW: "You mean you think he was feeding Garrison information, but he was also feeding, you know, the FBI or something?"

ANDREWS: "Look, since my father did things for the government, you know, he went up there to Washington and met with people or something. He never told us what it was, you know? On a regular basis. Whether he did it afterwards, he did it by himself…. I believe that my father was a middle … like a field guy, and a hands-on field guy with Marcello, and things of him … things within his world, Marcello's world, which was drugs, fish, produce…. Now, if the government wanted something done, I believe that that's what was going on. That my father was going there, and he was getting orders on what they wanted to have done or something."

LAW: "So, you think that he was basically reporting on Marcello for the government at the same time while being friends with Marcello?"

ANDREWS: "Yeah. I've got that right. I think that's it. But mainly, also, just to, you know, well, we want a favor from him. This is the favor, you know? We'd not like to get him convicted, but to use him as an asset to do things, you know, nefarious things that they couldn't do themselves. I don't know what. That's just a feeling I got."

LAW: "So what was your home life like during this period (once Jim Garrison's investigation went public)?"

ANDREWS: "Well, I tried to carry, you know, my father said, 'don't worry about it, just carry on your normal life.' But, you know, it's always floating in your back of your mind, 'oh, my God, my father's indicted for perjury. You know, what are my friends going to say?' … You know, it definitely bothered me. I mean, you know, my father, you know, he acted like nothing was wrong, but obviously things were wrong, you know."

LAW: "Did it ruin his career, his business?"

ANDREWS: "Well, he wanted to be a judge, and it was feasible. You know, he would have been backed by certain individuals that you need to get elected, and under the table you had Marcello, Buddy, and all that was thrown out of the window thanks to Jim Garrison."

LAW: "Did he remain friends with Marcello after this?"

ANDREWS: "Oh, yeah, absolutely. Up until he died, yeah. So...Wait a minute. No, my father died first. My father died in 1981, up until my father's death.... I think Marcello lived into the middle 80s.... I think he died maybe five years after my father..."

LAW: "Now, your dad had a secretary named Eva Springer, whom he called 'Train.' Do you remember anything about her?"

ANDREWS: "Yeah. She was a very gregarious lady. She was very organized. My father needed her. She put a lot of organization to the office. You see, it had various secretaries, but none like Train. My father had a big heart. He would try to rehabilitate hookers and drug addicts and give them something to do. Give them a job outside of their comfort zone. If you don't want to be a hooker, you don't work in a bar. You don't work in a racetrack or anything like that. You learn how to type and you get a job in your office."

LAW: "So tell me, was Train one of these people that he took in?"

ANDREWS: "I don't know. Train was a very fat woman. Huge. How he got her, I don't know. She certainly wasn't a drug addict or a stripper or anything like that.... She came into his life. She was there for a number of years.... So she was a fairly good secretary for him."

LAW: "So there's something about Oswald's files disappeared. Can you tell me about that?"

ANDREWS: "Well, again, this is just my theory on it. I mean, my father could have told her to lose the file, and she would have done it. Without question.... But that could have been a possibility. The cover is, could have been a meeting revolving around the Fair Play for Cuba committee or something else. Who knows? I mean, you got Garrison involved in this, you got Clay Shaw, you got Clem Bertrand, who, you know, was an alias used by, you know, Clay Shaw, sometimes, my father said. But, you know, when he was in court, he said, 'it's not the same guy.' Clem Bertrand said it was a different guy."

LAW: "I was just going to ask you to describe your father's testimony before the Warren Commission, which seems to be conflicted."

ANDREWS: "Well, all I know about the Warren Commission is that everything he said was unsubstantiated, so they just said it's not reliable.... I'm going to have to look around next time, and I'll find that report from the Secret Service. Partial report on my dad. Everything is, you know, it's unsubstantiated, and, you know, so they can't rely on it. But, I mean, the way I look at it is, if he was doing some sort of nefarious stuff or, you know, 007 type of, you know, stuff, then why would he, you know, he wouldn't have a legal conviction. You know, I mean, people could maybe put Oswald in the office, but without a record of it, they couldn't prove it."

LAW: "Now, when your dad, you know, the investigation, the Garrison investigation, you know, really took off and your dad was enmeshed in all the goings-on, do you have any real recollections of what was going on at the time? The whole world was watching your family."

ANDREWS: "Well, when that thing popped, it was just, you know, just... The heat was on, man. I mean, they staked out the house. They staked out.... And when this happened, we moved from a house into a condo, a nice condominium that was just built. You know, it was like a nice courtyard."

LAW: "Because they were watching your house and stuff."

ANDREWS: "Well, no, we moved there.... For whatever reason, I don't know why, but we moved from Bonneville Boulevard to 17 Bonneville Boulevard to Whitney Place Condominiums. And it had a nice courtyard, which was manicured, and they had a nice pool.... They had a big barbecue.... Well, I don't know, barbecue area. It was a nice building, screened-in building where you could have parties outside."

LAW: "Did your dad's income seem to be more at that period? Because that sounds like a really nice place to go."

ANDREWS: "Well, it was a nice place. I mean, it was a three-bedroom apartment. But it was two baths.... I mean, it wasn't that exclusive. I mean, you had Saints football players living there. You had accountants living there. You had businessmen living there. I mean, it wasn't ... I don't know. I personally would have rather stayed in the house. Maybe his finances were wrong. Maybe he lost money. My father was up and down with money, you know what I mean? … I mean, you know, like when he died, a lot of people owed my dad money, and my mother would get checks for years, people paying him off slowly, you know."

LAW: "Now, I know you've seen the movie *JFK*. So what did you think of John Candy's performance as your dad?"

ANDREWS: "Well, I mean, nobody else did it, so I had nothing to compare it to. But physically, I thought he was a good match, you know. I thought he was a nice physical resemblance. He got the jive stuff down pretty good. He got great for passable. I thought, you know, I mean, 'the right hee-hee, the wrong ho-ho,' he got all that kind of stuff pretty right. You know, he's told Garrison that you can't win. You're going up against the federal government. You can't win. You don't have the resources, and you're going to be embarrassed. But, you know, Garrison was probably, you know, not demeaned or whatever you want to call it in some circles, you know."

LAW: "Did you feel from watching the film that Stone captured the basics of what transpired overall in the events of the murder of JFK?"

ANDREWS: "I think so. I mean, you know, anybody who read books about it, you know, he covered the basis, the basic issues, what was wrong with the assassination, the shots fired and all that, the New Orleans connections. You know, like David Ferrie, who was a pilot, and he's a guy who picked up Carlos Marcello from Guatemala and brought him back to New Orleans. He also did weird work for the CIA, you know, and he went there around the time of the assassination, and then he flew back, I believe. Did he bring, was he dropping off shooters? Who knows, you know. That was implied by somebody. They thought he dropped off shooting shooters.…
I mean, how do you get to the truth about it? I mean, all these people involved were just the type of people that the CIA or NSA or FBI like to have doing field work for them because there's so much plausible deniability. They were such characters."

LAW: Now, tell me, you had a chance to be part of the Oliver Stone film. Tell me about why you chose not to be part of that and not to speak to Stone.

ANDREWS: "I mean, as a consultant, my mother didn't want anything to do with it. She didn't want us to have anything to do with it. I felt that I had to honor my mother's request. I mean, she would have been very,

very upset if I decided I wanted to do it because they were going to pay, you know."

LAW: "If you don't mind my asking, what did they offer you? Was it a big sum of cash?"

ANDREWS: "Well, I was told by this lady lawyer who was sitting. Me and my cousin went to Snug Harbor, a restaurant and jazz club on Frenchford Street, New Orleans, and I saw this lady who knew my father. She was a criminal lawyer as well. And Oliver Stone was there and came. He was with Costner, Kevin Costner, whatever his name was. And she said, you know, they contacted your mother. They wanted to interview her. They were going to pay her. They offered her $20,000. And my mother turned it down. And they would like to talk to you, but I don't know exactly what they would pay. And she said, 'it would probably be less than $20,000 because you were a child at the time. But it would probably be, you know, more than $10,000.' And it doesn't matter because my mother doesn't want me to do it.... So I didn't talk to Oliver Stone. They were there. I got up from there. We went inside the musical. We came out. They were there talking to her. And I didn't go over there for no reason, too. And my cousin was at the bar drinking after the concert. And we got up to go to the bathroom. And those two bastards took our seats. Oliver Stone. I wanted to get in their face about it, but my cousin said, 'no, don't do it. They're big people. We're little people. And we're the ones who are going to go to jail. I mean, come on. You're going to start a fight with Oliver Stone and Kevin Costner? How drunk are you, you know?' ... Actually, you know, we got up and went to the bathroom. Therefore, the seats were supposed to be public establishment. The seat didn't have my name on it.... They may or may not give you the seat. Depending on your size and their size. If they're bigger than you, they might say, tough shit.... If they're little[r] than you, they might say, okay, here's your seat back."

CHAPTER FIVE

WILLIAM LAW 1993 INTERVIEW WITH PERRY RAYMOND RUSSO

I knew "Leon Oswald," who was whiskered, dirty, and had rumpled hair. I did not know a Lee Harvey Oswald.

– Perry Raymond Russo

WILLIAM LAW: "And [I] wanted to ask you, just, you know, you read a lot of things about Jim Garrison."

PERRY RAYMOND RUSSO: "Sure."

LAW: "You know, and everything that I've been able to read, it's like they really try to discredit what he's done."

RUSSO: "Well, yeah, that's accurate. The CIA went into high gear in 1967 and devised a game plan to discredit Garrison. I had a CIA contact all the way to '79, and that's when the last time I dealt with the CIA on a direct basis, until 1991. They called me at that time when the movie, *JFK*, by Oliver Stone, was being made."

LAW: "Right. Did that cause you any problems?"

RUSSO: "Yeah, it did. They said they wanted the movie stopped. I said, 'look, fuck yourself.' I said, 'we don't do business anymore.' I haven't done any business since '79. So I said, 'you know, there's just no point in it. So why do we got to stop the movie? You know what it's going to do?' On and on and on and on. I said, 'I have no allegiance to your people. Our business deals, that doesn't cover anything.' I said, 'so what are you talking about?' So they said they were sending people down here. I said, 'I don't give a fuck. Send whoever the fuck you want. I'm dead anyway.' Anyway, so yes, they did devise it, but it was unsuccessful in it, you know."

LAW: "Well, it seems to be. I mean, everything I've ever picked up, I mean, from books way back to recent books, you know."

RUSSO: "Have always stopped and ridiculed or jested. And it had its effect. In August of 1968, I was labeled a drug addict. And I'm Sicilian. I never even smoked grass. So I was labeled a drug addict. So here's someone in Portland who's reading *Time* magazine's law section. And essentially, this is the essence of the article, "Garrison's Act of Fantasy." And it says, Jim Garrison has posited a new theory, or perhaps an old theory, concerning the assassination of John F. Kennedy. And this is an assassination that comes from CIA and industrial and all that kind of stuff. So let me base this theory upon the testimony of one Perry Raymond Russo, known, capital K-N-O-W-N, known, a drug addict, capitalized. Who says such and such? Now, of course, you're reading it in Portland – Portland drug addict. You know, he's hallucinating at best. Or he's doing it for mischievous or devious reasons. Or self-gaining reasons. So what the fuck? They paid me $15,000 for that. They claimed it was a typographical error. They really meant to revert it. So they paid, but they said they could not issue a retraction. And they gave me an ultimatum. They said if I didn't want to take the $15,000 and drop the action, they had all the money in the world. They may lose in a district court, they would win in an appellate court. If they lost in an appellate court, they'd win in a Supreme Court. A reversal because of the Sullivan case and the libel laws of William O. Douglas. That's all about William O. Douglas. And so on. And that has proved to be the case in my essence. So I was a public target. The purpose of this attack on me would be to invalidate the reasonableness or sensibility of anything that I would say. And therefore, you thus crushed Garrison. Well, that worked. It worked very well."

LAW: "Well, it seems to have worked."

RUSSO: "Yeah, sure."

LAW: "Could you recount for me a little bit about being at the party and what was said?"

RUSSO: "Well, a lot of things were said. Garrison, Oswald, and I didn't get along. There was no chemistry between us. Ferrie was a central mover, and he was a rogue CIA agent who did a lot of things on behalf of the CIA. He had been involved in the Bay of Pigs. He eventually was to fly Marcello back into the country. He was well-positioned to do a few works and little games of intrigue on behalf of the CIA. He was very, very intelligent, almost to the point of being a genius. And he was very creative in his approaches to different things. It showed best, well, in that movie, *JFK*, which was sort of choreographed, if that's the correct word, that conspiracy room scene. A lot of it is exactly the way it occurred."

LAW: "So that was a pretty fair..."

RUSSO: "Yeah, a pretty fair statement by Oliver Stone as far as how that occurred that night. It wasn't nearly as boisterous as it's done there, and such. They didn't use Ferrie's apartment, which, when people come to New Orleans, if they want to go on Overdriver Cab now, if they want to ride around, I'll ride around to all these different locations, and we can go to Ferrie's apartment."

LAW: "Do you really? Well, I'm thinking about going to New Orleans."

RUSSO: "Well, if you come down here, if you let me know when you're coming in, I'll meet you at the airport."

LAW: "That'd be great."

RUSSO: "And we could roam around, and I can give you the address and tell you how much time is involved. It is like a cab fare to me, what it is, you know. At night, it would be fun. I wouldn't ride you around in a cab fare, but at night, you can only see so much."

LAW: "That'd be great."

RUSSO: "So it'd be up to you. So what do you do for a living?"

LAW: "I work in a mill, believe it or not."

RUSSO: "Oh, out there?"

LAW: "Yeah. We're a little mill town."

RUSSO: "And so what is your point of this kind of assassination, the Garrison thing?"

LAW: "Well, I've studied it from one end. You know, I'm a guy that just got tired of reading books."

RUSSO: "Yeah."

LAW: "You know, I've read every kind of book I can get my hands on."

RUSSO: "Sure."

LAW: "And I thought, hey, you know, I've got to start talking to some of these people."

RUSSO: "Right. Well, there are some books out that are just totally false. I mean, there's one, 'Betrayed,' I think. 'Betrayed' or 'Betrayal.'"

LAW: "I've heard of it. I have not read it."

RUSSO: "Well, Robert Morrow, he says I died in 1977, and two other books that say I'm dead."

LAW: "That one I haven't read."

RUSSO: "Yeah, well, that's in there, and that's still just, you know, puts a very strange effect, aura. But there's a lot of testimony that I gave, of course that has never been indicated by anybody else's testimony, and has been corroborated by some. And Garrison's case will remain an enigma in that it is the only official tribunal that ever occurred where a person was charged with witnesses and adversarial system. And though that person was found innocent, it raised many serious questions about participation of various people that had governmental contacts. Oswald lived here, all the way, a good part of his life he lived here."

LAW: "And it's very difficult for you to accept the fact that he was a Marxist, even though he said it: 'And upon this, I am a Marxist.' 'Are you a communist, Mr. Oswald?'"

RUSSO: "He was asked that on radio after distributing leaflets, Fair Play for Cuba leaflets. He had joined our group and had become a member of this group. And he offered to teach guerrilla warfare to Cubans as they plotted for a second invasion. And that would make him a right-winger to me. That would make him a radical-right, you know. And then the government in August, and it's very documented down here, the governmental FBI in August made lightning raids under instruction from Bobby Kennedy. He was an asshole."

LAW: "Bobby Kennedy?"

RUSSO: "Yeah. Bobby Kennedy ordered the FBI, ordered J. Edgar Hoover, and then ordered the FBI to reconnoiter with these Cuban groups because John Kennedy had given the house away when he made a deal with Khrushchev in October of '62 in the Missile Crisis. Oh, we sit back, everybody said, 'Kennedy and Khrushchev looked eyeball to eyeball and Khrushchev blinked.' Well, that didn't fucking happen."

LAW: "That didn't come out until later, though."

RUSSO: "Yeah, I know it didn't come out until later, but we knew it. We knew there had been a betrayal."

LAW: "You guys were following that pretty closely."

RUSSO: "Very closely. The Cuban community here knew that there was a betrayal. There was a stab in the back. The effect of the Cuban Missile Crisis and the deal that was wrought was outrageous. It wasn't we're a big bad USA and the American Eagle's going to trounce, trample on the Russian path. The effect of it was this, that we made an agreement that six months after Khrushchev would take his missiles out, which were non-operational, we would remove our missiles from Turkey, which were operational. We would never put them back. We have never put them back. That's the law we follow. But that wasn't all that Kennedy gave. He was a bum of a president, a bum. The second thing he gave is that he guaranteed there would never be another invasion—that was the part that bothered the Cubans. That was the part that they suspicioned [sic], that in this secret deal that was made, they were sold out. There would never be another invasion from the U.S. mainland. And thirdly, which was sort of incidental, Khrushchev, I mean Kennedy guaranteed that we would never try to assassinate Castro. And we wouldn't care if his beard grew all the way to his toes. And so the effect of that was that the American Eagle became the co-guarantor of Castro's longevity and the communist revolution and Cuba's longevity along with the Russian Bear. Now the Russian Bear has moved out. It can't support him because it fell apart. But the truth is we're still keeping Khrushchev-Fidel in office. So the Cubans read that very clearly. I knew that in August of '63 that that was the case, that we, the Cubans had been sold out. And so the Cubans went from a rage over that summer.

They began saving money. They were going to invade again from Guatemala to the western shore of Cuba. And they were saving up all that money because in '63 you could, in fact, transship heavy artillery. You could transship guns of any sort. You didn't need all these Commerce Department licenses, State Department licenses and so on. You could buy it at the normal Army and Navy surplus or at governmental surplus sales. And then you could turn around and transship it to Guatemala and then you could buy it in a second invasion. They were going to do it again and not allow the United States to get involved, but they were going to do it much more prepared. And this was frustrating because on August 1st, 3rd, and 7th here in the New Orleans area, the morning *Times-Picayune*, a local newspaper here, had this funny headline, "FBI Makes Lightning Raids on Formbushey Ammunition Stuff." That's about 60 miles west of us. FBI makes lightning raids in Slidell and Covington and other places. The point of this was that you read the article and it says 6,000 rounds of this and 3,000 rifles and 1,000 grenades and 500 grenade launchers and bazookas and all that kind of crap were confiscated. And the owner of the farm was 'Lopez' or 'García' or 'Hernandez' or whatever, a Latin name. But yet nobody was arrested. All they did was confiscate it. This was an attempt by the FBI to frustrate, after they had received information about where they were storing the guns and the weapons, to frustrate the Cubans that they could not mount a second invasion no matter where it was from. Bobby Kennedy talked to Jack Kennedy, and this is all authenticated and documented, talked to Jack Kennedy and told him that, in fact, to make sure there was not a third world war, that the truth would be that not only would they not allow another invasion from the United States mainland, like it came from Florida for the Bay of Pigs, but they would not allow another invasion, period, from Guatemala or from any other place by any Cuban. That was a corollary of the second agreement made that Bobby Kennedy's interpretation, to keep the lid down, to keep it closed, because forever and after that, still to this day, Fidel Castro was considered a nuisance. He would vaporize in a third world war. He would vaporize. And we would vaporize Cuba right quick.

That was just a matter of known military tactics. We were going to vaporize Cuba if we went to a third world war. So this way, there would not be a trigger. Since we were writing off Cuba, to hell with the 175,000 Cubans that are now in Florida and Louisiana. So *just to hell with that.* So this was a very dastardly deed. This was a betrayal. So they frustrate them. They grab their rifles. They grab their grenades. And there's nothing else. What are you going to fight the fucking invading Cuba with? Bows and arrows? You can't do that. So therefore, they come back to New Orleans. And I go to a meeting, which I've been ridiculed and attacked and yelled at and screamed at. And I was lied to by people who would never go to court and say it. They would just say it in some fucking newspaper or something like that. And that couldn't be. Russo has to be lying or he has to be doped up or something. Or Garrison has to have something on him. That these guys sat around and they began plotting how to assassinate Castro. And then one of them got up and said, 'Fuck Castro. Assassinate Kennedy. Blame it on somebody like Castro.' And the guy that was perfect for that was Oswald. Because he was supposedly a Russian defector. He wasn't. He was a member of our group. He wasn't a fucking defector. He wasn't a monk. So in order for him to create a semblance and to plan to go into Cuba to assassinate Castro, he had to create a cover, CIA cover. Typical thing. He goes out and starts distributing leaflets. Fair Play for Cuba

Committee, New Orleans chapter. Send your donations 544 Camp Street. Well that's Guy Banister's office.... That's INCAS, that's the Information Council to the American's Office. That's right next door to the CIA. Right down the block from the FBI."

LAW: "That's so amazing."

RUSSO: "Yeah. This address that they're telling you to send us. Oh, but now. Where is Fair Play for Cuba? It's not in the building. No such chapter in New Orleans. This is just for public consumption... so it looked like we had a rip-roaring Marxist. If you had been in New Orleans in the 60's, you would know that if you created a front, you go on fucking Havana Radio the next day – Huey Newton was, Eldridge Cleaver did, Stokely Carmichael did, Ralph Brown did, these four bombed the United States, "Burn, baby burn. Soul on ice...." All these people attack the United States. And they go up on Havana Radio and blast the United States. Well this would allow Lee Oswald to get a visa. And to put in to effect Plan A – and that was to assassinate Castro. He and two other people would be in there."

LAW: "But was it going to be Lee Oswald?"

RUSSO: "No. It was going to be another man in his place – a man who spoke Spanish; a man who knew Cuba, who looked like Oswald. And if you read a lot, you'll know that there is always a reference to another Oswald running around wherever Lee was."

LAW: "Right."

RUSSO: "Remember Oswald said that, and so did Ruth Paine in Dallas – in New Orleans too. There's a second Oswald. Who was this second Oswald? I know who he was. I met him. He's a mean son of a bitch. But he was crazy. He was a Cuban who was going to go back to Cuba, who was wanted by the Cuban government. But he would have a visa."

LAW: "How did he get a visa?"

RUSSO: "Oswald would have to go to the Cuban Embassy in Mexico City. And he went September 26th. But he was turned down. How can he turn them down? He's a Russian defector with a Russian wife; an American defector *to* Russia with a Russian wife. A man who's gotten on WSU Radio or WWL Radio with Ed Scanlon Butler of Information Council. But the Americans then debated the relative merits of Marxism versus communism. I mean Marxism versus capitalism. He said, 'I'm a Marxist.' And this is beamed by the CIA. They found the right to disprove him.

And it's beamed down to Cuba. How? They knew no Cuban intelligence was listed. Why did they turn him down? Well, the USA won't tell you why, because they had the Embassy bugged. But they won't tell you why he was turned down. The official notification by the Cuban government: 'Application for visa.' 'Oswald Harvey Lee' – [he] put it backwards. 'Denied.' That's all. That's the official statement. Oswald came back, he moved to Irving, Texas. The second plan went into effect: *get Kennedy by someone like Oswald.* They tried two other places. I'll tell you where they are: Chicago and Miami."

LAW: "I heard about the one in Miami. Yeah, and one in Chicago too. They tried to get him with a rifle in the building."

RUSSO: "Yeah. And they were. They chickened out in Chicago. And they shot somebody in Miami. And then they finally got Oswald. They finally got Kennedy. Oswald didn't fire a shot. Listen, why don't you do this? I don't want to stay on the phone because I get up real early in the morning. If you care to, then we can chat another time."

LAW: "Sure."

RUSSO: "And if you want, you can record the conversations. I don't care… There's a lot of stories, side stories and all that kind of stuff, and it depends on how much you know about the New Orleans thing. You have to understand that the whole New Orleans thing is sensible as a possible group that assassinated Kennedy. The same people show up in Dallas, but yet it's difficult to say were they in Dealey Plaza. The same people show up in Dallas. Now, the question is, were they in Dealey Plaza? Oswald was standing down there amidst the motorcade or, you know, right around the doorway. That photograph sort of indicates that. And you have these other people that were around, that were New Orleans-based people. It is very logical that it [the assassination conspiracy] comes out of New Orleans, but it's also very, very reasonable to me that Oswald didn't fire a shot and was exactly what he said he was. He didn't kill Kennedy. He doesn't know anything about it, and he's 'just a patsy.' And that's what Stone believes."

LAW: "Right. I've seen it [Oliver Stone's *JFK*] so many times I drive people crazy. Yeah, I mean, this is a brief beginning."

LAW: "Right. You're the guy at the bar [in Stone's *JFK* film], right?"

RUSSO: "At the bar. Right. And 'Kennedy, he's a motherfucker—he deserves to die.' And then the guy in front of me says, 'Well, they should hang that son of a bitch' [Oswald]. And I say, 'Hang him? Hang him? They should give him a fucking medal!'"

LAW: "Right, right."

RUSSO: "You know, but that thing is done 70 times. And they have long versions and short versions. And there was one little episode—and then I have to get off the phone. But there was one episode where I didn't know how they made movies. I just thought, you know, they gave you a script. They never gave me any script. They just said, 'just say what you feel.' You know, and I told him, I said, so anyway.... So anyway, there's Kevin Costner getting out there: 'Come on, Jack, you can do it.' (You know, for Jack Kennedy to pull through his trauma and head injury.) The announcement had just come over the TV. There was a head injury and a priest had been called, which would indicate very serious wounds. And there was a possible ... sacrament of Extreme Unction [Last Rites], which is the final rites before death or immediately after death, before and after death ... [in the Catholic] church. And so Kevin Costner standing up, and it [is] ... about 30 takes. I mean, Stone was in the next room looking at TV. You know, that's how they do it now. I didn't know that. I thought they stood right there, but they don't. And he's in the next room looking at TV, seeing what it looks like. And so Kevin Costner gets up, 'Come on, Jack, you can do it. Come on, Jack, you can do it.' And so I'm watching him, and I said, 'sit down, asshole. I didn't vote for you.'"

LAW: "Oh, really?"

RUSSO: "Yeah."

LAW: "Oh, my God..."

RUSSO: "Cut. And Oliver Stone comes running. He comes face to face an inch away in the very quiet voice. He says, 'don't yell at Kevin. That was the $7 million man.' He said something like, 'I don't know what his contract was, but, you know, the rumor was that he signed off on $7 million and had a percentage and all that kind of stuff.'"

LAW: "[Costner's] ...going to need it. He's going through a divorce."

RUSSO: "But the point is that, 'don't yell at Kevin.' I don't blame him for anything he did. He didn't want Kevin to see that. And I was only three feet away. I said, 'sure, I won't yell at Kevin.' Kevin Costner was a very nice person. But I don't know where to get this Cornwall accent that they put on. But that's the movie chain. Anyway, listen, why don't we talk again?"

LAW: "I'd love to. I have lots more questions."

I called Perry Russo the next night.

Here he picked things back up, discussing James Kirkwood, author of *American Grotesque,* one of the most extreme of all the attacks on Jim Garrison.

RUSSO: "All the way up to this, I supposedly tell him that all the stuff that Garrison had me witness to in court – I don't know where that came from. 'I made it up under drugs.' 'I made it up under hypnosis.' 'I don't know how that occurred.' 'I never knew this.' 'I didn't understand that either.' Everything that was said in court, I confidentially told him *differently,* of which he wrote – look [in his book] *American Grotesque.* The American judicial system gone awry, you know, and 'grotesque.' So Russo asked, 'now that he is washed of his sin,' asked 'what he would say to Clay Shaw,' you know, as if I want to apologize and ask for his forgiveness. He said, 'what would Judas say to Christ?' That's a great line, except he got a little bit crazy. That line is a dramatic Broadway line. It comes out of his own imagination. It fits perfectly—if he can put words in my mouth—but *I* didn't say it."

LAW: "So you never gave him an interview anyway?"

RUSSO: "Oh, yeah, I did give him an interview. Gave him an interview with Garrison's awareness of it. But he just made up what he wanted. He made up what he wanted. He just got way off the fucking beam. Him to say that, like I was so overwrought. And now, 'what would Judas say to Christ?' That's dramatic. That's fucking cinema-graphic. That's 'Broadway-itis.' That's James Kirkwood."

LAW: "Yeah, I've read one of his books."

RUSSO: "Yeah, he's got all his apologies and all these trumpets and all these great sayings. More power to him, but it's a fictional world to him. He lost his sense of reality somewhere, and for what reason? He propositioned me for sex. I said, 'I don't get turned on by you,' (which I'm glad about now)."

LAW: "Yeah, really."

RUSSO: "And so on. But the point is, that is a melodramatic coined phrase of a melodramatic author. Not a fucking Tulane, Loyola, LSU jock who's a pervert like me. It comes from Broadway. 'What would Judas say to Christ?' Almost Shakespearean..."

LAW: "Kind of, yeah."

RUSSO: "And so he gets by with that. That becomes the mainstream press. The same type of press that Clinton gets. You know, the mainstream press. They don't find a thing wrong with him. The man's a fake. He's a sleaze-bucket. Somebody should blow his fucking brains out."

LAW: "Well, he's always coming up with something new, isn't he?"

RUSSO: "Yeah, he sure is. He's a fake. So anyway, that's sort of… hopefully you understand that. Read the Kirkwood book. It's fabulous. Read it in 'Fiction,' *American Grotesque*. You know, [it] just destroys the Garrison case. If you let his premises go, but his facts are *all wrong*. What he quotes for me is wrong. What he says I told him, I *never* told him. He told me, 'You couldn't have said Clay Shaw was this! I mean, how *would* you? You couldn't have heard him [Shaw] talking about the Kennedy Assassination. Why wouldn't you run out in the room and say, *you're plotting to murder Kennedy!*' I said, 'because *I didn't give a fuck.*'"

LAW: "Exactly."

RUSSO: "He doesn't put that in there. I told him, 'I didn't give a fuck.' I said I didn't like Kennedy. So those people [Clay Shaw, etc.] thrilled me when they talked."

LAW: "Well, the person that I've just been reading is Epstein. Have you heard of him?"

RUSSO: "Yeah, sure."

LAW: "Yeah. And he's real negative… But some of his own stuff was questionable. You know, he did his first book and things."

RUSSO: "Oh, right, yeah. What's his title?"

LAW: "He's got one; *Counter Plot*, is the one that I have."

RUSSO: "Yeah, right. Okay, all right…You know, he has his thoughts, you know. And his assumptions are that it, just so you know, not based on *anything*. At least Garrison—my testimony—could have been challenged by all kinds of witnesses, if it didn't occur. I *had* to have been right. Let me tell you something. In '67 and '68 and '69 and '70, everything I said, if I was making it up, I must have been the smartest son of a bitch ever walked on the streets of New Orleans. And everything I said about the facts of that period of '63, '62, and '61, factually *was correct*. Clay Shaw was around. Dave Ferrie was around. Lee Oswald was around. Now, remember, if Lee

Oswald had been in Texas, it couldn't have occurred. If Clay Shaw had been in Brazil, it couldn't have occurred. All he needed to do was show his hotel receipts for Brazilian hotels or Yugoslavian hotels. If Dave Ferrie had been in jail, it couldn't have occurred. But I just come out of the blue and start stating these things. And, yeah, I remember on September 13th, I was at a meeting where they discussed this."

LAW: "That's the party you were at."

RUSSO: "That's the date. And we discussed it. Anybody comes up and says that it didn't— listen, I was in Baton Rouge. I was making a speech that night at the LSU Assembly Center, Baton Rouge. I *couldn't* have been there. And Russo, well, that makes him at least that credible. But no one, no one was able to get up there and say differently. *No one.*"

LAW: "What you have to say is explosive stuff."

RUSSO: "Yes. Marina Oswald, when she did a great deal of damage, she was held incognito for about three months, two months, by the FBI after the Assassination. And she was a Russian woman. When she came out of incognito or detention, she proceeded to announce to the world that Lee had, in fact, talked about killing Kennedy and that he was, in fact, guilty—that she was sorry. And she was overwhelmed with her sympathy for Jackie and so on and so on."

LAW: "She's given so much conflict[ing testimony]."

RUSSO: "Yeah. In 1970, she announced that Lee Oswald had never, ever stayed away from her bed. So therefore, with Perry Russo saying that Lee Oswald was a roommate, and in question, you know, the term 'roommate' – that's just a quick gay way of saying that's your 'trick for the night.' Of Dave Ferrie, that Lee Oswald was, in fact, correct – that he never slept away from Marina, that their marriage was, in fact, a fairly decent marriage. It wasn't *until 1979* that she became a little more Americanized. She could say things without worry or regard that she could be kicked out of the country or put in jail. She announced before the House Select Committee on Assassinations that she, in fact, she and Oswald Lee used to fight all the time. He used to beat the fuck out of her, get drunk, beat the fuck out of her, and leave. He'd be gone for three or four days; a week at the longest. At this time, in New Orleans, he was gone over to Dave Ferrie's house – *exactly* what I said."

LAW: "That would make sense."

RUSSO: "You see? He had a fight with her, so he goes and sleeps over at this dude's house. That's not so very unusual. But of course, all the way up to when the trial's around, that makes me look bad."

LAW: "Right."

RUSSO: "I'm saying that the guy stayed over at this other guy's house. Well, the wife should know. How the fuck would this dude, Perry Russo, how would he know? Well, he didn't. And then she admitted that he used to beat the fuck out of her, and then run out on her. And he'd be gone for three or four days. And she's glad to see him go. And she said at 1970, telling her when we were in court, she said that he always was immaculately clean. Well, he wasn't when he was away from her. He was dirty and unshaven. Well and understandable, because he didn't bring his shaving stuff. He didn't bring his deodorant. He didn't give a fuck. He was mad at the world. I didn't get along with him. But I maintain that. I look like the Lone Ranger. No one could believe me. His wife said he slept every night with her. He took care of the kids. He was never dirty. He was always clean and meticulous about his appearance. I'm saying he's unshaven three days in. Now, that comes out in 1979. He used to beat the fuck out of her, leave for a week. And all of a sudden, it becomes reasonable that Lee Oswald went over to his friend's house, Dave Ferrie. Not that far from 4905 Magazine Street, where he lived, with her … in Louisiana."

LAW: "Well, that's the thing I was going to ask."

RUSSO: "Go ahead."

LAW: "That about Jack Ruby, do you think that he knew Oswald?"

RUSSO: "Yeah, I sure do. The thing about him knowing Oswald is if you will, there is a tape that you can go get, *Rush to Judgment*."

LAW: "I have that."

RUSSO: "You have the tape? You have the book?"

LAW: "Yeah, I get everything I can."

RUSSO: "There's a movie tape to that effect—and the *Rush to Judgment* thing. And in it, some of the people are interviewed that worked with Ruby. In that Carousel Club. And Garrison interviewed quite a few more. And the basic consensus of what they said was that Jack Ruby knew Oswald, knew Tippit, knew these people, and knew half the sheriff's office."

LAW: "Yes."

RUSSO: "And then the official version was by the police chief, Curry. (Is that what his name is? Curry?)"

LAW: "Yes, Curry, yeah."

RUSSO: "Curry ... [said] that there had only been twelve to fifteen incidents of police misdemeanor at the Carousel Club. And of that, on a 1,000-man police force, of that fifteen, maybe ten of them were on vice business, undercover, trying to get a broad to solicit them or something to that effect, you know? The police work. 15 out of 1,000. Well, let's say 50 out of 1,000. That's 5%. And that's three times what the police chief said. 300% more than what the police chief said. Well, who do you ask? You ask the people who work there. There's no axe to grind. They have nothing to grind, *nothing* to gain by this. They say, 'well, what do you suppose—that Jack Ruby knew any of these people?' Well, he knew about half the police force, by first name. Half is 500."

LAW: "That's a lot of people."

RUSSO: "Well, let's say this black piano player or the girl dancers were wrong by 50%. It's still 250."

LAW: "You bet."

RUSSO: "And that's still 250 versus 15 or 20 people."

LAW: "They were covering their asses with it."

RUSSO: "They were covering, yes. Now, getting back to Oswald, there are people that place Ruby and Oswald together, you see? That place them together.... Now, that's not to damn it at all, but there is something for an argument [to be made] that says that Oswald never looked at the gun when he was being shot. He looked straight at Ruby's eyes with that look on his face, *'what the fuck are you doing here?'* It was a look of recognition in his eyes. Play the tape over and over and over. He *never* looked at the gun."

LAW: "Right, right. I have."

RUSSO: "Because Ruby comes bolting through the group, and he pulls the pistol out, and shoves it about his stomach, [going] ...'bang, bang,' or whatever it is. And Oswald never looked at the gun. *'What the fuck are you doing here?'* Well, that doesn't prove anything. It's something you put into it there. And so on. So it would make sense that they did know each other."

LAW: "Well, it's like I think that it was written – that when Ferrie went to Houston. Was it Houston?"

RUSSO: "Yeah, Ferrie went to Houston. "

LAW: "He went to Galveston. Ruby made a phone call to Galveston, and they're putting that together. Ferrie went to Galveston. Ruby called Galveston that night, which would put him in contact with Ferrie."

RUSSO: "Okay, that could be a possibility there. Yeah, Ruby was in love with some of the clubs over here in New Orleans, in the French Quarter. Don't know about ownership, and maybe it may have been percentages over the ownership. But the Marcello family, they own most of the clubs around, you know, the big ones, the money-making clubs and so on. So that would then put him in very good contact or posed for contact with none other than Jack, I mean Carlos Marcello's "people," who are Dave Ferrie…"

LAW: "Right, he pops up all over the place."

RUSSO: "All over the place. Marcello, he in fact returned Marcello from Guatemala, flies him back into the country after Bobby Kennedy had deported him."

LAW: "Right, that's what I've heard."

RUSSO: "You see, that's a fact. You know, it's well-validated; authenticated. But the point is that Ruby then has a contact here, a mule – so to speak. Ferrie is a mule. And that telephone call that may have been placed … to Dave Ferrie. You know, it's time to update him, to make sure that everybody will be where they should be and so on. What I don't know, you see, you're speculating now. And of course, speculation, you know, we'll see. Well, we'll never see. This is now academic, because so much for him; it'd make him the bad guy.

LAW: "And he'd been trying very hard."

RUSSO: "And it should have gone, except Mark Lane came along and began *Rush to Judgment*. He had been hired to defend Lee Oswald, by Marguerite Oswald. And on the way to Dallas, Oswald was just shot. He no longer had the client. Marguerite Oswald said, 'well, my son worked for the government. How can they say he did it? And now, he'll be in the history books as a killer of a president.' But her son worked for the government. What does she mean by that? And so she asked Mark Lane to continue, and please go over that. He said, 'well, I will, only if I come up with an idea that he in fact didn't do it; that I can make an announcement that way.' And she said, 'Okay.' Well, he does an investigation. He comes up with exactly what it says. He [Oswald] didn't do it. It doesn't make Mark Lane correct. And I see him every once in a while here in town."

LAW: "Oh, do you really?"

RUSSO: "Yeah. And it doesn't make him correct. But what it does do is make his position of defending that man, you know, the arguments that he raises are very, very strong. You know, about the bullet, the gun, the paraffin test that's performed and so on. And why these things, you know, we've seen a couple of television productions over the years. *The Trial of Lee Harvey Oswald* – what was the jury rule? And we've seen one where they rule him guilty. And we've seen another where they don't rule at all and they leave it up to you, you know, the audience. And what the preponderance of evidence, which in a criminal case does not work. In a civil case it works, preponderance of evidence. See, that's what the preponderance of evidence makes you think – he's guilty. But the preponderance of evidence is a strictly civil law term. Do you understand?"

LAW: "Right."

RUSSO: "Okay. If you can produce enough witnesses that say that you had a green light and I had a red light and I ran through the red light, that's preponderance. We have 20 witnesses and I have five. Well, of course, Will has the green light and Perry has the red light, so Perry's at fault. But in a criminal case, it has nothing to do with that. You have the liability of an individual of, what did you say, of evidence in that instance. In the Warren Report, 99.9% of every page is of no use. A few pages then would be evidence of each volume. If you have 500 pages to a volume, let's suppose 10, 15 pages, would be worthwhile as evidence in a criminal matter – wouldn't be much of a case. You could bring in all the letters you had of Lee Oswald while he was in the Soviet Union. It has nothing to do with this particular case. You could bring in people's analysis of him in the Marine Corps. It has nothing to do with this particular case. Or his letter back to the State Department, which would grant a reentry into the United States – very strange – within a couple of weeks; a couple of months…"

LAW: "You know, you could say, I can buy that Oswald could kill the President of the United States, but when you've got all these other things. You know, Garrison's the one that, to my understanding, brought out about Ferrie and Guy Banister and things like that."

RUSSO: "He did. And you said all these things. Then you began to say, well, maybe Oswald should be taken on what he literally said."

LAW: "Well, when you listen to him, you believe him."

RUSSO: "Here's some other suspicious things that happened to the other players. I mean in Dallas. Oswald was interrogated. Of course Oswald was arrested. And then he won't talk to anybody. He said, 'I want to see the Special Agent in Charge, New Orleans FBI, and so and so.' I can't think of the guy's name. Now, let me tell you something. I *don't even know* an FBI agent's name. Do you, where *you* live? FBI?"

LAW: "No."

RUSSO: "You *don't.* Here's a guy who was arrested for shooting a sitting president of the United States in 1963. The FBI is much more secretive than it is now. We don't have television then like we do now. I don't know of *any* FBI agents. But *he* does.... He won't talk to anybody else but him."

LAW: "When he had the fight with Cubans."

RUSSO: "And that FBI agent showed up. He showed up in New Orleans for that particular fight. He also showed up in Dallas when he was arrested."

LAW: "Now, that I didn't know."

RUSSO: "Yeah. And he shows up there and he does the same thing he did in New Orleans. He listens for a half-an-hour or forty-five minutes. The most important thing in the world! And when he walks out of there, you figure he didn't say much. These notes are no good. He trashes them and burns them just like he did some of them before. *What kind of FBI work is this?*"

LAW: "Exactly."

RUSSO: "Okay. Now, here's another one. The autopsy is performed by Dr. Holmes. Is that his name?"

LAW: "Autopsy doctor? 'Humes.'"

RUSSO: "Okay, 'Humes.' And he says that he burned his notes."

LAW: "Burned his autopsy notes, yeah."

RUSSO: "Autopsy notes, yeah. Yeah. What the fuck is going on here? Now, you say, *what the fuck?* Why did you do those types of things? 'Oh, well, I just wasn't involved....' Oh, *wasn't involved??* Okay. Don't believe me. You're full of crap, man. You're full of crap. So, we know that there's something up. You're not dealing with an ordinary malcontent, Lee Oswald. You're dealing with a special person – a person who probably spied for the United States *and* the Soviet Union; a person who did basic training at Osaka, Japan. Which basic training school there [in Osaka] was not Fort Jennings; was not Paris Island, South Carolina. He did basic training in Japan. *That's a spy school.*"

LAW: "Right."

RUSSO: "That was where the U-2s took off over through Russia and then would land on the other side of the globe. So, what you're dealing with is a guy that does basic training over there. Now, I know that when I was in high school – and I'm 53 years old – we were given questionnaires. 'Would you like to work for the government? Why?' 'Would you like to do intelligence work?' 'Would you like to do analytic work?' 'Would you like to do counterfeit work?' You see, these are the FBI and so on and CIA questionnaire. No, no, no, whatever happened to them. I was asked the same questions in college. 'Would you like to join this?' 'Would you like a field in this?' These things were too (apparently) passed out, right? So, he's doing his basic [training] in Japan. So, you think he's a spy. So, we're dealing with a special person here. That's what I'm getting at; special why? I don't know. His whole background indicates something is not what it appears to be. In 1963, the CIA did what it essentially wanted to do. It didn't care. And if it wanted to take down a government, it tried to do it. If it wanted to assassinate Castro, it tried to do that. The [Salvador] Allende thing by President Nixon, very great move. That's the way you do things. That's the way the world rotates. Why do we have to play nice guy now? Allende was elected in Chile. Allende was elected in 1973 or '72. That's terrible. That's another rotten regime. That, coupled with Cuba, coupled with protests in Nicaragua, that [were] allowed. But we have cruel, fabulous regimes. So, Nixon orders the CIA to destabilize Chile. They go down there. They form a total revolution. Everybody is all excited. We're paying for the fucking insurrection. And, lo and behold, they capture the palace and they got Allende in there. And the CIA station chief walks in and tells everybody to get the fuck out. He walks in, tells everybody to get the fuck out. Those fucking liberals and left-wingers and fucking fools of the world, debate why Nixon is such a bad person. That's leadership there. Yeah, that's leadership there! And so, we are left with that situation. So, we don't have to collect more money. That Pinochet takes over. So, he screws over the people. And I don't give a fuck about that. That's not my concern. That's one of my own allies. Well, anyway. So, we'll go about, like, any other questions for right now?"

LAW: "Well, just the death of Dave Ferrie. Did you know about that immediately?"

RUSSO: "Well, I knew about it. I went to his newspaper in Baton Rouge on a Thursday, I think. And when I went down to see Garrison on a Friday or a Saturday or whatever it was, I saw that Ferrie had, in fact, told me some years or months before that, that he said, number one, he said, we were talking about law and proof in courtrooms, but he knew about a lot of subjects, well-read, well-thought-through. And he said this, and why it was dramatic, because he used one word that coupled it to his own death. He said, 'did you want to pull a perfect murder?' I said, 'well, how would that be, Dave?' He said, 'well,' he said, 'you would need to...' And he had a tendency to get a chalkboard or a big piece of paper, and he began writing down his chemical equations, which I don't know if it was accurate or truthful or not. He said, '$C^6 H^{12}...$' you know, read all these other letters, and I don't know how they work. And he said, 'if you get this,' and he said, 'now what this does,' he said, 'you either inject it or ingest it,' and he said, 'if you inject it over a period of time, it doesn't damage; and if you inject it, it'll do it rather quickly...' He said, 'the person then dies,' and he said, '... and the chemicals will break down in the system.' He said, 'what if he dies? He dies of an aneurysm in the brain.' I said, 'what is an aneurysm, Dave?' And he said, 'well, it's when you have an artery and it explodes and floods the brain. It's a weak wall in the artery. This causes the weak wall.' And I said, 'well, what if it would show up in autopsy?' And he said, 'after 72 hours, the chemicals would have broken down and it would appear to be a normal, unless they had it injected. They could find a hole for an injection.' But he said, 'if it was ingested,' he said 'it would cause an aneurysm,' and he said, 'the person would look like he's dying of natural causes.'"

LAW: "Isn't that something?"

RUSSO: "On his death certificate, he died of a stroke brought on by an aneurysm of the brain, blotting of the brain, drain of the wall, you know, the chamber..."

LAW: "But his death happened not too long before it hit the papers, right, that he was involved in this thing?"

RUSSO: "Yeah, oh yeah. And so Johnson then quickly called Dr. Chetta, who was a coroner, and asked for a second autopsy. And they went through elaborate toxicology tests that they had at the state of the art of 1963, not exactly 1993. Okay, so they did another autopsy and [it] didn't show anything. So officially he died of natural causes. The movie claims the fact that he was murdered as a possibility, and it was a possibility that someone forcibly forced him to take this, or they forced this stuff into his system. And there are types, they have a typewritten suicide note, very convenient because it wasn't signed, but it had a typewritten suicide note, which I could type it up right there on his typewriter. So anyway...

LAW: "Yeah, well, I'm going to, I'm in the midst of trying to get some of that stuff."

RUSSO: "I don't know. I have access to Johnson's files through his family, his personal files of this thing. And I'm sure I can get you – if I know in advance when you come in."

LAW: "Oh, that's great."

RUSSO: "I know the ones that are part of, you know, my background. And so if you were to plan to come with a camera, a video camera and some sound equipment and just something that we can talk."

LAW: "When is the Mardi Gras down there? Well, I don't know exactly this year, but it's always 41 days before Easter. So if you look at that year's calendar, and you see Easter also there, stack it up 41 days and you have Halloween, I mean, Mardi Gras Day itself, and then for two weeks before that, it's generally around February."

LAW: "Well, I'm planning to go down there. So I hope I do."

RUSSO: "And then we'll work something out and so on."

LAW: "Okay."

CHAPTER SIX

CONCLUSION:
THE CONSPIRACY IS CLEAR

Telling the truth can be a scary thing sometimes.
                                                    —Jim Garrison

A s our dear friend, show business legend John Barbour likes to say, "Jim Garrison solved this case!" Sifting through the records that are available to the public, it is remarkable to consider the extent of the work Garrison and his office did. The fact that Garrison remains a pariah to so many in the research community is frustrating and inexplicable.

The evidence connects Clay Shaw to a myriad of powerful figures and organizations. He was not simply a kindly philanthropist who loved President Kennedy. Much as the record shows that Jack Ruby wasn't inspired to kill Oswald because of an emotional attachment to the Kennedy family, it's clear that Shaw and every other member of the ground level conspiracy despised JFK, with one exception: Lee Harvey Oswald. There is not a single anecdotal account of the alleged assassin ever saying a negative word about the man we are supposed to believe he killed. In this regard, he must have stood out like a sore thumb in that small, manipulated band of Kennedy-haters.

John Barbour became the first person to interview Jim Garrison after the Clay Shaw trial, for three-and-a-half hours on September 5, 1981. Barbour explained, "But we talked for another 6 hours. Often he would tell me to turn off the camera and the mics because he didn't want to speculate on camera." Barbour has told the story many times of how the media managed to defame Garrison, right under his own nose. "I was fired from my own show, *Real People,* by George Schlatter, after I had tried unsuccessfully to tell the story of Jim Garrison, on one of Schlatter's shows, called *Speak Up, America.*" Barbour told us. "And George Schlatter had reedited part of the Garrison story, to deliberately libel Jim Garrison. And what it was he did, when I interviewed Mr. Garrison, I asked him how many shooters there were in Dealey Plaza. He said, 'John, there were three teams. Probably two men to a team. Two of the teams in front, one in the back. Probably the Dal-Tex Building, none at the Book Depository. The Book Depository is just where they pre-located the patsy.' He said that because it was an important killing, they probably had a third who was a radio operator.... And then I asked, 'how many people do you think actually knew he would not come out of Dallas alive?' And he said, 'Well the plan to kill him began on the day that John Kennedy refused to provide air support at the Bay of Pigs. That's the day it started." He said, "And it's all on a need-to-know basis, since this was the most important killing of a head of state... So I would say 32 people knew, including some in the media. Because they were infiltrated by the CIA and Project Mockingbird.' And, of course, that turned out to be CBS, with Walter Cronkite, Mike Wallace, and Dan Rather...."

Barbour continued, "So, anyway, I put the story together, and Marjoe Gortner, who was the host of the show, it was called *Speak Up, America,* was to ask the question.... This was a part two. Part one was an enormous hit, because it was the first time Garrison had ever been seen on national television in prime time unhindered. So it was the highest rating the show [we] ever got. And people were crowding around the studio to come in and see part two. Anyway, when we get to Marjoe Gortner, asking Mr. Garrison how many shooters were there, unbeknownst to me, George Schlatter took Donna Kanter who was my field producer, down into the editing room midnight the night before, and reedited it, to make Garrison look bad. So when Marjoe Gortner said, 'How many shooters were there?' they cut to Garrison, and Garrison says, '32.' And then the phone rings, and it's George Schlatter, laughing and giggling, because he had made a fool of Jim Garrison. Of course, I tried to talk Mr. Garrison into suing Schlatter, because I'd accidently recorded his phone call, and Mr. Garrison said, 'John, if I ever went into court, I would never see my family for all the people who are libeling me. Just send me a *Real People* t-shirt.'"

During one of their off the record discussions, Garrison told Barbour that "one of the ruling families had to give the go ahead for the hit. And the person chosen was Averell Harriman." Harriman, an ultimate DC insider whose government career started as Ambassador to the Soviet Union in 1943, was Ambassador-at-Large and then Under Secretary of State for Political Affairs during the Kennedy administration. The man whose codename was "Crocodile," a fitting name for this life-long swamp creature, consistently urged JFK to escalate things in Vietnam. Harriman had supported a coup against South Vietnam President Ngo Dinh Diem, along with others working against Kennedy's interests from within his administration. Diem was toppled and killed on November 2, 1963, an event which greatly distressed JFK.

John Barbour also recounted how Jim Garrison had talked to a police officer he didn't name, that was in on the unrecorded interrogation sessions with Lee Harvey Oswald. He claimed that Oswald was never asked about the assassination inside of Will Fritz's office. This perhaps explains Oswald's befuddlement at the midnight press conference, where he replied to the question, "Did you kill the president?" by stating that the first he'd heard about that was when the newspaper reporters in the hall questioned him. Barbour still regrets that he never learned the identity of this officer from Garrison.

John Barbour would go on to make the most important documentary ever done on the Garrison investigation, *The JFK Assassination: The Jim Garrison Tapes*, in 1992. The film featured pertinent excerpts from those hours of interviews with the former New Orleans District Attorney. He followed this up with the sensational *The American Media and the Second Assassination of John F. Kennedy*, in 2017, which remains the best documentary ever done on the mainstream media's shameful performance.

John Barbour shared a touching anecdote with us, which we feel illustrates just what kind of character Jim Garrison possessed. As he was on his deathbed, Garrison requested that his wife, who'd abandoned him when he needed her most, as he was beleaguered and attacked by the entire Establishment, be brought in to visit him. He then demanded that they be remarried, so that she could collect his lucrative pension. That incident alone says a great deal about just what kind of person Jim Garrison was.

On June 27, 2023, Don Jeffries visited with Dean Andrews III. Confined to a wheelchair, Dean waved him in through the patio door, which was unlocked. The apartment was small, what you'd expect given Dean's financial situation. But he felt fortunate to have obtained a Section 8 unit, and also to qualify for a modest food stamp supplement. There was an aide who comes and assists him every day. In spite of the rather harsh hand life had dealt him, Dean maintains his dignity and his intellect. Jeffries had to move a foldable table from Dean's bedroom into the living room, so they would have a place to eat the Chinese carryout. While not displaying overt bitterness, Dean was a bit preoccupied with what might have been. He noted that, if not for Garrison's investigation, "I'd probably be loaded." There is every reason to think that, if his father's legal career hadn't been sidetracked by the events of November 22, 1963, he might have left young Dean a nice inheritance. Just as importantly, without his family and personal life being disrupted by the national attention Garrison received, it's very probable that he would have finished law school and become a lawyer himself. Dean started to nod off after they finished eating. "I can only get like two hours of sleep at night," he explained. "It's not you." He shared pictures of his father, including some from the New Orleans Jazz Festival he ran. It was obvious that, even though Dean III had every reason to resent his father, he instead reveres his memory "If they hadn't tried to assassinate my father in the hospital, I think he might have helped Garrison." Dean said. Leaving Dean, Jeffries was struck by how the Assassination had touched a life so tenuously connected to it, inflicting emotional and financial damage upon a man whose father had happened to take a phone call from the wrong person.

We have demonstrated in this book that Clay Shaw was no unfairly targeted innocent citizen. On the contrary, he had ties to powerful individuals and organizations going back to WWII. The connections between Lee Harvey Oswald and Clay Shaw, David Ferrie, Guy Banister, Jack Martin, Kerry Thornley, Sergio Arcacha Smith, Carlos Bringuier, Jack Ruby and others at the "ground level" of the plot are undeniable. All of these individuals seem to have had some kind of ties to intelligence agencies, and were probably undercover assets themselves. So they may have all been played off each other, separately and individually told to report back on the brewing conspiracy to kill Kennedy. Oswald being chosen as the patsy should surprise no one, since he'd seemingly been impersonated since 1961, and questions had been raised about him being impersonated, by the likes of J. Edgar Hoover, since then as well.

Our efforts in this book have been to scrutinize these ground level conspirators, who while not being the primary movers behind the assassination, might have been able to identify at least some of the more powerful forces in the Pentagon and the intelligence agencies, which directed them like pawns on a chessboard. The foundation of Jim Garrison's case against Clay Shaw, the last surviving member of this ground level conspiracy whom he was able to prosecute, was the Clay Bertrand alias. As Dean Andrews III told us in no uncertain terms, Clay Shaw *was* Clay Bertrand. Too many people have died prematurely in an effort to suppress the truth. We hope to have revealed the unvarnished truth in this book.

AFTERWORD

By Jack Roth

When I decided to write my book, *Killing Kennedy: Exposing the Plot, the Cover-up and the Consequences*, my goal was to document a broad range of interviews that provided compelling new insight into the assassination of John F. Kennedy. I wanted to get readers thinking critically, asking more questions and doing their own research. I was incredibly fortunate to interview both Donald Jeffries and William Madsen Law, the authors of *this* book, who provided fascinating insight based on their individual research. I felt a kinship to these men, who have dedicated years of their lives to uncovering the truth about the JFK assassination and other dastardly deeds perpetrated by our leaders.

When they asked me to write the Afterword for this book, I was honored, and I wanted to do their research justice bynot only summarizing their key points but also by enhancing the spotlight on New Orleans by sharing what I gleaned from writing my book.I hope this chapter succeeds in doing that.

Four years ago, as I began to interview researchers, academic scholars,eyewitnesses and family members of those who were part of the tangled web of U.S. Intelligence operations associated with the Cold War and the assassination of JFK, I quickly realized two things: 1) Lee Harvey Oswald was much more than either the lone-nut assassin or patsy most of us have come to know him as,and he was most definitely a U.S. Intelligence asset, and 2) Understanding what happened in the city of New Orleans during the summer of 1963 is the key to understanding many critical aspects of the JFK assassination.

One researcher I interviewed called New Orleans the"Casablanca of the Cold War"and the hub of U.S. Intelligence because of the Port of New Orleans and the city's proximity to and trade withCuba, Central America and South America. I liken New Orleans during the Cold War to a boiling pot of U.S. Intelligence gumbo, the main ingredients being the CIA,

FBI, Secret Service, NSA and Naval Intelligence, seasoned liberally with the likes of spies, assassins, mobsters, double agents, military operatives, soldiers of fortune, Cuban exiles, crooked politicians, con men, shadowy multinational organizations and businesses (read: United Fruit Company), secret societies and their global elitists,and finished with a pinch of nefariouscharacters and ne'er-do-wells looking to make a name for themselves.

Also, and this is critical, New Orleans is a "small town big city." Once you realize much of what occurred in the summer of '63 as it relates to the Kennedy assassination occurred within a very small radius (Lafayette Square, the Central Business District and the French Quarter), you begin to see a clearer picture develop. For example, the Reily Coffee Company (where Oswald "worked" that summer) and its adjacent "U.S. Intelligence garage" were two blocks away from Guy Banister's office (544 Camp Street AND 531 Lafayette Street), which is directly across the street from Lafayette Square, in which you can get a panoramic view of several federal buildings that in 1963 housed the main ingredients of the gumbo I mentioned above.

Picture this: An FBI agent (perhaps Warren de Brueys) with an office on the third floor of the building across from Reily Coffee Company watches from his window as Oswald "goes to work" in the morning and meets his CIA handler (perhaps David Smith) in the adjacent garage during lunchtime. This same agent then reports this activity to his boss, J. Edgar Hoover, by the time Oswald gets back from lunch. That same day, a U.S. Naval Intelligence operative walks out the door of his building and into Lafayette Square, eats the bagged lunch his wife made for him while watching Cuban exiles (perhaps Carlos Quiroga) enter Guy Banister's office from one entrance and Lee Harvey Oswald exit from the other entrance (different address, same building) with Fair Play for Cuba Committee flyers, with which Oswald then walks just a few blocks to hand out on Canal Street at the edge of the French Quarter. And on his leisurely stroll to complete his assignment, Oswald walks by the offices of the United Fruit Company and the New Orleans International Trade Mart, where Clay Shaw has spent a few morning hours before meeting a Permindex associate at Antoine's restaurant for lunch in the French Quarter. There, they run into Carlos Marcello and a few of his associates and/or Dean Andrews and fellow attorney Clem Sehrt (childhood friend of Marguerite Oswald), who are enjoying some Café Brûlet and Baked Alaska.

Once you realize Oswald and the other main players "applying their craft" that summer did so within this tiny radius, you realize it's akin to placing a number of indoctrinated and well-trained soldiers and a pack of rabid, hungry wolves into an 8' x 10' enclosed ring and "seeing what happens." It's not going to end well for most of them.

In this book, Jeffries and Law mention the many actors in the Shakespearean tragedy that played out in the summer of '63 who met violent deaths, died under mysterious circumstances or simply disappeared never to be seen again. This is no coincidence, because when you play in the wolves' den, you often die in the wolves' den. These men knew what they signed up for. When you're a marine, or a spy, or a soldier of fortune, you know your job is dangerous, and you understand the risks involved. Oswald knew the dangers, as did David Ferrie and other foot soldiers, but perhaps the more powerful, insulated high-society types like Clay Shaw believed they were above the fray and immune from harm. This was merely wishful thinking, because unless you were at the very top of the pyramid, you were expendable.

The people I have empathy for are those who happened to be in the wrong place at the wrong time and saw or heard something they weren't supposed to see or hear. Due to its small size and tight-knit social constructs, New Orleans was, and still is, a city where everyone either knows or knows of each other, so it's not surprising that residents who ran in particular circles knew Clay Shaw and Clay Bertrand were one and the same person. It's also not surprising that many residents saw Lee Harvey Oswald with David Ferrie, Clay Shaw, Carlos Marcello and/or Guy Banister at some point either in the French Quarter or Central Business District.

Some of these individuals, including Dean Andrews, were subpoenaed to testify as part of Jim Garrison's investigation, which put them in a rather precarious situation. Tell the truth, and the bad guys kill you. Lie, and the good guys charge you with perjury. Andrews tried to cleverly toe the line on this matter, but he ultimately couldn't and was eventually charged with perjury. He probably would've been killed by the bad guys at some point as well if it wasn't for his friendship with Carlos Marcello.

Other innocents included those who, as a result of their profession or unique talents, were engaged in one of the intelligence community's sanctioned and funded black projects. Such was the case with Dr. Mary Sherman, who I will talk more about later in this chapter.

I call these people "innocents," but very few if any were boy or girl scouts. It was hard to be squeaky clean in New Orleans, especially in 1963.

New Orleans has always been a tough and dangerous city filled with unsavory, fringe and edgy individuals. Ironically, this is what gives the city its rich and unique character. Dean Andrews was a perfect example of one such individual. By all accounts, he was larger than life, a good father, and a smart, capable lawyer, but he also played loose with the law and associated on the fringes of society. If you knew Clay Shaw and Claw Bertrand were the same person, you most likely ran in secretive and/or unsavory circles. If Jim Garrison subpoenaed you, you probably ran in clandestine and/or unsavory circles. There were a few exceptions, but not many.

I agree with the authors of this book that many in the JFK research community have judged Jim Garrison way too harshly, and the mainstream has also done a yeoman's job discrediting him, labeling him any combination of publicity whore, egomaniac, self-serving careerist, closet homosexual, degenerate pedophile and more. This character assassination may be based in some truth, but it remains largely irrelevant to the case he put together against Clay Shaw. The truth is, Jim Garrison did more than just about anyone else to shine a bright light on some of the JFK assassination conspirators, and it can be argued that when you take the full extent of Garrison's work into account, John Barbour is correct in saying, "Jim Garrison solved this case!"

However, I also believe that by pursuing his investigation with extreme vigor, Garrison got a few individuals killed … a prime example of this being David Ferrie. Some may have been assassination conspirators, but others weren't. This didn't matter. Garrison reopened a still-fresh wound four years after the assassination, exposing some of the ground-level conspirators, which could've led to exposing the high-level conspirators living in the penthouse. This, of course, was deemed unacceptable by very powerful men, who eliminated some of these ground-level individuals with extreme prejudice.

This book provides considerable insight into Dean Andrews, an important player in the events of the summer of '63. Like most of us, he had both admirable qualities and serious flaws, but as is always the case when researching the Kennedy assassination, it's important to see these people as human beings… complete with hopes, dreams, insecurities and all the other trimmings that come with being human. Andrews wasn't simply a colorful New Orleans attorney who was portrayed admirably by John Candy in the movie *JFK*; he was a real person, a husband and father who cared for his children and was philanthropic in the community he loved so much. And one day he took a phone call from the wrong person, and his life was irrevocably changed and ultimately destroyed.

In *Killing Kennedy*, I talk about the emotional damage associated with being a child of a CIA operative and how CIA families, while the picture of Blue Blood perfection on the outside, were absolutely broken on the inside. In this book, we see the emotional damage inflicted on Dean Andrews III and his mother. Horace, the Roman poet, wrote, "For the sins of your fathers you, though guiltless, must suffer." This appears to be true, although in the case of Dean Andrews, "sins" may be a bit harsh. He wasn't perfect, but his life (and his family's)was seriously damaged because of the things he did and the people he associated with.

Part 2 of my book – titled "New Orleans: The Summer of '63" – includes eye-opening interviews with Ed Haslam Jr., Judyth Vary Baker and Victoria Sulzer. I also included an interview with New Orleans tour guide Jeffrey Holmes in the section titled "Keeping the Story Alive". The information gleaned from these interviews ties directly into the characters and events the authors talk about in this book, and, as such, I want to present some of that information to further highlight the tangled web being weaved in New Orleans that summer.

Ed Haslam Jr.'s father taught at Tulane Medical School in New Orleans, and, as a child, he got to know one of his father's colleagues, Dr. Mary Sherman, who was later found murdered in her apartment in 1964. In 1990, Haslam began to investigate her death and her relationship with David Ferrie. In 2007, he published *Dr. Mary's Monkey*, in which he examines the connections between Sherman, Ferrie, Dr. Alton Ochsner, Lee Harvey Oswald, covert cancer/bioweapon research, and the assassination of John F. Kennedy.

I asked him what he concluded as a result of his research.

"I researched a murder and discovered an epidemic," he said.

It all goes back to the Jonas Salk polio vaccine, which was approved in 1955 and contained SV40, a live, infectious, cancer-causing monkey virus. At the time, there was serious pushback from doctors who feared that continued inoculation of the polio vaccine into humans would result in a human cancer epidemic. Nevertheless, between 1955 and 1963, some 98 million Americans were exposed. When I asked Haslam if we now have a cancer epidemic, he asserted confidently that we have an enormous cancer epidemic, particularly in elevated rise in soft-tissue cancers – breast, prostate, melanoma and lymphoma – in the last 50 years.

The U.S. Government knew about the virus in 1955, so in 1963 it set up a top-secret medical project with a linear particle accelerator (located in the U.S. Public Health Service Hospital in New Orleans) to mutate monkey viruses and develop a vaccine that would stop SV40 from causing a cancer epidemic, but they also commissioned covert projects through the CIA with the purpose of weaponizing cancer to eliminate political enemies such as Fidel Castro, which was what Dr. Alton Ochsner, Dr. Mary Sherman, Judyth Vary Baker, David Ferrie and Lee Harvey Oswald were working on in various capacities during the summer of 1963.

Based on his research, Haslam asserted, "I believe Mary was working on both projects.... She was electrocuted at the laboratory, and I believe it was sabotage.... Whether sabotage or not, the linear particular accelerator project could not be exposed, so that's when it was decided to bring her body back to her apartment and make it look like an intruder killed her there."

To summarize for readers, I asked Haslam, "So, during the summer of 1963, you have a covert, CIA-sponsored biological weapon project, a covert linear particle accelerator project, and the Kennedy assassination chicanery with David Ferrie, Clay Shaw, Guy Banister and Lee Harvey Oswald (and many more) ALL happening in New Orleans. Is it fair to say the Crescent City was a busy place?"

"Absolutely," he said.

Judyth Vary Baker confirmed much of what Haslam's research revealed, and she also provided a great deal of insight into Lee Harvey Oswald. In high school, Baker, a brilliant woman, received national attention for her cancer research. In 1963, she was offered a summer medical internship in New Orleans through Dr. Alton Ochsner and Tulane Medical School. There she met Oswald, Ferrie, Ruby and others. She and Oswald became lovers, and she worked with him and others to develop an aggressive strain of cancer as part of a CIA plan to assassinate Fidel Castro.

She also got to know David Ferrie quite well and described him as "a nervous and very conflicted man." She shared a story about when she and Lee "got together with some very suspicious people, including Jack Ruby and others who were going to visit Clay Shaw." She confirmed that all of these men knew each other and ran in the same circles.

By the fall of 1963, Oswald had been sent to Dallas by his CIA handlers, and Baker had been dismissed by Dr. Ochsner when she voiced her displeasure about testing the biological weapon on which they had been working on prisoners from a Louisiana state penitentiary. She was in Gainesville, Florida when she spoke to Lee for the last time, just weeks before the assassination. That last phone call was an hour and a half long, and it was very emotional because Lee had ascertained that instead of being part of an effort to protect Kennedy from Cuban exiles, he was actually being set up as the patsy in a much larger and more insidious assassination plot being called the "Big Event."

"Lee told me he didn't think he was going to make it out of the situation alive, and I begged him to leave Dallas and fly to Mexico," she remembered. "I told him I'd meet him there, but he was convinced there was no way out at that point because they would kill his entire family, including his children, if he aborted. Besides, he told me if he stayed in Dallas, there would be one less gun pointed at President Kennedy. He still believed he could help stop the Big Event from happening, but in retrospect, this was wishful thinking on his part."

Victoria Sulzer is a long-time New Orleans resident who was a student at P.G.T. Beauregard Jr. High School at the same time as Oswald. In 1963, she and her family lived at the Patio Apartments, the same apartment complex where Dr. Mary Sherman lived and was found murdered in 1964. "I would see Mary coming and going, and we would often say hello to each other.... She was always polite and asked me about my daughter and pregnancy now and again. I knew she was a doctor.... She appeared to be nice and kind, and she definitely had an aura about her that was professional."

Sulzer also lived next door to a man named Juan Valdez, "a rather mysterious man" who would sometimes visit Dr. Sherman and who, Sulzer later learned, worked at the New Orleans International Trade Mart. Sulzer would often hear conversations in Spanish coming from his apartment, and from time to time she could hear his toilet flushing repeatedly. This seemed odd to her, as it occurred from about 10 p.m. to the early morning hours. Juan Valdez disappeared after Dr. Sherman's murder.

Sulzer also reconnected with Oswald at the Patio Apartments, when, one day, she heard a knock at her patio door, and there stood Oswald holding a small box in his hand and asking her if this was Juan Valdez's apartment. Sulzer recognized him immediately and said they went to Beauregard Jr. High School together. They had a polite exchange, and then he walked next door to meet with Valdez, who wasn't there.

"He came back and asked if I could keep the box in my refrigerator until Juan returned," Sulzer recalled. "He asked me to do this at least a few times over the course of several weeks, and at the time I didn't think anything of it."

Sulzer and her family moved out of the Patio Apartments about a month before Dr. Sherman's death. She remembers that a few days after her body was found in her apartment, she received a phone call from someone she is convinced was Juan Valdez, who told her, "Have you heard about Mary Sherman? She was murdered. I just want you to be careful about what you say and who you say it to." He then hung up.

"Juan was always a very kind person to me and my family. ... so I think he was trying to protect me," she shared. "There were a lot of rumors going around at the time about many people who knew Dr. Sherman either disappearing or dying mysteriously. It wasn't a good situation at all, and you could tell there was some kind of cover-up going on."

Jeffrey Holmes is co-owner of a tour company in New Orleans who does the highly educational and enlightening *Oswald's New Orleans Tour*, which follows in the footsteps of Oswald during the summer of 1963. His tour reveals a few fascinating things, including how small New Orleans is and how everyone knows everyone else's business. I had the pleasure of experiencing the tour, and it changed my entire tactical understanding of how things may have played out that summer.

"I try to make people understand how close everything is and how there are no coincidences in this story," Holmes shared. "The tour starts at 544 Camp Street in Lafayette Square, where in the movie *JFK* Jim Garrison tells his guys it's the center of U.S. Intelligence for the entire southern United States. It's literally one square city block. When you're standing there, you can clearly see the federal building that houses the CIA, FBI, Secret Service, U.S. Marshals Service, and even the Office of Naval Intelligence. Reily Coffee Company, where Lee worked that summer, was literally around the corner on the other side of the courthouse from the square."

When giving the tour, he concludes: "...there's no way anybody could've walked these streets, been engaged in this kind of activity, and been involved with people of this caliber in *this* city and have it *not* been something more than what it seemed."

When I asked what he wanted to accomplish with the tour, he replied, "All these people, all these families are still here. But it's never been talked about; it's always been hush-hush. ... It's fascinating. Especially the death of Dr. Mary Sherman. ... Where do you even start with that? And nobody knows about this. It isn't common knowledge. I've just been trying to help piece the big picture together."

So, what do we know about New Orleans in the summer of 1963? It is safe to say it represented a major hub of U.S. spy craft and various clandestine operations during the height of the Cold War. As such, it was an extremely dangerous place where the stakes were incredibly high. This cannot be overstated. The men who plied their trades that summer lived on the edge... not knowing from one minute to the next if they were going to survive the cruel game of espionage, counterespionage and subterfuge.

Dean Andrews, Lee Harvey Oswald, Clay Shaw, David Ferrie, Guy Banister, Jack Martin, Kerry Thornley, Perry Russo, Sergio Arcacha Smith, Carlos Bringuier, Jack Ruby and others most certainly were all ground- to mid-level players with ties to the intelligence community, the Cuban exile community and/or the mob. They also were most certainly manipulated on some level by their masters – men like Averell Harriman, Allen Dulles, Gen. Edward Lansdaleand other elitists willing to do anything to maintain their power and control. Andnobody was more manipulated than Lee Harvey Oswald, a soldier and patriot who became the ultimate patsy and a pariah for the history books. These men were all in the right (or wrong) place at the right (or wrong) timemere months before the most heinous crime in American history was perpetrated.

That summer in New Orleans was a conglomeration of pieces and ingredients, of events and individuals, that triggered a nuclear reaction, an act so violent and so unimaginable that it changed the course of American history – and certainly not for the better.

Such is the story of New Orleans in the summer of '63. This book clarifies much of that story ... and hopefully compels readers to think more critically and conduct further research to get to the entire truth regarding the JFK assassination. Why? Because it still matters ... the truth still matters ... justice still matters. And we cannot move forward as a free and democratic society until the truth is revealed and justice is served.

APPENDIX A

WARREN COMMISSION TESTIMONY OF DEAN ANDREWS, JR.

We feel that this remarkable testimony, which in our view stands above all the others in the 26 volumes of mostly meaningless material, deserves to be read in full. We are including it here for interested readers. As Harold Weisberg wrote, "As a lawyer Andrews was true to the ethics and responsibilities of his profession, taking unpopular cases, including those of political and sexual deviates. This is what makes him part of the story of the assassination and of Oswald in New Orleans. It is doubtful if there was ever a lawyer in any kind of official proceeding who employed fewer legal phrases or more slang. At times he had to translate himself, so Liebeler could understand him. On the stand or in court, he speaks as he does in private life, in the language of his less conventional clients. His speech is exotic, pungent and direct, having its own kind of rare expressiveness. Although flamboyant as Bourbon Street, his testimony was pointed, consistent, hard and unretracted despite the unhidden government dissatisfaction with it, apparent in Liebeler's questioning as it was in the suppressed and unsuccessful FBI effort to get associates to retract."

TESTIMONY OF DEAN ADAMS ANDREW& JR. (WARREN COMMISSION HEARINGS & EXHIBITS, VOL. XI, PP. 325-339)

The testimony of Dean Adams Andrews, Jr., was taken on July 21, 1964, at the Old Civil Courts Building, Royal and Conti Streets, New Orleans, La., by Mr. Wesley J. Liebeler, assistant counsel of the President's Commission. Dean Andrews, having been first duly sworn, was examined and testified as follows:

Mr. LIEBELER: Mr. Andrews, as you know by now, I am an attorney on the staff of the President's Commission. I have been authorized to take your deposition pursuant to authority granted to the Commission by Executive Order No. 11130, dated November 29, 1963, and joint resolution of Congress, No. 137. I understand that the Secret Service served a subpoena on you last week to be here today, so you have had the requisite notice for the proceeding. As you are a member of the bar-as you know, of course, you are entitled to counsel, but you can probably forego that if you want to. You also know that you have all the usual privileges not to answer questions on the grounds of incrimination and whatever other privileges you might have and want to exercise. Would you state your full name for the record, please.

Mr. ANDREWS: Dean, and the middle initial is A, A for Adams, Andrews, Jr.

Mr. LIEBELER: I am correct, am I not, that you are a member of the Bar of Louisiana?

Mr. ANDREWS: I am a member of the bar of the State of Louisiana.

Mr. LIEBELER:. And you regularly practice law in the city of New Orleans?

Mr. ANDREWS: That's my office; yes.

Mr. LIEBELER: Where do you live?

Mr. ANDREWS: 207 Metairie Lawn Drive. That's in Metairie, La.

Mr. LIEBELER: Metairie Lawn Drive in Metairie?

Mr. ANDREWS: Yes.

Mr. LIEBELER: Where do you maintain your offices?

Mr. ANDREWS: 627 Maison Blanche Building, New Orleans. *608 North St. Paul, one block from Ervay and YMCA. 325

Mr. LIEBELER:. I am advised by the FBI that you told them that Lee Harvey Oswald came into your office some time during the summer of 1963. Would you tell US in your own words just what happened as far as that is concerned?

Mr. ANDREWS: I don't recall the dates, but briefly, it is this: Oswald came in the office accompanied by some gay kids. They were Mexicanos. He wanted to find out what could be done in connection with a discharge, a yellow paper discharge, so I explained to him he would have to advance the funds to transcribe whatever records they had up in the Adjutant General's office. When he brought the money, I would do the work, and we saw him three or four times subsequent to that, not in the company of the gay kids. He had this Mexican with him. I assume he is a Mex because the Latins do not wear a hutch haircut.

Mr. LIEBELER: The first time he came in he was with these Mexicans, and there were also some gay kids. By that, of course, you mean people that appeared to you to be homosexuals?

Mr. ANDREWS: Well, they swish. What they are, I don't know. We call them gay kids.

Mr. LIEBELER: Had you ever seen any of those kids before?

Mr. ANDREWS: None of them.

Mr. LIEBELER: Have you seen any of them since?

Mr. ANDREWS: Since the first time they came in?

Mr. LIEBELER: Since the first time they came in?

Mr. ANDREWS: Yes.

Mr. LIEBELER: You have?

Mr. ANDREWS: Yes.

Mr. LIEBELER: Did they ever come back with Oswald?

Mr. ANDREWS: No; Mexicanos came back.

Mr. LIEBELER: Where did you see these gay kids after the first time?

Mr. ANDREWS: First district precinct. Police picked them up for wearing clothes of the opposite sex.

Mr. LIEBELER: How many of them were there?

Mr. ANDREWS: About 50.

Mr. LIEBELER: They weren't all with Oswald, were they?

Mr. ANDREWS: No; Oswald-you see, they made what they call a scoop and put them all in the pokey. I went down for the ones I represented. They were in the holding pavilion. I paroled them and got them out.

Mr. LIEBELER: You do represent from time to time some of these gay kids, is that correct?

Mr. ANDREWS: Yes.

Mr. LIEBELER: You say that some of the gay kids that you saw at the time the police arrested this large group of them for wearing clothes of the opposite sex were the ones that had been with Oswald?

Mr. ANDREWS: Yes.

Mr. LIEBELER: Were you able to identify them by name?

Mr. ANDREWS: No; you see, they just-we don't even open up files on them. We don't open a file. We mark what we call a working file. We make a few notes and put it in the general week's work. If you come back and the office is retained, we make a permanent file and-but these kids come and go like-you know.

Mr. LIEBELER: When were these people picked up by the police as you have told us?

Mr. ANDREWS: Let me think. Some time in May. I went and checked the records. I couldn't find nothing on it. I believe it's May of 1963.

Mr. LIEBELER: They were picked up in May of 1963?

Mr. ANDREWS: On Friday.

Mr. LIEBELER: That was after Oswald had been in your office?

Mr. ANDREWS: After Oswald's initial contact. I think he had come back with this Mexican0 one more time.

Mr. LIEBELER: Before these people were arrested?

Mr. ANDREWS: Yes; then the second time he came back, we talked about the yellow paper discharge, about his status as a citizen, and about his wife's status.

Mr. LIEBELER: Now before we get into that, let me try and pin down how long 326 it was after the first time Oswald came in that these kids all got arrested. All 50 of them for wearing these clothes?

Mr. ANDREWS: I don't know it was 30. That I can't remember.

Mr. LIEBELER: Was it a month? Two months? A week?

Mr. ANDREWS: No ; it wasn't that. Ten days at the most.

Mr. LIEBELER: I suppose the. New Orleans Police Department files would reflect the dates these people were picked up?

Mr. ANDREWS: I checked the first district's blotter and the people are there, but I just can't get their names. You see, they wear names just like you and I wear clothes. Today their name is Candy ; tomorrow it is Butsie ; next day it is Mary. You never know what they are. Names are a very improbable method of identification. More sight. Like you see a dog. He is black and white. That's your dog. You know them by sight mostly.

Mr. LIEBELER: Do you remember what date it was that that large arrest was made?

Mr. ANDREWS: No; every Friday is arrest day in New Orleans. They clean them all up. The shotgun squad keeps the riots, the mugging, and all the humbug out. They have been doing that very effectively. .You can pick just any Friday.

Mr. LIEBELER: This was on a Friday?

Mr. ANDREWS: It had to be a Friday or Saturday.

Mr. LIEBELER: In May of 1963?

Mr. ANDREWS: Yes.

Mr. LIEBELER: After you saw these kids at this big pickup on Friday or Saturday, did you ever see any of them again after that?

Mr. ANDREWS: No ; still looking for them. They owe me a fee.

Mr. LIEBELER: They are always the hardest ones to find.

Mr. ANDREWS: They usually pay. They are screwed in.

Mr. LIEBELER: What did Oswald say to you about his own citizenship status? You say that he mentioned that the second time he came back. What did he talk to you about in that regard?

Mr. ANDREWS: They came in usually after hours, about 5, 5:15, and as I recall, he had alleged that he had abandoned his citizenship. He didn't say how; he didn't say where. I assumed that he was one of the people who wanted to join The Free World and-1 represented one or two of them. They had belonged to The World Citizenship1 explained to him there are certain steps he had to do, such as taking an oath of loyalty to a foreign power, voting in a foreign country election, or snme method that is recognized defectively as loss of citizenship. Then I told him, "Your presence in the United States is proof you are a citizen. Otherwise, you would be an alien with an alien registration with a green card, form 990."

Mr. LIEBELER: Had he told you he had been out of the country?

Mr. ANDREWS: Yes.

Mr. LIEBELER: Did he tell you where he had gone?

Mr. ANDREWS: No.

Mr. LIEBELER: Since he had been out of the country, the fact that he was back and didn't have an alien card was proof he was a citizen?

Mr. ANDREWS: Yes.

Mr. LIEBELER: Do you remember any other part of the conversation?

Mr. ANDREWS: When he asked the questions-I don't know which visit it was-about citizenship of his wife, I asked the birthplace or origin cited for citizenship purposes-that's what counts-and he said Russia, so I just assumed he had met someone somewhere, some place, either in Russia or in Europe, married them, and brought them over here as a GI, a GI bride, and wanted to g0 through the routine of naturalization, which is 3 years after lawful admission into the United States if you are married, and five years if you are not, maintain the status here in the States cumulatively for 5 years.

Mr. LIEBELER: Did he indicate that he wanted to institute citizenship proceedings for his wife?

Mr. ANDREWS: Yes; I told him to go to Immigration and get the forms. Cost him $10. All he had to do was execute them. He didn't need a lawyer. That was the end of that. 327 731-2.27 0-64-vol. XI-22

Mr. LIEBELER: How many times did he come into your office?

Mr. ANDREWS: Minimum of three, maximum of five, counting initial visit.

Mr. LIEBELER: And did you talk about different subjects at different times? As I understand it. the first time he came there, he was primarily concerned about his discharge, is that correct?

Mr. ANDREWS: Well, I may have the subject matter of the visits reversed because with the company he kept and the conversation-he could talk fairly well-1 figured that this was another one of what we call in my office free alley clients, so we didn't maintain the normalcy with the file that-- might have scratched a few notes on a piece of pad, and 2 days later threw the whole thing away. Didn't pay too much attention to him. Only time I really paid attention to this boy, he-was in the front of the Maison Blanche Building giving out these kooky Castro things.

Mr. LIEBELER: When was this, approximately?

Mr. ANDREWS: I don't remember. I was coming from the KBC building, and I walked past him. You know how you see somebody, recognize him. So I turned around, came back, and asked him what he was doing giving that junk out. He said it was a job. I reminded him of the $25 he owed the office. He said he would come over there, but he never did.

Mr. LIEBELER:. Did he tell you that he was getting paid to hand out this literature?

Mr. ANDREWS: Yes.

Mr. LIEBELER: Did he tell you how much?

Mr. ANDREWS: No.

Mr. LIEBELER: Do you remember telling the FBI that he told you that he was being paid $25 a day for handing out these leaflets?

Mr. ANDREWS: I could have told them that. I know I reminded him of the $25. I may have it confused, the $25. What I do recall, he said it was a job. I guess I asked him how much he was making. They were little square chits a little bit smaller than the picture you have of him over there [indicating].

Mr. LIEBELER:. He was handing out these leaflets?

Mr. ANDREWS: They were black-and-white pamphlets extolling the virtues of Castro, which around here doesn't do too good. They have a lot of guys, Mexicanos and Cubanos, that will tear your head off if they see you fooling with these things.

Mr. LIEBELER: What were they like?

Mr. ANDREWS: They were pamphlets, single-sheet pamphlets.

Mr. LIEBELER:. Just one sheet? It wasn't a booklet?

Mr. ANDREWS: No.

Mr. LIEBELER:. What color were the pamphlets ? You say it was white paper?

Mr. ANDREWS: White paper offset with black.

Mr. LIEBELER: Could it have been yellow paper?

Mr. ANDREWS: I am totally colorblind. I wouldn't know. But I think it is black and white.

Mr. LIEBELER: You are colorblind?

Mr. ANDREWS: Yes. Most of them wanted it around there. You give it to them, the people look at it and they drop it, right now.

Mr. LIEBELER: Do you remember what day of the week this was that you saw him handing this stuff out?

Mr. ANDREWS: It was in the middle of the week, around Tuesday or Wednesday.

Mr. LIEBELER: What is the Maison Blanche Building? What street is it on?

Mr. ANDREWS: !321 Canal Street. It is on this side. It is bounded by Dauphine and Burgundy.

Mr. LIEBELER: How far is it from the International Trade Mart?

Mr. ANDREWS: It depends on what route you take. If you come up Camp Street, it would be two blocks to Canal and four blocks toward the cemetery; so it would be about six blocks. It would be six blocks no matter which way you went, but you would walk four blocks on Common Street or Gravier, and then two blocks over the other way.

Mr. LIEBELER: [handing picture to witness]. I show you a picture that has been marked as "Garner Exhibit No. 1," and ask you if you recognize the individual in that picture and the street scene, if you are familiar with it.

Mr. ANDREWS: This is Oswald.

Mr. LIEBELER:. That's the fellow who was in your office?

Mr. ANDREWS: Yes.

Mr. LIEBELER: Do you have any doubt about that in your mind?

Mr. ANDREWS: I don't believe; no. This is him. I just can't place it. This isn't where I saw him. This is probably around the vicinity of the International Trade Mart.

Mr. LIEBELER [handing picture to witness]: I show you another picture that has been marked for identification as "Bringuier Exhibit So. 1," and ask you if you recognize anybody in that picture and the street scene.

Mr. ANDREWS: Oswald is marked with an X, and a client of mine is over here on the right-hand side.

Mr. LIEBELER: Is that a paying client or what?

Mr. ANDREWS: No; paying client [indicating]. And this dress belongs to a girl friend.

Mr. LIEBELER: Which one is your client?

Mr. ANDREWS: It should be three. There's two sisters and this young lady [indicating].

Mr. LIEBELER: What's her name?

Mr. ANDREWS: I don't remember.

Mr. LIEBELER: You are referring to the woman that appears on the far right hand side of the picture with a handbag on her arm?

Mr. ANDREWS: Yes.

Mr. LIEBELER:. Now you say Oswald is marked with an X, and you identify that as the man that you saw in your office and the same man you saw passing out pamphlets?

Mr. ANDREWS: Yes.

Mr. LIEBELER:. I call your attention specifically to the second man who is standing behind Oswald to his right and facing toward the front wearing a white, short-sleeved shirt 'and necktie, who also appears to have some leaflets in his hand. Have you ever seen that man before?

Mr. ANDREWS: The Mexican that I associate Oswald with is approximately the same height, with the exception that he has a pronounced short hutch haircut. He is stocky, well built.

Mr. LIEBELER: The fellow that I have indicated to you on "Bringuier Exhibit No. 1" is too slightly built to be associated with Oswald; is that correct?

Mr. ANDREWS: He is stocky. Has what they call an athletic build.

Mr. LIEBELER:. Was this other fellow taller than Oswald or shorter than Oswald?

Mr. ANDREWS: Very close. Not taller. Probably same height; maybe a little smaller.

Mr. LIEBELER:. How much would you say the Mexican weighed, approximately?

Mr. ANDREWS: About 160, 165.

Mr. LIEBELER: You say he was of medium build or heavy build?

Mr. ANDREWS:. Well, stocky. He could go to "Fist City" pretty good if he had to.

Mr. LIEBELER:. How old would you say he was?

Mr. ANDREWS: About 26. Hard to tell.

Mr. LIEBELER:. Do you remember what he was wearing when he came into the office with Oswald on these different occasions?

Mr. ANDREWS: Normally, different colored silk pongee shirts, which are pretty rare, you know, for the heat, or what appeared to be pongee material.

Mr. LIEBELER:. Did you ever talk to this other fellow?

Mr. ANDREWS: Well, he talked Spanish, and all I told him was poco poco. That was it.

Mr. LIEBELER:. Do you speak Spanish?

Mr. ANDREWS: I can understand a little. I can if you speak it. I can read it. That's about all.

Mr. LIEBELER [handing picture to witness]: I show you a picture which has been marked "Frank Pizzo Exhibit No. 463-C," and ask you if that is the same man that was in your office and the same man you say was passing out literature in the street.

Mr. ANDREWS: It appears to be.

Mr. LIEBELER:. Would you recognize this Mexican again if you saw him?

Mr. ANDREWS: Yes.

Mr. LIEBELER: Do you remember telling the FBI that you wouldn't be able to recognize him again if you saw him?

Mr. ANDREWS: Probably did. Been a long time. There's three people I am going to find : One of them is the real guy that killed the President ; the Mexican ; and Clay Bertrand.

Mr. LIEBELER: Do you mean to suggest by that statement that you have considerable doubt in your mind that Oswald killed the President?

Mr. ANDREWS: I know good and well he did not. With that weapon, he couldn't have been capable of making three controlled shots in that short time.

Mr. LIEBELER: You are basing your opinion on reports that you have received over news media as to how many shots were fired in what period of time; is that correct?

Mr. ANDREWS: I am basing my opinion on five years as an ordnanceman in the Navy. You can lean into those things, and with throwing the bolts-if I couldn't do it myself, 8 hours a day, doing this for a living, constantly on the range, I know this civilian couldn't do it. He might have been a sharp marksman at one time, but if you don't lean into that rifle and don't squeeze and control consistently, your brain can tell you how to do it, but you don't have the capability.

Mr. LIEBELER:. You have used a pronoun in this last series of statements, the pronoun "it." You are making certain assumptions as to what actually happened, or you have a certain notion in your mind as to what happened based on material you read in the newspaper?

Mr. ANDREWS:. It doesn't make any difference. What you have to do is lean into a weapon, and, to do three shots controlled with accuracy, this boy couldn't do it. Forget the President.

Mr. LIEBELER: You base that judgment on the fact that, in your own experience, it is difficult to do that sort of thing?

Mr. ANDREWS: You have to stay with it. You just don't pick up a rifle or a pistol or whatever weapon you are using and stay proficient with it. You have to know what you are doing. You have to be a conniver. This boy could have connived the deal, but I think he is a patsy. Somebody else pulled the trigger.

Mr. LIEBELER: However, as we have indicated, it is your opinion. You don't have any evidence other than what you have already told us about your surmise and opinions about the rifle on which to base that statement; is that correct? If you do, I want to know what it is.

Mr. ANDREWS: If I did, I would give it to you. It's just taking the 5 years and thinking about it a bit. I have fired as much as 40,000 rounds of ammo a day for 7 days a week. You get pretty good with it as long as you keep firing. Then I have gone back after 2 weeks. I used to be able to take a shotgun, go on a skeet, and pop 100 out of 100. After 2 weeks, I could only pop 60 of them. I would have to start shooting again, same way with the rifle and machineguns. Every other person I knew, same thing happened to them. You just have to stay at it.

Mr. LIEBELER: Now, did you see Oswald at any time subsequent to that time you saw him in the street handing out literature?

Mr. ANDREWS: I have never seen him since.

Mr. LIEBELER: Can you tell us what month that was, approximately?

Mr. ANDREWS: Summertime. Before July. I think the last time would be around-the last could have been, I guess, around the 10th of July.

Mr. LIEBELER: Around the 10th of July?

Mr. ANDREWS: I don't believe it was after that. It could have been before, but not after.

Mr. LIEBELER: Now, you mentioned this Mexican that accompanied Oswald to your office. Have you seen him at any time subsequent to the last time Oswald came into your office?

Mr. ANDREWS: No.

Mr. LIEBELER: Can you tell us approximately how long a period of time elapsed from the last time Oswald came into your office to the last time you saw him in the street handing out literature?

Mr. ANDREWS: I would say about 6 weeks, just guessing.

Mr. LIEBELER: And you have never seen the Mexican at any other time since then?

Mr. ANDREWS: No. He just couldn't have disappeared because the Mexican community here is pretty small. You can squeeze it pretty good, the Latin community. He is not known around here.

Mr. LIEBELER: Have you made an attempt to find him since the assassination?

Mr. ANDREWS: Yes.

Mr. LIEBELER: And you haven't had any success?

Mr. ANDREWS: No. Not too many places they can go not being noticed.

Mr. LIEBELER: Was there anybody else with Oswald that day you saw him handing out literature?

Mr. ANDREWS: Oh, people standing there with him. Whether they were with him or not, I wouldn't know.

Mr. LIEBELER: Did it appear that there was anybody else helping him hand out literature?

Mr. ANDREWS: There was one person, but they had no literature. They weren't giving anything out. Let me see that picture of that little bitty guy, that weasel before.

Mr. LIEBELER: [handing picture to witness]. This is Bringuier Exhibit No. 1.

Mr. ANDREWS: No; he resembled this boy, but it is not him. It is a pale face instead of a Latin.

Mr. LIEBELER: When you talked to Oswald on the street that day, did he give you any idea who was paying him to hand this stuff out?

Mr. ANDREWS:. No; he just said, "It's a job."

Mr. LIEBELER: My understanding is of course, that you are here under subpoena and subpoena duces tecum, asking you to bring with you any records that you might have in your office indicating or reflecting Oswald's visit, and my understanding is that you indicated that you were unable to find any such records.

Mr. ANDREWS: Right. My office was rifled shortly after I got out of the hospital, and I talked with the FBI people. We couldn't find anything prior to it. Whoever was kind enough to mess my office up, going through it, we haven't found anything since.

Mr. LIEBELER: You have caused a thorough search to be made of your office for these records?

Mr. ANDREWS: Yes.

Mr. LIEBELER:. You haven't been able to come up with anything?

Mr. ANDREWS: No.

Mr. LIEBELER: Did there come a time after the assassination when you had some further involvement with Oswald, or at least an apparent involvement with Oswald; as I understand it?

Mr. ANDREWS: No ; nothing at all with Oswald. I was in Hotel Dieu, and the phone rang and a voice I recognized as Clay Bertrand asked me if I would go to Dallas and Houston-I think-Dallas, I guess, wherever it was that this boy was being held-and defend him. I told him I was sick in the hospital. If I couldn't go, I would find somebody that could go.

Mr. LIEBELER: You told him you were sick in the hospital and what?

Mr. ANDREWS: That's where I was when the call came through. It came through the hospital switchboard. I said that I wasn't in shape enough to go to Dallas and defend him and I would see what I could do.

Mr. LIEBELER: Now what can you tell us about this Clay Bertrand? You met him prior to that time?

Mr. ANDREWS: I had seen Clay Bertrand once some time ago, probably a couple of years. He's the one who calls in behalf of gay kids normally, either to obtain bond or parole for them. I would assume that he was the one that originally sent Oswald and the gay kids, these Mexicanos, to the office because I had never seen those people before at all. They were just walk-ins.

Mr. LIEBELER: You say that you think you saw Clay Bertrand some time about 2 years prior to the time you received this telephone call that you have just told us.about?

Mr. ANDREWS: Yes ; he is mostly a voice on the phone.

Mr. LIEBELER:. What day did you receive the telephone call from Clay Bertrand asking you to defend Oswald?

Mr. ANDREWS: I don't remember. It was a Friday or a Saturday.

Mr. LIEBELER: Immediately following the assassination?

Mr. ANDREWS: I don't know about that. I didn't know. Yes; I did. I guess I did because I was-they told me I was squirrelly in the hospital.

Mr. LIEBELER: You had pneumonia ; is that right?

Mr. ANDREWS: Yes.

Mr. LIEBELER: And as I understand it, you were under heavy sedation at that time in connection with your treatment for pneumonia?

Mr. ANDREWS: Yes ; this is what happened : After I got the call, I called my secretary at her home and asked her if she had remembered Lee Harvey Oswald's file. Of course, she didn't remember, and I had to tell her about all the kooky kids. She thought we had a file in the office. I would assume that he would have called subsequent to this boy's arrest. I am pretty sure it was before the assassination. I don't know.

Mr. LIEBELER: You don't mean before the assassination-don't you mean before Oswald had been shot? After the assassination and before Oswald had been shot?

Mr. ANDREWS: After Oswald's arrest and prior to his-

Mr. LIEBELER: His death?

Mr. ANDREWS: His death.

Mr. LIEBELER: Now my recollection from reviewing reports from the FBI is that you first advised the FBI of this, telling them that you recall that Clay Bertrand had called you at some time between 6 o'clock and 9 o'clock in the evening and spoke to you about this matter. Do you remember telling the FBI about that?

Mr. ANDREWS: I remember speaking with them. The exact words, I do not, but that's probably correct.

Mr. LIEBELER: Do you remember what time approximately that Clay Bertrand did call you?

Mr. ANDREWS: I will tell you : They feed around 4 :30. By the time I got fed, it was about 5 o'clock. They picked the tray up. So that's about the right time. It's around that time.

Mr. LIEBELER: Now you said that after Clay Bertrand called you, you called your secretary and asked her if she remembered the Oswald file ; is that correct?

Mr. ANDREWS: Yes; she didn't remember Oswald at all. She knows that occasionally these people walk in and out of the office and she had remembered something, but nothing of any value.

Mr. LIEBELER: And do you remember that after you got out of the hospital, you discussed with your secretary the telephone call that you made to her at home?

Mr. ANDREWS: Yes.

Mr. LIEBELER: And do you recall that she said that she remembered that you called her at approximately 4 o'clock on the afternoon of November 23, 1963?

Mr. ANDREWS: Yes.

Mr. LIEBELER: Now have you-let's take it one step further : Do you also recall the fact that your private investigator spent most of that afternoon with you in your hospital room?

Mr. ANDREWS: Yes ; he was there.

Mr. LIEBELER: He was there with you?

Mr. ANDREWS: Yes ; Preston M. Davis.

Mr. LIEBELER: Do you remember approximately what time he left?

Mr. ANDREWS: No.

Mr. LIEBELER: Would it have been before you called your secretary or afterwards?

Mr. ANDREWS. Yes.

Mr. LIEBELER: Before you called?

Mr. ANDREWS. No ; after.

Mr. LIEBELER: After you called your secretary?

Mr. ANDREWS: Let's see. He wasn't there when I made the phone call. He wasn't there when Clay Bertrand called me, I am pretty sure, because he would have remembered it if I didn't.

Mr. LIEBELER: You discussed it and he doesn't, in fact, remember that you received the telephone call from Clay Bertrand?

Mr. ANDREWS: He wasn't there. While he was there, we received no call from Clay Bertrand or no call concerning the office or business because I would have talked to him about it.

Mr. LIEBELER: You say that he left before you called your secretary?

Mr. ANDREWS:. I think he left around chow time, which, I think, is around 4 o'clock. I could be wrong.

Mr. LIEBELER: Now after giving this time sequence that we have talked about here the consideration that I am sure you have after discussing it with the FBI, have you come up with any solution in your own mind to the apparent problems that exist here? That is to say, that your recollection is that you called your secretary after you received the call from Clay Bertrand and you called your secretary at 4 o'clock, which would indicate that you must have received the call from Clay Bertrand prior to 4 o'clock, but you did not receive the call from Mr. Bertrand while Mr. Davis was there, and he left at approximately 4 o'clock or shortly before you called your secretary, in addition to which, you first recall receiving the call from Clay Bertrand some time between 6 o'clock and 9 o'clock in the evening.

Mr. ANDREWS: Well, the time factor I can't help you with. It is impossible. But I feel this: I wouldn't have called my secretary-if I couldn't get her to verify it, I would tell you that I was smoking weed. You know, sailing out on cloud 9.

Mr. LIEBELER: But, in fact, she did verify the fact that you did call her?

Mr. ANDREWS: Yes; I often thought it was a nightmare or a dream, but it isn't. It's just that I can't place-other than what I told Regis Kennedy and John Rice, the exact time I can't help you on. But if it hadn't been for calling her and asking her-

Mr. LIEBELER: To look up the Oswald file or if she remembered the Oswald file?

Mr. ANDREWS: Yes ; I would just say I have a pretty vivid imagination and let's just forget it. Anything other than the law practice-1 would say that what Regis suspects is that I was full of that dope, but I normally take certain steps, and this is the way I would have done it is what I did. I called her. Had Davis been there when the call came in, Davis would have been told, and he would have left the hospital, went down to the office, and shook the office down for the file, and called me from there before he went home. I know it couldn't have come in while he was there. The only media of time that I can use is either medication or food. Of course, being fat, I like food. I wasn't much interested in food. They weren't feeding me too much, and I am pretty sure it was after medication and food and the tray had been picked up that the call came in.

Mr. LIEBELER: Of course, they fed you more than once up there?

Mr. ANDREWS. They feed three times a day, but they don't feed you enough to keep a sparrow alive.

Mr. LIEBELER: Well, in any event, you are not able to clarify for us the sequence of what happened?

Mr. ANDREWS: Well, the sequence of events had to be this : Davis spent Saturday afternoon with me. He probably left just before chow, and then I ate, and the phone call came in some time after chow. I am positive it wasn't as late as 9 o'clock. I think the latest it could have been is 6, but Miss Springer says I called her some time around 4, 4 :30 I don't know which.

Mr. LIEBELER: Miss Springer is your secretary?

Mr. ANDREWS: Yes.

Mr. LIEBELER: Now do you recall talking to an FBI agent, Regis L. Kennedy, and Carl L. Schlaeger on November 25?

Mr. ANDREWS: I don't remember-Kennedy, yes; Schlaeger, no. I don't even know if he was in the same room. I don't think I have even seen him, much less talk to him.

Mr. LIEBELER: Kennedy was; yes?

Mr. ANDREWS: Yes.

Mr. LIEBELER: They usually go around in pairs?

Mr. ANDREWS: Well, they work in teams, so he's got to have been there.

Mr. LIEBELER: Now Kennedy came and visited you at the hospital; is that correct?

Mr. ANDREWS: Right.

Mr. LIEBELER: Now-

Mr. ANDREWS: I remember that pretty good because I called the Feebees, and the guy says to put the phone, you know, and nothing happened.

Mr. LIEBELER: The Feebees?

Mr. ANDREWS: That's what we call the Federal guys. All of a sudden, like a big hurricane, here they come.

Mr. LIEBELER: Do you remember telling him at that time that you thought that Clay Bertrand had come into the office with Oswald when Oswald had been in the office earlier last spring?

Mr. ANDREWS: No ; I don't remember.

Mr. LIEBELER: Was Bertrand ever in the office with Oswald?

Mr. ANDREWS: Not that I remember.

Mr. LIEBELER:. Do you have a picture in your mind of this Clay Bertrand?

Mr. ANDREWS: Oh, I ran up on that rat about 6 weeks ago and he spooked, ran in the street. I would have beat him with a chain if I had caught him.

Mr. LIEBELER: Let me ask you this: When I was down here in April, before I talked to you about this thing, and I was going to take your deposition at that time, but we didn't make arrangements, in your continuing discussions with the FBI, you finally came to the conclusion that Clay Bertrand was a figment of your imagination?

Mr. ANDREWS: That's what the Feebees put on. I know that the two Feebees are going to put these people on the street looking, and I can't find the guy, and I am not going to tie up all the agents on something that isn't that solid. I told them, "Write what you want, that I am nuts. I don't care." They were running on the time factor, and the hills were shook up plenty to get it, get it, get it. I couldn't give it to them. I have been playing cops and robbers with them. You can tell when the steam is on. They are on you like the plague. They never leave. They are like cancer. Eternal.

Mr. LIEBELER: That was the description of the situation?

Mr. ANDREWS: It was my decision if they were to stay there. If I decide yes, they stay. If I decide no, they go. So I told them, "Close your file and go some place else." That's the real reason why it was done. I don't know what they wrote in the report, but that's the real reason.

Mr. LIEBELER: Now subsequent to that time, however, you actually ran into Clay Bertrand in the street?

Mr. ANDREWS: About 6 weeks ago. I am trying to think of the name of this bar. That's where this rascal bums out. I was trying to get past him so I could get a nickel in the phone and call the Feebees or John Rice, but he saw me and spooked and ran. I haven't seen him since.

Mr. LIEBELER: Did you talk to him that day?

Mr. ANDREWS: No; if I would have got close enough to talk to him. I would have grabbed him.

Mr. LIEBELER:. What does this guy look like?

Mr. ANDREWS: He is about 5 feet 8 inches. Got sandy hair, blue eyes, ruddy complexion. Must weigh about 165, 170, 175. He really took off, that rascal.

Mr. LIEBELER: He recognized you?

Mr. ANDREWS: He had to because if he would have let me get to that phone and make the call, he would be in custody.

Mr. LIEBELER: You wanted to get hold of this guy and make him available to the FBI for interview, or Mr. Rice of the Secret Service?

Mr. ANDREWS: What I wanted to do and should have done is crack him in the head with a bottle, but I figured I would be a good, law-abiding citizen and call them and let them grab him, but I made the biggest mistake of the century. I should have grabbed him right there. I probably will never find him again. He has been bugging me ever since this happened.

Mr. LIEBELER: Now before you ran into Clay Bertrand in the street on this day, did you have a notion in your mind what he looked like?

Mr. ANDREWS: I had seen him before one time to recognize him.

Mr. LIEBELER: When you saw him that day, he appeared to you as he had before when you recognized him?

Mr. ANDREWS: He hasn't changed any appearance, I don't think. Maybe a little fatter, maybe a little skinnier.

Mr. LIEBELER: Now I have a rather lengthy report of an interview that Mr. Kennedy had with you on December 5, 1963, in which he reports you as stating that you had a mental picture of Clay Bertrand as being approximately 6 feet 1 inch to 6 feet 2 inches in height, brown hair, and well dressed.

Mr. ANDREWS: Yes.

Mr. LIEBELER:. Now this description is different, at least in terms of height of the man, than the one you have just given us of Clay Bertrand.

Mr. ANDREWS: But, you know, I don't play Boy Scouts and measure them. I have only seen this fellow twice in my life. I don't think there is that much in the description. There may be some to some artist, but to me, there isn't that much difference. Might be for you all.

Mr. LIEBELER:. I think you said he was 5 feet 8 inches before.

Mr. ANDREWS: Well, I can't give you any better because this time I was looking for the fellow, he was sitting down. I am just estimating. You meet a guy 2 years ago, you meet him, period.

Mr. LIEBELER:. Which time was he sitting down?

Mr. ANDREWS: He was standing up first time.

Mr. LIEBELER: I thought you met him on the street the second time when you-

Mr. ANDREWS: No, he was in a barroom.

Mr. LIEBELER:. He was sitting in a bar when you saw him 6 weeks ago?

Mr. ANDREWS: A table at the right-hand side. I go there every now and then spooking for him.

Mr. LIEBELER: What's the name of the bar you saw him in that day, do you remember?

Mr. ANDREWS: Cosimo's, used to be. Little freaky joint.

Mr. LIEBELER: Well, now, if you didn't see him standing up on that day-

Mr. ANDREWS: No.

Mr. LIEBELER: So that you didn't have any basis on which to change your mental picture of this man in regard to his height from the first one that you had?

Mr. ANDREWS: No.

Mr. LIEBELER: I am at a loss to understand why you told Agent Kennedy on December 5 that he was 6 feet 1 to 6 feet 2 and now you have told us that he was 5 feet 8 when at no time did you see the man standing up.

Mr. ANDREWS: Because, I guess, the first time-and I am guessing now-

Mr. LIEBELER: Is this fellow a homosexual, do you say?

Mr. ANDREWS: Bisexual. What they call a swinging cat.

Mr. LIEBELER: And you haven't seen him at any time since that day?

Mr. ANDREWS: I haven't seen him since.

Mr. LIEBELER: Now have you had your office searched for any records relating to Clay Bertrand?

Mr. ANDREWS: Yes.

Mr. LIEBELER: Have you found anything?

Mr. ANDREWS: No; nothing.

Mr. LIEBELER: Has this fellow Bertrand sent you business in the past?

Mr. ANDREWS: Prior to I guess the last time would be February of 1963.

Mr. LIEBELER: And mostly he refers, I think you said, these gay kids, is that right?

Mr. ANDREWS: Right.

Mr. LIEBELER: In discussing this matter with your private detective, Mr. Davis, and Miss Springer, your secretary, have you asked them whether or not they have any recollection of ever having seen Oswald in the office?

Mr. ANDREWS: Davis does; Springer doesn't.

Mr. LIEBELER: Davis does have a recollection?

Mr. ANDREWS: Yes; he recalls. He usually stays with me until about closing time. We review whatever he is doing, and he remembers them as a group.

Mr. LIEBELER: So he was there then the first time they were there? The only time that he was with a group is the first time, is that right?

Mr. ANDREWS: Right.

Mr. LIEBELER:. Have you discussed with Miss Springer and Mr. Davis the whereabouts or any recollection they might have about Clay Bertrand?

Mr. ANDREWS: They weren't with me, I believe, at the time I knew Bertrand.

Mr. LIEBELER: Have you discussed it with them?

Mr. ANDREWS: Yes; but they weren't employed by me at the time I knew him.

Mr. LIEBELER:. So they have no recollection of Bertrand?

Mr. ANDREWS: No.

Mr. LIEBELER: When Oswald came into your office, of course, he told you what his name was, didn't he?

Mr. ANDREWS: Lee Oswald. I don't know whether that's his name or not.

Mr. LIEBELER:. But that's what he told you?

Mr. ANDREWS: That's what he told me.

Mr. LIEBELER: Do you remember discussing or mentioning his name to Davis at any time prior to November 23, 1963?

Mr. ANDREWS:. What the procedure is-1 am in a different office now than I was then, and it was a very small office, and they would come into it-well, what I would call my office-and they just had the reception room out in the front, and Davis would go out there, and on those matters, it's not a matter that he would be discussing, but probably some words passed as to the swishing and the characteristics that they had, but other than that in the business, unless something is assigned to him, he knows nothing in that office unless it is assigned to him.

Mr. LIEBELER: So you say you probably did not mention Oswald's name to Davis?

Mr. ANDREWS: I probably did not, other than we commented on the group in general, but none of the business that was involved or any names.

Mr. LIEBELER: Is it an extraordinary thing for a bunch of gay kids to come into your office like that, or did they come from time to time?

Mr. ANDREWS: Well, let's see. Last week there were six of them in there. Depends on how bad the police are rousing them. They shoo them in. My best customers are the police. They shoo them into the office. God bless the police.

Mr. LIEBELER: Did you ever know a man by the name of Kerry Thornley as one of these gay kids?

Mr. ANDREWS: No.

Mr. LIEBELER: Have you ever heard of Thornley?

Mr. ANDREWS: No; I represent them and that's about all there is to it. When they owe me money, I know where to go grab them, and that's about as far as it goes. Is he supposed to be down here?

Mr. LIEBELER: Thornley?

Mr. ANDREWS: Yes; I can find out if he ever made the scene here real easy.

Mr. LIEBELER:. No; he is not in New Orleans, I don't think, at the moment. When Oswald told you about his discharge, did he tell you what branch of the service he had been in?

Mr. ANDREWS: No.

Mr. LIEBELER: Did he tell you why he got discharged?

Mr. ANDREWS: No.

Mr. LIEBELER:. Did he tell you what kind of a discharge he had?

Mr. ANDREWS: He told me he was dishonorably discharged. That's what I call a yellow sheet discharge. I told him I needed his serial number, the service he was in, the approximate time he got discharged, and, I think, $15 or $25, I forget which, and to take the service, his rate or rank, the serial number, and to write to the Adjutant General for the transcript of the proceedings that washed him out so that they could be examined and see if there was any method of reopening or reconsideration on the file.

Mr. LIEBELER: But he did not tell you any of those things?

Mr. ANDREWS: No; he said he would come back, and he came back, but I still didn't get his serial number and I still didn't get the money.

Mr. LIEBELER: Do you remember specifically that he stated he had a dishonorable discharge as opposed to some other kind of discharge? Do you have a specific recollection on that?

Mr. ANDREWS: We call them in the Navy, B.C.D.'s and I associated that. He never mentioned the specific type discharge. It was one that was other than honorable, as we would put it in the legal sense. I just assumed it was a B.C.D. if he was in the Marines br Navy. If he was in the Army, it's a yellow discharge.

Mr. LIEBELER: Did he tell you if he was working at that time or if he had a job when he first came into your office?

Mr. ANDREWS: Never asked him.

Mr. LIEBELER: Did he associate his other than honorable discharge with difficulty in obtaining employment?

Mr. ANDREWS: I just don't remember. He had a reason why he wanted it reopened. What, I don't recall. He had a reason. I don't recall. He mentioned a reason, but I don't recall. I was trying to remember where they were seated to see if that would help, but no.

Mr. LIEBELER: Tell me approximately how tall Oswald was.

Mr. ANDREWS: Oh, about 5 feet 6 inches, 5 feet 7 inches, I guess.

Mr. LIEBELER: And about how much did he weigh?

Mr. ANDREWS: About 135, 140.

Mr. LIEBELER: I don't think I have any more questions. Do you have anything else that you would like to add?

Mr. ANDREWS: I wish I could be more specific, that's all. This is my impression, for whatever it is worth, of Clay Bertrand: His connections with Oswald I don't know at all. I think he is a lawyer without a brief case. That's my opinion. He sends the kids different places. Whether this boy is associated with Lee Oswald or not, I don't know, but I would say, when I met him about 6 weeks ago when I ran up on him and he ran away from me, he could be running because he owes me money, or he could be running because they have been squeezing the quarter pretty good looking for him while I was in the hospital, and somebody might have passed the word he was hot and I was looking for him, but I have never been able to figure out the reason why he would call me, and the only other part of this thing that I understand, but apparently I haven't been able to communicate, is I called Monk Zelden on a Sunday at the N.O.A.C. and asked Monk if he would go over-be interested in a retainer and go over to Dallas and see about that boy. I thought I called Monk once. Monk says we talked twice. I don't remember the second. It's all one conversation with me. Only thing I do remember about it, while I was talking with Monk, he said, "Don't worry about it. Your client just got shot." That was the end of the case. Even if he was a bona fide client, I never did get to him; somebody else got to him before I did. Other than that, that's the whole thing, but this boy Bertrand has been bugging me ever since. I will find him sooner or later.

Mr. LIEBELER: Does Bertrand owe you money?

Mr. ANDREWS: Yes; I ain't looking for him for that, I want to find out why he called me on behalf of this boy after the President was assassinated.

Mr. LIEBELER: How come Bertrand owes you money?

Mr. ANDREWS: I have done him some legal work that he has failed to pay the office for.

Mr. LIEBELER: When was that?

Mr. ANDREWS: That's in a period of years that I have-like you are Bertrand, YOU call up and ask me to go down and get Mr. X out. If Mr. X doesn't pay on those kinds of calls, Bertrand has a guarantee for the payment of appearance. One or two of these kids had skipped. I had to go pay the penalty, which was a lot of trouble.

Mr. LIEBELER: You were going to hold Bertrand for that?

Mr. ANDREWS: Yes.

Mr. LIEBELER: Did Oswald appear to you to be gay?

Mr. ANDREWS: You can't tell. I couldn't say. He swang with the kids. He didn't swish, but birds of a feather flock together. I don't know any squared that run with them. They may go down to look.

Mr. LIEBELER: When you say he didn't swish, what do you mean by that?

Mr. ANDREWS: He is not effeminate : his voice isn't squeaky ; he didn't walk like or talk like a girl ; he walks and talks like a man.

Mr. LIEBELER: Did you notice anything about the way he walked? Was there anything striking about the way he carried himself?

Mr. ANDREWS: I never paid attention. I never watched him walk other than into and out of the office. There's nothing that would draw my attention to anything out of the ordinary, but I just assumed that he knew these people and was running with them. They had no reason to come. The three gay kids he was with, they were ostentatious. They were what we call swishers. You can just look at them. All they had to do was open their mouth. That was it. Walk, they can swing better than Sammy Kaye. They do real good. With those pronounced ones, you never know what the relationship is with anyone else with them, but I have no way of telling whether he is gay or not, other than he came in with what they call here queens. That's about it.

Mr. LIEBELER: You have never seen any of these people since that first day they came into your office with Oswald, that first day and when you saw them down at the police station?

Mr. ANDREWS: The three queens? The three gay boys? No; I have never seen them.

Mr. LIEBELER: There were just three of them?

Mr. ANDREWS: The Latin type. Mexicanos will crop their hair and a Latin won't, so I assume he is a Mex.

Mr. LIEBELER: So altogether there were five of them that came into the office?

Mr. ANDREWS: Five. The only other thing that shook me to my toes-you have the other part-the Secret Service brought me some things. They don't have the complete photograph. They have another photograph with the two Realpey sisters. They are actually in the office, and that shook me down to my toes pretty good.

Mr. LIEBELER [handing picture to witness]: The 'picture you refer to might be Pizzo Exhibit No. 453-B. Is that the one?

Mr. ANDREWS: Yes, this is it. Victoria Realpey-Plaza and her sister Marguerite Realpey-Plaza, and I can't recall this young lady's name here at all [indicating].

Mr. LIEBELER: You are pointing to the three women who are standing.

Mr. ANDREWS: The one facing, standing as you look at it.

Mr. LIEBELER: That's the one you can't identify?

Mr. ANDREWS: Yes; I have her file in the office. Uncle is a warden at the Parish Prison here in New Orleans.

Mr. LIEBELER: And you are referring to the three women that are standing at the right side of Pizzo Exhibit No. 453-B?

Mr. ANDREWS: The girl carrying the pocketbook.

Mr. LIEBELER: That's the one whose name you can't remember at the moment?

Mr. ANDREWS: Right.

Mr. LIEBELER: Now this little fellow standing on the far left side of the picture, have you ever seen him before? Is he one of those gay boys who were in the office?

Mr. ANDREWS: No; these were all Americanos, these boys. He may be, but he is Latin looking.

Mr. LIEBELER: He looks like a Latin?

Mr. ANDREWS:. Right. This boy should be able to be found. I wanted to look for him, but I didn't have a picture of him.

Mr. LIEBELER: Who is that?

Mr. ANDREWS: The one you just asked me about. If you put some circulars around to have the Latin American people squeezed gently, he has got to be found. They are very clannish. There are only certain places they go. Some body has to remember him. He can't just come into New Orleans and disappear. As long as he walks the street, he has to eat and he has to have some place to sleep and-but I didn't have a picture of him, and nobody-you just can't do it. But a lot of water has run under the stream. He may or may not be here, but it wouldn't be too hard to locate him, you know, with the proper identification.

Mr. LIEBELER: Well, your friends down the street have been trying to find him and haven't come up with him yet.

Mr. ANDREWS: de Brueys?

Mr. LIEBELER: Yes.

Mr. ANDREWS: Sometimes the stools on that are not too good. They need Latin stools for that boy.

Mr. LIEBELER: Off the record. (Discussion off the record.)

Mr. LIEBELER: Did you just indicate that you would like to find Mr. Bertrand and he did run off? Did you see him run off?

Mr. ANDREWS: Yes ; I chased him, but I couldn't go.

Mr. LIEBELER: This was when you saw him 6 weeks ago?

Mr. ANDREWS: Yes: this barroom is right adjacent to-the street-as you go in, there are two entrances, one on the block side and one on the corner. I had no more idea of finding him than jumping off the bridge. I went in there hoping, and the hope came through. I was so surprised to see him there. I kept working my way there to go to the front when he recognized me and he sprinted out the door on the side of the street and was gone. I had to go past him to go to the phone. I should have conked him with the beer bottle.

Mr. LIEBELER:. He took off as soon as he saw you?

Mr. ANDREWS: No; but I was moving to go to the phone. He thought I was moving towards him.

Mr. LIEBELER: [handing picture to witness]: I show you Pizzo Exhibit No. 453-A, and ask you if you can recognize anybody in that picture.

Mr. ANDREWS: The one that has a brief case under his arm, fullface towards the looker, appears to be Lee Oswald. This boy back here [indicating] appears to be familiar, but I would have to blow his face up to be sure. He is in between. See, this one here [indicating]? I have never seen this picture before.

Mr. LIEBELER: Between Oswald, who has the cross mark over his head, and the man who has the arrow over his head?

Mr. ANDREWS: He is a local boy here, a face I recall. It would take me a while to place it, but the face appears to be familiar.

Mr. LIEBELER: You haven't seen this picture before, is that correct?

Mr. ANDREWS: I don't believe.

Mr. LIEBELER: The Secret Service and the FBI have shown you various pictures, but you don't recall this one?

Mr. ANDREWS: I don't recall seeing that one. There was one of a series where-one of an attorney in town was there where we all knew him. They may have shown me this, but I don't remember. We used to have a club back in 1946 called Lock (?) Fraternity, and he resembles a boy that was a member.

Mr. LIEBELER: I don't think I have any more questions, Mr. Andrews. I want to thank you very much for coming in and I appreciate the cooperation you have given us.

Mr. ANDREWS: I only wish I could do better.

Quoting Harold Weisberg again, he blasted the Warren Commission for "not naming the man who used what the Attorney General himself, on March 2, 1967, said is the alias of Clay Bertrand ... Knowing who Clay Bertrand really was – and this knowledge was the entire defense of the government when Garrison made the identity public – the Commission could not with honor and honesty avoid confronting Andrews with him.... Nowhere in the millions of printed words is there the name of the man who went as Clay Bertrand. Nowhere in the 900 pages of the Report is his real name or his alias mentioned. Not once in the 15 printed pages of Andrews's interrogation and testimony (11H325-39) did Liebeler hint at government knowledge of the identity." Weisberg is, of course, referring here to Clay Shaw.

APPENDIX B

LETTER FROM FLETCHER PROUTY TO OLIVER STONE, SEPTEMBER 2, 1990

This intriguing letter explores information that has not been generally found in the assassination literature.

Dear Oliver, You asked, "Who did it?", "How was it planned?" Read on. Society's murders are sophisticated. No one person did it. No one person planned it. I'll show you how it was done. Your idea of using Jim, the honest, hard-working law man, as the main character is magnificent. Then we have to fill in the real data. What made his job so difficult? What made it so dangerous? These are not data of the "researchers." These are data from the Pentagon, from Board Rooms, from major law offices, from the Executive Suites of major banks... all of this US and foreign.

> NOTE: So you'll know this is in bed rock. I happen to have kept almost every daily "Pentagon News Clips" of that period. The "Clips" is a rare 36-40 page summary of world-wide news and other items put together daily by the Intelligence services and distributed to a small group of top pentagon officials. Thus, I have the key "Clips" of interest to that top echelon of men from about 1959-1963. It is a fabulous resource. Now on to the guts of the matter.
> -- End NOTE --

During the latter part of the Eisenhower administration the top people prepared for a Nixon Victory and a Nixon Administration, and another high-flying eight years. The biggest dollar deal they had going was the "Everest Fighter", a design created under Gen Frank Everest as the "Ultimate" aircraft. On purpose that money was reserved from year to year so that, after the Nixon inaugural, it could be allocated in one contract ... the biggest ever written ... to the hard-core Military-Industry Complex. Nixon lost. All that money and planning came crashing down. JFK inherited, what was now called, the "TFX" i.e. Tactical Fighters Experimental, billions.

By the time the contract was awarded in 1962, that amounted to some $6.7 billion for openers.

All the insiders knew that this contract would go to Boeing. Lockheed withdrew from contention. This left Boeing and General Dynamics/Grumman in the contest. McNamara, who did not know new aircraft from mushroom soup, leaned on a specialist, Al Barbour who had been a Navy Test pilot of great experience, i.e. like my old friend Chuck Yeager. McNamara had brought in the Whiz Kids and they were good; but Barbour was the only pilot, except for me, on his staff... and I was not in that business. Many thought this mighty TFX selection would be made by Barbour for McNamara. In this scenario, Barbour can be made into a role almost the equal of Garrison ... the competent guy beaten down and ignored by the system.

With that enormous sum of money in the pot, the JFK 'Irish Mafia' began to intrigue, 'How best to put those billions to work?' JFK had squeaked through the 1960 election. It could be made a run-away in 1964. Master of the scheme was Sec. Labor Arthur Goldberg. He had McNamara set up a suite near his office (happened to be near mine) on the Third Floor-Pentagon. This office, headed by Ron Linton, was "decorated" by a set of maps from every state showing the counties... the basic political unit. Then, as these huge contract proposals came in from the contractors, every place where a contractor, or sub-contractor, was located was physically marked out on the maps. These maps had been specially treated with the 1960 vote data. The JFK-carried counties were one color. The Nixon counties were another. The Marginal Counties were the battlefield. This is where the money would go first.

In such deals there are always corporate spies and sympathizers. Litton's office became the target. Word leaked out. They wanted it to leak out. The contractors could see the game. They began to put offices in Podunk, that little county that JFK lost by 50 votes. They scheduled new factories in "Sandy Hill, NV." Each new, marginal county gave that contractor another chance. The hell with the airplane ... McNamara's band got a bright idea. They said the TFX would be both an Air Force and a Navy aircraft. This poured more money into the pot. And raised temperatures everywhere.

Al Barbour began to see what was happening. He tried to call the attention of McNamara and the Whiz Kids to the 'Aeronautical' advantages and disadvantages of each of the proposals. He wanted the decision to be made on technical grounds for the finest aircraft. Al was worried, and began to see what was coming – He was no politician. Naturally he began to leak this to his friends. Pressures rose as the newspapers showed. Finally, into 1962 I believe – I have the exact dates – McNamara announced that the TFX decision was around the corner. It was now a hotly contested $6.7 billion (I have the exact data). On the Friday before the final announcement there had been a 'last' meeting in McNamara's office – Eugene Zuckert, a major Washington lawyer and then-Secretary of the Air Force, along with General Curt LeMay, left that office elated and told a few close friends that night while closeted for a dinner celebration that they felt certain 'Boeing had won it!'

JFK and the Irish Mafia, Goldberg and McNamara had played it cool. (This following information is something that I know from my personal acquaintance with Roger Lewis. then-president of General Dynamics ... the eventual winner.) McNamara was concerned. He wanted to he absolutely certain that his 'political' choice of General Dynamics would fly. He had called Lewis and asked who he would recommend to make one final study of the TFX plans. Lewis a clever old aircraft builder, formerly Asst. Sec. Air Force, told McNamara, "Send the plans to Kelly Johnson head of the famous U-2 'Skunk Works' at Lockheed. He'll give the plans a last review and then give you his expert advice." What could be better? (Lewis had worked for Lockheed years ago and knew Kelly Johnson well. He was taking no chances. His bet on Kelly was a sure thing.) McNamara had done that secretly. He did not even discuss the plans with Barbour. Kelly said the TFX plan from General Dynamics was fine. On Saturday, while all offices were closed, McNamara announced that the 'TFX Contract Has Been Awarded to General dynamics/Grumman.' Boeing lost!

In Boeing there was an 8 Megaton explosion. In major Board Rooms across the country there were enormous waves of that explosion. For example, and this is a partial listing, on Boeing's Board were representatives from:

- Bank California-Tri State Corp.

- Citibank N.A. and CITICORP and Crocker National Corp.

- Cracker National Bank, and Hewlett Packard Co.

- Gulf United Corp.

- Manufacturers Hanover Corp, Manufacturers Hanover Trust

- Minnesota Mining & Manufacturing Corp. (3M)

- New York Stock Exchange and Pacific National Bank and the RAND Corp

- Seattle First National Bank and SRI Int'l (Stanford Univ.)

223

- Standard Oil Co. of California
- Mobil Corp.
- Nordstrom Inc.
- Pacific Northwest Tel.
- Texas instruments Co.
- United States Steel
- Weyerhauser Co.

That's just Boeing. There were a whole family of sub-component manufacturers such as the engine builder, etc. all with their own Boards, Bankers and Lawyers. This sat off a tsunami wave throughout the Military-Industry Complex. McNamara sent Roswell Gilpatric, his Deputy and a Wall Street man to calm things. That next Monday, the entire suite of offices, where the Goldberg and Linton maps had been, was empty. Their job done. Al Barbour had resigned. A new era had begun. This was 1962.

Over the horizon the ground work for the Vietnam War was well under way. There were signs, since the disastrous failure of the Bay of Pigs operation and the drastic firing of Allen Dulles, Gen. Charles Cabell and Richard Bissell among others, that JFK was thinking of a new direction there. He had listened to Lansdale, but the Bay of Pigs took the bloom off that rose. He was listening to a new set of voices in place of Lansdale and the old "Southeast Asia" gang. This too reverberated in the highest places. There they knew about the enormous amounts of oil on that peninsula and its offshore areas. By early 1963 same of this talk was turning harsh and bitter. JFK had even thwarted a move into the education field by the Catholic Church. His old friend from Whitman, Massachusetts Cardinal Spellman, dean of Military Chaplains and head of the Church in New York (a long time friend and associate of Joe Kennedy) was shocked by JFK's "independence."

In the highest places they were looking at the calendar. It was early 1963. Elections would come in 1964. From Boardroom to boardroom things got more tense. Such things as "We've got to keep him out of the White House in 1965-1966" were heard frequently. Then one day a major, almost informal meeting was held quietly, perhaps in New York, in the elegant offices of – we'll say – the Baker, McKenzie Law Firm. Following heated debate and emotional discussion that group came to the conclusion that "JFK had to go." No single voice said that. The group evolved it. There was no vote. This was a most sophisticated, social decision "for the good of everyone." At that meeting there had been a special agent—a man with direct access to the upper echelons of the CIA. In former days, he might have been called the "Bag Man." As the meeting broke up, this experienced man knew that he had received his orders.

This is crucial … in accordance with this social system that is as old as the Crucifixion, no one had said "He must die". There had been no vote. There was absolutely no one to blame. The man who left with orders, had received no orders. But he knew. In Washington he told no one. Someone in that meeting would have told John McCone, Allen Dulles' replacement as head of the CIA through the "old boy" network. Allen Dulles would have been told. Gradually, like an oil spot spreading over the surface of a pond, others at that level would know, even others would feel it. They seemed to know what was underway, but it had no face. Some began to see Goldwater as the sacrificial lamb to be. The "bag" man made one call to a most experienced agent who had participated in other such actions. "A job has been scheduled for this Fall. You will use men from our best group. We shall provide you with the date, the time and the place later. YOU WILL HAVE COMPLETE RESPONSIBILITY FOR GETTING THEM IN AND OUT QUICKLY AND SAFELY, AND YOU WILL BE TOTALLY AND COMPREHENSIVELY RESPONSIBLE FOR THE COVERING ARRANGEMENTS. BOTH BEFORE AND AFTER, THAT MUST BE MADE THEN AND FOR ALL TIME. YOU ARE TO USE CLEARED MEDIA RESOURCES IN AMERICA AND WORLD WIDE. MONEY IS NO PROBLEM. YOU HAVE THE CHECK BOOK."

JFK's schedules were studied with care. Dallas, the home of Gen. Cabell where his brother was Mayor, was selected as ideal. This was to be a power play. There were deception moves, but there was be no need to hide. No one would ever be arrested, tried and prosecuted. This was a coup d'état; not a simple murder. They would be in charge as soon as this was done. Teams of experts were formed for the Job. They were totally cellularized. Few ever met each other. The technical side of the job was easy. The "mechanics" were already trained. They live in an over-seas site, and are available anytime and anywhere. They need no particular briefing: just how to get in and get out.

Up close. The central operator is put in charge of a large and ostensibly TOP SECRET project: we'll say, something like a CIA/Military Operation to assassinate Castro. It is called "MONGOOSE." This gives that same operator a reason for those who become whiting of the project to do many things that otherwise might raise questions. (Witness the Contra deal for Drugs). A special part of MONGOOSE is based in the New Orleans area. This is because it was in the Lake Pontchartrain region that an element... the renegade element of the old Bay of Pigs Brigade was isolated and trained. The tough Marines who trained them are there. The top CIA infrastructure is there from Bertrand, the senior official in that region to that individual Oswald who has been selected to be the "Fall Guy" or "Patsy." New Orleans becomes a bee-hive of clandestine "Anti-Castro" activity. It is "clandestine" but it is leaked to media sources and to the police for later use as cover stories.

The Dallas area is placed under other experts who know only that something they are doing may involve "Castro" or someone like that. They meticulously arrange the "Scenario of the Patsy." At the same time they skillfully brief the Dallas Police, the Sheriff, the local FBI men and all the rest. They bring in a gang of the old "Bay of Pigs" Cubans and CIA guys to add color. Down through top society in Dallas, in the Petroleum Club, word trickles out that something important is afoot. They learn the President is coming. "Of course. That's what it is." There are mixed emotions because they do not know "The Plot."

In Washington the more intricate plans are underway. JFK has been crafting his plan to get out of Vietnam. Earlier, after the Bay of Pigs fiasco, he had issued a directive (NSAM # 55) that would end the CIA's role in Covert Operations and turn "Peacetime Operations" i.e. covert, over the Chairman of the Joint Chiefs of Staff. This had angered the CIA and its allies.

Then in early September 1963, after a summer of careful planning, the President sent a skilled team (Gen. Krulak from the Joint Staff and Joseph Mendenhall of the Dept. of State) to Saigon on an important mission. No sooner had they returned than he dispatched Secretary McNamara and General Maxwell Taylor to Saigon. It was the "Taylor-McNamara Report" of their visit that led to President Kennedy's declaration that he was going to bring 1000 troops home for Christmas 1963 and have all US personnel out of Vietnam by the end of 1965. This was the opening gun of his 1964 Campaign.

These pressures converged. Kennedy's plans were underway. Meanwhile, the plot was moving skillfully. An unusual action was taken to assure that Vice President Lyndon Johnson would be in the Presidential procession as it traveled through Dallas. Other plans were made to assure that Richard Nixon, then-Counsel to the Pepsi Cola Co. was in Dallas on Nov 22. Both men would be "indoctrinated under fire." More intricate plans were made to have most of Kennedy's Cabinet en route to Tokyo in an unusual group visit to Japan.

Quiet calls were made to Secret Service units shifting them around so that it would happen that few if any were on duty in Dallas. At the same time, the usual military units used to augment the Secret Service as "Presidential Protection" had been told that they were not needed that day, since another unit would take care of Dallas.

Great care had been taken in the preparation of the "Patsy." He had been put under the wing of a prominent oil man and member of the Prestigious Petroleum Club of Dallas. With this type of care, it was not difficult to place the "Patsy" in a most propitious place working in the Texas Book Depository Building. The next step was to arrange the Presidential processional route to pass below that building and on a street with defilade fire on the President's car from two directions. There is no need here to progress with this draft.

It is important to note that the first official meeting President Lyndon Johnson had in the White House after the duties of the Kennedy funeral and the visit of all the foreign dignitaries was over, was held on Friday Nov 29, 1963. That first official visitor was the Att. General of the State of Texas, Waggoner Carr. The discussion, no doubt, was simple. Carr was informed that the President had decided to appoint a Commission to investigate the assassination and THERE WOULD BE NO NEED TO HOLD A MURDER TRIAL IN TEXAS, EVER. Carr understood.

President Johnson's second guest was his old friend, and 19-year neighbor in Washington, J. Edgar Hoover. He could hardly wait to speak with Hoover. His first question to Hoover was:

"Were they shooting at me?"

Lyndon had heard those bullets as they whistled close above him from the DAL-TEX building. He knew the sound of gun fire. He knew his good friend Governor Connally had been hit. He wondered had they shot at him? Was there a chance he might be shot at some other day? LBJ had been "indoctrinated" and the sword of Damocles hung directly over that Texans brow and he knew it.

Hoover's reply was quickly spoken:

"No, Mr. President, they were not!"

With that question and that answer we have ended our story.

Lyndon knew THEY had fired the guns. Hoover knew THEY had not fired at the Vice President. They both knew that THEY had done it. "THEY" could not have been that "Lone Gunman" Lee Harvey Oswald. Both Johnson and Hoover knew that then. That is all we need to know.

That afternoon, after obtaining Hoover's concurrence, LBJ announced the make-up of the Warren Commission. The heavy work had begun. The cover-up that had been so carefully planned began to march across the sands of time

This is what the District Attorney in New Orleans saw. He had seen that covering action in Louisiana. He knew there had been some major activity; but his was a local and parochial view. There is no way he could have known what had taken place in the "Faceless" Board Room when an act of spontaneous evolution had taken place. Therefore he did what he had been so ably trained to do. He began the difficult and—in this case—impossible process of seeing that Justice be done.

This is the Jim Garrison story. It is, in a particular sense the Al Barbour story. This is an all American story. This country has not been the same since, and never shall be.

Lyndon died wondering about those shots. Shortly before his death he told an old acquaintance with the media that "The CIA has a Murder Inc. in the Caribbean." He was right; but he did not know that a Murder Inc. can be maneuvered suddenly to perform its deeds in any direction. All it takes to set this enormous train in action is the word of one single man, the Focal Point operator, who is totally anonymous and who knows that he has that special authority from on high and that he will never be punished or uncovered ... unless, like the men who buried Capt. Kidd's gold, it becomes necessary to silence him.

He never would have been uncovered had it not been for a chance, random photograph taken during those hectic minutes at the Dallas Text Book depository building that afternoon of the 22nd of November, 1963.

This is stuff to sleep on. Then, if it helps to sort out the answers you sought with your direct questions, think it all over carefully and draw up all the questions you can think of. I have tons of source data and, given the direction of your inputs, I can polish and elaborate on this rough work.

Why have I done this? You are the first person in a position to be able to do something serious with this rare data, who has asked me point blank the right questions. I don't see why we can't answer them and in so doing memorialize the crime of the Century by creating the story of an epoch. Mere "solving" the crime would be a shallow goal. We must create a monument.

Sincerely,
L. Fletcher Prouty

APPENDIX C

ANNE DISCHLER

Anne Dischler was an investigator who worked initially with the police. She and Louisiana State Lt. Francis Fruge investigated reports that Lee Harvey Oswald had been seen in Baton Rouge and other places across Louisiana. People were so scared to talk to them that Dischler often adopted the persona of a local newspaper reporter. Included in these slew of instances was an altercation at a Holiday Inn, where Oswald had signed the bar tab "Hidell," before fleeing without paying. Alex Hidell was the mysterious alias dubiously tied to Oswald. These seemed to have been less publicized instances of the more familiar Oswald impersonations that Warren Report critics have noted provide strong evidence of conspirators framing the patsy ahead of time. There were the same kinds of suggestive remarks from "Oswald," with one being, "a lot of Catholic rulers are going to be killed in a few months." More than one witness saw Oswald with Jack Ruby, and Barbara Messina claimed to have had dinner several times with Jack Ruby, when she would be picked up in a Cadillac being driven by a gray haired man, who could presumably have been Shaw, and a young man she recognized on television after the assassination as Oswald. She became frightened, and disappeared. Perhaps more than just Oswald was being impersonated. William Law had interviewed Marina Oswald three of four times in the early 2000s, and she once told him that she'd gone to a store that she'd never been in, and the proprietors said she'd been there before.

The following is excerpted from a speech before a November 18, 2006 JFK Lancer conference by Anne Dischler, who went on to work for Jim Garrison. It is most of, but not all the interview, since the audio on the archived tape stopped working. The questioner is Lancer conference host Jim Oliver. As mentioned previously, Dischler had worked with Louisiana State Police Lt. Francis Fruge, who was in the center of the case of Rose Cheramie, who told him and others that JFK was going to be assassinated, before it happened. Here Dischler concentrates mostly on the allegation that Oswald, Ferrie, and Clay Shaw were involved together in getting voters registered in Clinton, Louisiana. Clinton Town Marshall John Manchester would tell Jim Garrison that he saw a Cadillac, parked close to the Voter Registrar's Office, and "I remember finding out in some way that the car was from the International Trade Mart in New Orleans." He saw two people in the front seat, and the driver "resembled CLAY SHAW quite a bit." Manchester would later tell the HSCA that the man provided his name as "Clay Shaw, which corresponded with his driver's license." Three other witnesses tied Shaw to the Cadillac: Corrie Collins, Henry Palmer, and William E. Dunn, Sr. Palmer's connection to the Ku Klux Klan was used to undermine his testimony. He was the first to put Oswald there, claiming he had applied for a job and was told to register to vote. The sightings of the Cadillac took place while Oswald was supposedly standing in line at the Congress for Racial Equality voter drive. Palmer would tell Anne Dischler that Oswald had signed the register when he registered to vote. He then revealed that Oswald's name and signature had been erased, and another name written over it. When Dischler attempted to get a copy, Palmer told her that the page was missing. Collins would later name the three men associated with the Cadillac as Shaw, Ferrie, and Oswald. From Dischler's speech:

ANNE DISCHLER: "What I was doing was working with an officer undercover. I knew nothing about fixing to be in on the JFK assassination. I was already working as an investigator so I knew what to do. And so when Garrison called, I should say Mr. Garrison, called the State Police and asked for someone to help investigate the area in our state, around Clinton and Jackson.

"Colonel Red Rat said, 'Bratty's project should be able to go.' And he asked if I could go and go with him and do this legwork because we had been doing undercover work and we both knew how to work together. So they said that should make a fine team. Mr. Garrison, I met him at his office when we went. But he approved of our work, and they just put us on the job and sent their investigators to work with us. In fact, us working at their direction is how it was supposed to be."

JIM OLIVER: "And what was the first task that you took on, you and Francis? What was the first area of investigation that you did?"

DISCHLER: "Mostly, as I remember, Mostly the first thing that we did was go around and meet people that we were going to have to interview, like the registrar of voters... What happened when we went there without cameras or anything, because we were used to filming what we worked with as much as we could, or we had no camera with us.

"So we looked at the registrar of voters' book. And there was Oswald's name, Lee Harvey Oswald, where he had registered, and you could see it had been erased. I saw that. It had been erased and written over, but it was very plain that L and the O, they were very, very plain. That L was written over and we went back the next morning to film—no book. Disappeared. So we knew we had a trail of something that we should go on looking for that. Let's backtrack just a little bit. Lee Harvey Oswald would have been registering to vote in Clinton for what reason? So he could go to work at Jackson.

"They wanted him to go to work at Jackson. Now, we didn't find out all the details about why all this was taking place. We were looking for specific things that Jim Garrison was working for. "

OLIVER: "And one of those other things was trying to tie Lee Harvey Oswald together with Clay Shaw from the International Trade Mart, people like David Ferrie. And tell us about that and how you came to learn that those three were spotted together in Clinton."

DISCHLER: "Well, Mr. Garrison gave us pictures to work with of several people. And one of them was the Black Cadillac with people in it. And we were to look and see if anybody knew these people. And we did. We were able to identify this old document, and you can find it. In fact, a lot of that is in Joan Mellen's book, *Farewell to Justice*, and she wrote it correctly that morning…"

OLIVER: "There was speculation at some point that the gentleman with the gray hair and the black Cadillac may have been Guy Banister, but that you did a test with photographs that proved differently. People who identified the man, the gray haired man in the Cadillac was not Guy Banister."

DISCHLER: "Well, there was speculation that there was a third person there who was Guy Banister, but Clay Shaw and Levar Bionzwell were identified in those photographs."

OLIVER: "Those who were identified were witnesses of Clinton who actually saw them?"

DISCHLER: "Yes, and one of them wound up dead, which is, you know, the story of that."

OLIVER: "And the time frame, Anne?"

DISCHLER: "This is 1967. This is '67, just prior to the months, about 8 or 9 months prior to when Jim Garrison started his trial of Clay Shaw. Well, it went decades beyond that, that the government, FBI, those people would not admit the fact that Clay Shaw and Lee Oswald were together in Clinton, but you found this out in 1967 for sure. We found witnesses who said they knew that that was him in that court. They had seen him there."

OLIVER: "And then when you tie that into the fact that Oswald had signed in to register for voting privileges in that area, Representative Morgan Reeves; Morgan Reeves, who Oswald had gone to see to ask for a job at the Louisiana State Hospital, Jackson, was told if you want to get a job in this area you're going to have to be registered to vote and so therefore sending down to the voting line and the fact that the name was erased from the book 1967 you saw Oswald's name and it had been erased and someone else's name written over and then the next day you come to take a picture of the book and the book is missing altogether."

DISCHLER: "The book is missing altogether and we never saw it. We were never able to get ahold of anybody who would let us have that book."

OLIVER: "Right, tell us a little bit about Jackson. What's been on in Jackson? Did you do interviews in Jackson as well?"

DISCHLER: "We did a lot of interviews in Jackson."

OLIVER: "Okay, those were concerning what?"

DISCHLER: "Well, Lee Harvey Oswald did his haircuts at Lee McGee's water shop. And this is—you're wanting me to say things that is, that are 40 years old. And in what order? It's in my records."

OLIVER: "It's in Joan's book in the proper order. But where Lee Harvey Oswald was, was he up there or not?"

DISCHLER: "We've established that. Was Clay Shaw up there? He was. We've talked about that. We had witnesses. They couldn't bring any of them to the front for Garrison to use because they killed one of them and the others backed off. Some of the others backed off."

OLIVER: "So basically the Jackson and Clinton interviews had to do with solidifying, you know, who were these people, identifying these people in this black car that came to both towns, and that for sure the witnesses told and that Clay Shaw and Lee Harvey Oswald were together in Jackson and Clinton. To me, that's a very, very significant thing and should be I'm sure to many of you who have researched the New Orleans aspect of the assassination."

DISCHLER: "Can I say something else? I know a person personally who told me that someone he knew from the area had been in contact with Lee Harvey Oswald had also himself seen Clay Shaw in that car. I will not name that person. He has a family. They were powerful. I will not name him, but read what's written more, what's written [is] better than Joan's. I'm not promoting Joan's book, but I wouldn't. She was factual. She was factual. Yeah, with what you said. Yes, with the facts. And you decide, you know? Because nobody's going to convince you of anything. You're going to believe whatever that you find to be truth. And that's all I ask you to search for is truth, because truth is what's going to reveal the truth about what happened to our person."

OLIVER: "Okay, can we talk about Rose Cheramie a little bit? Can you tell us a little bit about what you know about Rose Cheramie and Francis Fruge, Lieutenant Fruge. How, what do you know about that?"

DISCHLER: "What I know is that I was not on the job with him when Rose Cheramie came into the picture, But he did tell me when we started on the case, he told me everything that he wanted me to know about what had happened, and you probably all know the story, don't you?"

OLIVER: "Okay, well, can you tell us again just briefly what he told you with Francis?"

DISCHLER: "Well, she was thrown out of the car because of what she knew. She was thrown out of the car because of what she knew. She was thrown out of the car about five miles from the city of Eunice on the highway. She was thrown in with the antenna ... running over her. And they didn't succeed. She was so doped up that she was unable to even get up from where she was and they found her on the road and they brought her, now I'm skipping some of the details, but they brought her to the City Police in Eunice to the police department."

OLIVER: "There was no state police jail, so to speak. So they would use the local jail house. In Eunice is where they brought her, where Francis brought her."

DISCHLER: "Yes, and Dr. Durwin ministered to her. He was the (unintelligible) at the time. And he gave her a shot to calm her down. He did calm her down. They sent her off to Jackson. And she was screaming all this time, 'he's going to be killed!' And when she got to Jackson State Hospital, she was standing in front of the TV. Now, this is related from Francis. She was standing in front of the TV. And she said, watch. They're going to shoot him. And they did shoot him. Well, this raised a few of them in the State of Louisiana, I'm telling you.

"They told Francis to come and get her. I won't mention another name because I don't think the Premier's Center mentioned this, I'm not sure. But that Francis should come and get her and get her out of the state. Well he did. And as you probably know the demise of Rose Cheramie happened almost exactly like that. They did succeed in killing her, but in Big Sandy, Texas…

"And we all know that the motorcade downtown where the actual shooting took place was not carried live on television. But at some point in that day when the replays came on, on television is when she made the comment to some of the doctors in there that, well she had actually told them beforehand, as she told Francis Fruge that she had come down from Miami with a group of Cubans. They were on their way to Houston for a drug deal. She had a two-year-old son in Houston that she was going to pick up, and they were going to make their way to Dallas. She had done some work for Jack Ruby at his lounge previously. And she said to Francis Fruge, 'they're going to Dallas to kill Kennedy.' And for so many years, that was the story that we had told to us by Francis Fruge. He even testified before the House Select Committee on Assassinations. I was doing a talk in Lafayette one day when a former police officer walked up to me and said 'if you'd like to learn more about the Rose Cheramie thing, there's a former state policeman that you can talk to.' He gave me his name, Donald White. I went over to talk to Donald White and he says to me that he actually picked up Rose Cheramie first. There was a lounge in Basile, Louisiana, which is about maybe seven or eight miles from Eunice. And back in 1963 in that area the lounges had call girls working for them. And they… had a history of drug problems and alcohol. She obviously was found meandering along that highway, all drugged up several times, but was actually picked up initially by former trucker Donald White. Donald took her to the lockup in Eunice and I think they medicated her somewhat there. Obviously let her go at some point. Then Lieutenant Francis Fruge sometime later comes down that same highway and sees her meandering in the center of the highway again. When he picks her up, Donald White tells me that Francis Fruge called him and said, come on over here to the jailhouse, I got your girlfriend here, which is just a, that's the way those guys talked back then.

"And so Donald went to the lockup at Eunice, and Francis said to, he brought him into the cell and said to Rose Cheramie, 'now tell Trooper White what you just told me.' And she repeated the story to Donald White about coming from Miami with the Cubans, the drug deal, picking up the child in Houston, and the fact that these guys were going to kill Kennedy. So you know all of a sudden the lights come on because now we have a corroborating witness. All this time it was Francis Fruge's story, but now Donald White was actually in that jail at the same time as Francis and she told him the same thing. They traveled with her to Jackson, Louisiana Mental Hospital and you know Anne and I were talking about this on the way over here it's probably in those days two-hour, maybe three-hour drive and I would be most interested in knowing what the conversations were. One of the things that she told me on the way here was that a former state trooper by the name of Wayne Moran, who is now a sheriff in one of our parishes back home, accompanied Francis Fruge to take her to Jackson and actually to the hospital…

OLIVER: "To take her out of Jackson, flying her out of Jackson to Houston."

DISCHLER: "Okay, they brought her to Jackson and remember that Francis Fruge already called the state police the day after the assassination and said, 'hey, I picked up this woman a few days ago and this is what she said to me, she's now at the Louisiana State Hospital and the FBI's comment to Lieutenant Fruge was, 'hey, we've already solved the case, we've got the thing under don't worry about it, you know.' And so when Francis Fruge contacted the head of the state police, which was the head of the Department of Public Safety and Transportation. I'll say his name. His name was Thomas Burbank. And Donald White says to me that Thomas Burbank told Francis Fruge, 'get this woman to hell out of Louisiana.' I mean, she had been telling authorities and people at the hospital for 3 or 4 days that Kennedy was going to be hit. All of a sudden he's hit. Burbank didn't walk her anywhere around.

"So they boarded a plane, Wayne Moran and Francis Fruge, and flew her to Houston. Supposedly he kind of checked out the drug deal. There was a boat or a name of a ship or something coming in with drugs on it. They checked that out and found out that there actually was a ship by that name that was coming into the port at Houston. And then of course, she's in Big Sandy and we know the rest of the story.

"I want to insert right here that her mother lived in Houston. I spoke to her mother on the telephone. And found out that she was already dealing with her. Is that what you're asking? That's when Francis and I and Frank Loesch, Harrison's investigator, went to Houston. "

OLIVER: "And you met with her mother?"

DISCHLER: "Yes, on the phone. I talked to her on the phone, under the same name. And she answered me and said that she was already dead. And then Francis and I went and found that death certificate. And proved that she had lived two days after they tried to kill her. They said she was dead already. It wasn't true. The records, the hospital records reflect that she lived two days and she tried to talk. Then they said she died of these hemorrhages and stuck with it.

"Yeah. I saw from Joe West at some point and Gary Shaw that had a copy of the autopsy report. There was a bullet wound to the skull. They, you know, they gave the story that there were a bunch of suitcases. Well, the guy who ran over her actually testified and said that there were a bunch of suitcases in the middle of the road to avoid the suitcases. He hit the shoulder, that's where she was lying, and accidentally ran over her. But she did have a bullet wound in the head, according to the autopsy report. You know, the things that you're going to hear or have heard from Ann will not keep you here all day. I can tell you something about this lady. I contacted her in 1989. She was not seeking any publicity of any kind. Her family did not know that she was involved in the Garrison investigation until I came along. She had to tell them why this man was visiting her.

"Our children didn't know hardly anything about what I was doing, and that's part of why I'm here today. It was because Jim said that he would like to. Then my family, found out exactly what happened. You know, while I was working, because I never would let them. I wouldn't talk to them about it. I was told not to. And they, um, so they didn't, they didn't press and so now they don't know and now they want to know. They're all in their 40s and 50s. There's one of them sitting right here, Jan."

OLIVER: "I think at this point we would do some questions and answers. Again, if Anne does not know something, she's not going to embellish it or whatever. She was just telling she doesn't know."

OLIVER: "Stu?"

AUDIENCE MEMBER: "Let me say from the outset I don't endorse either of these ideas but I want you to encounter them because they're offered online by people who try and shoot down the Clinton case which is... I would rather get certain people's vote. The two claims are one, that the Ku Klux Klan intimidated all these people for whatever reason. I'm not particularly sure. They intimidated the Clinton witnesses to claim that Oswald was there.

DISCHLER: "I'm not going to use the name 'Ku Klux Klan.' Don't enter that into anything else. Oh no no…"

AUDIENCE MEMBER: "It's nothing you said. It's what the people who try and take away from the Clinton witnesses argue. They argue two things: they argue that the Klan intimidated the witnesses into making up the Oswald story. And … the second thing they always argue is somehow Garrison coached the Clinton witnesses over time to make their stories better. This is in Lambert; Lambert offered the Klan thesis and people like John McAdams offer… [that] Garrison coach[ed] them. I think that's another name she would rather not use."

DISCHLER: "Can I elaborate since you brought her up?"

AUDIENCE MEMBER: "Yeah, done."

DISCHLER: "I am thoroughly ashamed that I allowed her [Lambert] to put my work, my honest and truthful efforts to try to find out what happened to our president. She misused and I don't mean to be, but this is part of why I stayed quiet and wouldn't let Joan use my work for a while. Sent her [Lambert] back to New Jersey twice. Anyway, she misinterpreted what I gave her. I gave her the same thing that I gave Joan Mellen. And she twisted it. That Lambert, Patricia Lambert twisted my work. And I am ashamed that I am in her book. It is so degrading. So I don't want to comment on that."

OLIVER: "To answer one of the things that Stu just said, did Garrison at any time go with you and Francis on these interviews at all?"

DISCHLER: "Oh no, we saw him one time. I saw him one time. Francis was in touch with him. It wasn't always Francis. But he was always there. But Jim Garrison never came. It was always his investigators that came to us. And they finally just turned it over to him saying, 'y'all have done such a good job. Y'all make y'all work easy.' So they took my notes, and they took them back to Garrison. And he was there.

"Thank you, sir, for asking."

OLIVER: "Lady, here."

AUDIENCE MEMBER: "Since this lady was talking about 'they're gonna kill the president, they're gonna kill the president.' Did she not say any names of anybody? Because she was in the car with a gun..."

DISCHLER: "I think Jim had a feeling who she said she knew.

"She and Larry Hancock had asked me this several years ago. Jim Garrison had photographs that he gave to Lieutenant Francis Fruge and said, 'take this to the Silver Slipper Lounge in Bassey,' which is a lounge that she and her companions had been thrown out of for being rowdy and loud and drunk and drugged up and whatever. And Garrison, in trying to find out who these men were that she was with, gave photographs to Lieutenant Fruge. And he went over to the lounge, the manager Hadley and Matthew, you and I both know, thinking of deceased men, And showed him pictures and he actually picked out a couple of photographs. Now I have to go back to some notes. I believe one of these pictures was according to Garrison. Gee, and I hate to even say it because I'm not sure."

OLIVER: "Larry's gonna tell you ..."

AUDIENCE MEMBER: "Okay. Well, and I'll give you an answer..."

DISCHLER: "And by the way, Francis Fruge's testimony, his HSCA testimony is on the website, so if anybody wants to read his actual testimony. (Arcacha Smith and Emilio Santana as the pictures that most closely match the ones that he had in the investigation.)

"So the two faces that were recognized were Sergio Arcacha Smith and Emilio Santana. And I think if you'll click on this website, *JFK Lancer,* you can certainly find some information about these guys. Or Larry Hancock, You can contact Larry in his book but just type in their names in Google search and you're going to come up with some kind of rationale as to what their role may have been."

TAPE ENDS AT THIS POINT

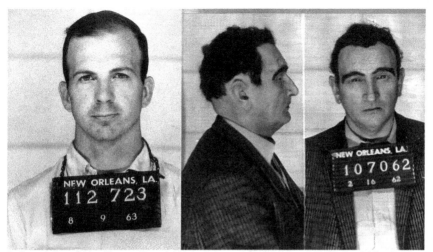

Left to right are:Lee Harvey Oswald New Orleans arrest photo, 8/9/63, David Ferrie New Orleans arrest photo, 2/16/62.

David Ferrie (far left) and Lee Harvey Oswald (far right) at a Civil Air Patrol barbecue

Lee Harvey Oswald Dallas arrest photo on 11/23/63, David Ferrie New Orleans arrest photo..

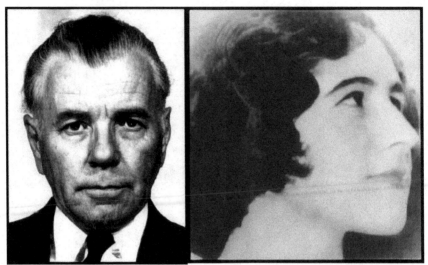

Guy Banister, Banister's secretary and mistress Delphine Roberts

(Left to right) FBI agent Regis Kennedy, Eladio del Valle

240

(Left to right) Sergio Arcacha Smith, Alvin Beaubouef

(Left to right) Kerry Thornley, Layton Martens

(Left to right) Gordon Novel, New Orleans Assistant District Attorney Lou Ivon

Perry Raymond Russo

Clay Shaw (center) celebrates his March 1, 1969 acquittal, defense attorney F. Irvin Dymond is on the right, unidentified figure on the left.

Clay Shaw (second from right in rear) and male friends

Clay Shaw (in wig, second from right) with male friends

(Left to right) Edward Voebel, Lee Harvey Oswald's best friend in high school, Voebel's twin sisters Doris "Sweetie Pie" Voebel Kuntz and Teddi "Cookie" Voebel Segal.

(Left to right) Multi-Emmy award winning entertainer and filmmaker John Barbour, Jim Garrison and family.

BIBLIOGRAPHY

William Davy, *Let Justice be Done: New Light on the Jim Garrison Investigation*, Reston, Virginia, Jordan Publishing, 1999

James DiEugenio, *Destiny Betrayed: JFK, Cuba, and the Garrison Case*, New York, Skyhorse Publishing, 2012

Paris Flammonde, *The Kennedy Conspiracy: An Uncommissioned Report on the Jim Garrison Investigation*, New York, Meredith Press, 1969

Jim Garrison, *A Heritage of Stone*, New York, Putnam, 1970

Jim Garrison, *On the Trail of the Assassins: One Man's Quest to Solve the Murder of President Kennedy*, New York, Warner Books, 1991

Edward T. Haslem, *Dr. Mary's Monkey: How the Unsolved Murder of a Doctor, a Secret Laboratory in New Orleans and Cancer-Causing Monkey Viruses Are Linked to Lee Harvey Oswald, the JFK Assassination and Emerging Global Epidemics*, Oregon, Trine Day 2014 updated version

Marrs, Jim, *Crossfire: The Plot That Killed Kennedy*, New York, Carroll & Graf, 1989

Joan Mellen, *A Farewell to Justice: Jim Garrison, JFK's Assassination, and the Case That Should Have Changed History*, New York, Skyhorse Publishing, 2013

Jack Roth, *Killing Kennedy: Exposing the Plot, the Cover-Up, and the Consequences*, New York, Skyhorse Publishing, 2022

Richard E. Sprague, *The Taking of America 1-2-3*, New York, Richard E. Sprague, 1976

Index